MEMOIRS OF

FINDING MY SOVEREIGNTY

Tina Djuretic

ISBN paperback: 978-1-0689564-0-9
ISBN ebook: 978-1-0689564-1-6

Published by Tina Djuretic

He who blames others has a long way to go on his journey
He who blames himself is halfway there
He who blames no one has arrived

Chinese Proverb

Growing up we never heard words like Empath or narcissistic behaviour. I'm not even sure those words existed until my forties. Today, you hear them all the time. In fact, they're so overused they've lost their power. People constantly accuse their partners of being narcissistic, having no idea what an actual narcissist looks like, but they DO exist. They're the stuff nightmares are made of.

In the seventies, we didn't have words, just emotions. Lots and lots of buried emotions. They were never voiced because if you did you were told to be quiet . . . to toughen up . . . so that's what we did. We toughened up. We did everything ourselves and relied on no one. We're what they call Generation X.

This book is dedicated to anyone who's ever been lost in the dark, anyone who's attracted to narcissists and doesn't know why, and for those looking back on their lives . . . wondering how the hell they got here.

ONE

August 2019

I'm not gonna lie, Luna. I'm seriously pissed at the Universe right now, and I don't know if that's bad juju or what, but I'm way past caring. I'm so frustrated I could scream. I've had one toxic relationship after the other, and I don't understand why. *Why?*" I practically yelled at the stranger sitting in front of me.

"I'm a good person, so why does the Universe keep punishing me? Why do I keep repeating this ridiculous pattern with narcissists? Please help me understand what's happening, because at this point I'm so incredibly lost, and I'm *so sorry* for taking it out on you."

"Oh . . . my," she said with an airy laugh. "Yes, I understand, but I promise you, Sage, the Universe isn't doing this *to* you. It's doing it *for* you. When the Divine has a message, it knocks on the door, so to speak. If we don't listen, it knocks louder. Then it blows the house down. I'm guessing that's where you're at."

That's exactly where I was at. After my last breakup, I'd finally seen a pattern when it came to my relationships, and it wasn't good. I've always been attracted to extremely handsome men but apparently only if they're emotionally unavailable.

As a woman in her late forties, I wanted to break this pattern, except I didn't know *how.* So last week I asked a friend if she knew any spiritual teachers, and she sent me to this woman—a channeler named Luna Rain. She wanted to meet in a busy café in Vancouver, which I thought was odd, but the noise didn't seem to bother her.

"Let's get started, shall we?" she said, interrupting my thoughts. "First I'm going to wrap us in a protective bubble so we can shut everyone in this cafe out of our energy field. Give me a minute . . . excellent. Now, we'd like you to say your name three times."

She looked at me expectantly, so I complied.

"Good. We never give information from the Akashic Records unless we have permission from your soul, and since we have that, we're looking initially at this lifetime."

"What are the Akashic Records?" I asked. "I've never heard that term before."

"They're basically a record of your soul's journey through every lifetime, but today we'll be looking at the time starting with the birth of Christ until now because that's really what your soul remembers. Now, there are four primary patterns that we all get stuck in: rejection, abandonment, betrayal, and loss. Yours is betrayal."

This wasn't a surprise. I've experienced a lot of betrayal in my life. *A lot.*

"We also want to know the essence of your soul, and yours is that of the teacher, the storyteller. You are, in all experiences of your soul's evolution, a teacher and a great communicator."

This was interesting because I've always been good at storytelling, even when I was a child. As for teaching, I used to teach the choir and dance classes when I worked on cruise ships. I guess that counts.

"We're looking specifically at this betrayal pattern. We're going into your past experiences to see when this became a *repetitive* pattern. When the betrayal was so profound it *stuck.* I'm traveling back through your . . . wow . . . you've been betrayed by male after male after male." She paused for a second. "Of course, we want to express that in all your lifetimes you've been fifty percent (give or take) male and female. Which means, whatever has been done to you, you've done to others."

"So, as many times as I've been betrayed, I've also been the betrayer? Well, that brings things into perspective, doesn't it?"

"Yes. That's what karma is. Now, what's getting in the way is the memory of this one lifetime in Mongolia. You were . . . hmmm . . . there's no *marriage* at this time, but there was a betrothal when you were . . . *nine.*"

"Woah. That's young."

"You were betrothed to a man who was at least forty years older than you, and he used you. Not only as a slave but as a breeding vessel."

I made a face, but I didn't interrupt. I could tell she was seeing this in her mind. I also assumed that the "we" she kept referring to were her spirit guides.

"This lord was very respected in the community, but he beat you, and he initiated sex on the eve you turned . . . *ten.* He gave you a year to be a child, although you were *never* a child."

She gives me a knowing look, like she knows I was never a child in this lifetime either.

"He started using you as a breeding vessel because he wanted sons. You basically had one pregnancy after the other. Many of the daughters were murdered. You had around fourteen children, but only seven survived. In the end, you died—not in childbirth, but from a *disease,* and it was *not* pleasant."

"Well, that sounds like a shitty lifetime," I said sardonically.

"Yes, these were not good times for women. The betrayal was by your father. Not your husband, but your father."

"Because he made the deal."

"Yes! And you were his favorite girl. Oh, there were four girls in your family! That's amazing. At that time, only one or two would have been allowed to live, but your mother was *very* strong and very smart. She hid things from him."

This *was* interesting. There are four girls in my current family, which she couldn't possibly have known.

"You were his favorite girl because he was intellectual and you were a great storyteller. Oh, look at that! The storyteller, you see? You entertained him and you believed that he'd betroth you to someone like himself, except he didn't. He sold you to the highest bidder and took the money. Like cattle."

"Bastard," I said under my breath.

"So, let's take a look at your journey in this lifetime. Can you give us your mother's name three times?"

I complied.

"Good. We need to trace her and get permission so we can see the relationship between the two of you." She was quiet for a minute while she did this. "Oh my! She's a pretty strong character!"

"That's one word for it," I deadpanned.

"There wasn't anything traumatic about your journey in the uterus. She was very careful. Hmmm . . . remember, she's of a different generation that lives almost fully in pain and suffering, so for that generation to put any amount of love into anything . . . wasn't easy."

Love? This is the last word I'd associate with my mother. In fact, I was pretty sure she wasn't capable of love. I don't remember being hugged, praised, encouraged, or even acknowledged as a child.

"We're looking at your birth until nine years old. Hmm . . . you were nine, almost ten, when you had this shutting out. Ka-boom! It's like a lightning bolt. Oh, look, there's that nine again. Very synchronistic. Tell me, what's that story? Do you remember what happened at that age?"

I smirked. "I most certainly do. That's when my parents joined a cult. A fanatical Christian cult."

"Oh my goodness! OK . . . wow. It was a lightning bolt. It changed how you *thought,* how you *felt,* and how you looked at life. You were struck dumb. That's the word we'll use so you can understand that, yes, that happened. It was real, and it was profound." She looked at me, and I nodded to acknowledge that I understood.

"The question we have is, who was it for? Was it for her? Was it for him? Was it for the family?" She paused for a second. "It was for *them.* It was all about them. Do you have siblings?" she asked suddenly.

"Yes, I have three sisters."

"Oh my gosh, would you look at that! There's the four girls again! And she feels a lot like that mother you had in Mongolia. You've had *many* mothers like her."

"Of course I have," I said dryly, but what she didn't say was that my father was also like that father from Mongolia. He was intellectual, and he betrayed me. The parallels were crazy.

"So ten, eleven, twelve . . . at twelve you were like, *what the? I don't want to be here. I don't want to be here. I* don't *want to be here.* I just keep hearing that over and over again. This was a significant time in your life."

I made a mental note to ask my sister what happened when I was twelve. I couldn't remember because I'd buried my childhood a long time ago. I knew the broad strokes (and they weren't pretty), but I'd always figured the rest was best forgotten. My sisters, who remembered everything and weren't better for it, agreed.

"Twelve, thirteen . . . there was a lot of shifting. It's like you were trickling your power back, and by the time you were fifteen, you were getting stronger. In your stubbornness, your strength, your . . ." She drifts off as she tilts her head. "It's not rebellion. It's like a volcano."

I remember my father throwing me down the stairs when I was twelve, and then he told me to pray for forgiveness so I wouldn't burn in hell for disobeying him. I remember how much I feared him in those days. How much I hated him.

"Yes! You've been percolating for a loooooong time and you were NOT ALLOWED to speak. NOT ALLOWED to express yourself. NOT ALLOWED to be who you are. Ninety-nine percent not allowed. That's only one percent freedom!"

She shakes her head like it's too crazy to believe, but I remember exactly what it felt like. It felt like prison.

"So, lots of trying to allow that one percent out, but it was met with a consistent squashing. In spiritual terms, you had just rolled over. The Divine was working with you and trying to activate you so you'd wake up and become who you were meant to be."

Which was who, exactly? I still didn't know.

"By the time you were twenty, you became very rebellious." She giggled. "Holy smokes. It was big, and it went on for years. Buck the system. Fuck the system. Good for you."

I smiled. I remembered the nineties fondly. It was an era of gay clubs and fabulous parties fueled by drugs, youth, and alcohol. I lived in the west end of Vancouver, and I was deeply embedded in the gay community. After growing up so isolated (the church didn't allow us to associate with anyone outside of the church), I embraced this new world as fiercely as it embraced me.

"When we look at those early twenties, there was a rumbling going on. It was volcanic at times, and then when you were twenty-seven, it was like, *I've had enough. I'm tired.* The rebelliousness started to dissipate as you asked yourself: *What am I doing? Where am I going? Who am I?*"

Twenty-seven. That's around the time I moved to Japan. When I got back, I met my first boyfriend and she was right, my life definitely changed.

"The next major experience for you was thirty-seven. You made a lot of decisions at that time, and you created boundaries. Any questions?"

"I'd like to go back to something you said earlier. My issues have always been with my mother, so it surprised me when you said they're with men."

"Men, or women with predominantly male energy, like your mother."

"Right. That makes sense. Over the years, I've learned that my trigger is bullies. My mother is a bully. She's bipolar, and I get that she's ill . . . but she's still a bully."

"Do you understand—no, we *know* you understand—that a bully usually exhibits sociopathic tendencies, which are exacerbated by narcissistic childhood experiences. So, they're not just damaged, but broken. You were broken. She was broken. "

I thought about that as I picked at my muffin. My mother never talked about her childhood, but we always knew it was bad. I'll never forget when she called me one day when I was eighteen years old. She was absolutely hysterical. Her mother had called, knowing my parents were broke, and offered her a lot of money on the condition that she divorce my father—or "that foreigner" as she liked to call him.

When my mother refused, she didn't give her a dime. She did, however, call every couple of years to make that same offer. Not once did she ever call my father by name. He was always "that foreigner. "

I listened to my mother bawl as she went on and on about how awful her mother was, but what truly shocked me was that the whole time she was describing her own mother, she was also describing herself, yet she clearly didn't see it. She could have called anyone that day, yet there she was, calling me, a victim of her own abuse.

I realized two important things that day: First, my grandmother was obviously bipolar like my mother (which meant it was hereditary); Second, my mother grew up with the same abuse she inflicted upon us. Because of that phone call, I finally understood my mother, and for the first time, I actually felt sorry for her. She clearly suffered from mental illness, and that realization helped me let go of my anger. It's also one of the reasons I decided not to have children.

"Yes, it's in the lineage," said Luna, as if reading my thoughts. "On the mother's side and the father's. When we look at your mother's ancestry, it goes back to your great grandmother. Woah! That's the tour de force that destroyed your grandmother and your mother. On your father's side, it goes back to the sixth-great-grandfather. That's a repetitive pattern of abuse: physical, emotional, and mental that goes back six generations."

So that's what people mean when they talk about generational trauma. Broken people raise broken people. No wonder my parents never talked about their childhoods. In fact, the only thing I knew about my father was that he came from Yugoslavia, and his family escaped when he was fourteen. He had a younger brother, was raised on a farm, and his family was Orthodox.

Growing up, they were very poor, and when times were tough, all they had to eat were lard and sugar sandwiches. He liked to remind us of this whenever we complained as children. My grandfather had a mean temper, and whenever his sons misbehaved, he sent them to the yard to cut a switch, then he took them to the shed for a beating. If they picked a switch that wasn't strong enough, he cut one himself and the beating would be twice as hard. This was another story my father liked to tell, especially when we misbehaved.

As for my mother, I knew even less about her, except that she had been born out of wedlock, and her stepdad was an alcoholic. She was French Canadian and was raised strictly Catholic, which is why my grandparents disowned my father for marrying her. His parents hated Catholics. I smiled when I thought about that. My father liked to poke the bear. I was a lot like him.

"You're not abusive," Luna said out of nowhere, and then she deliberately looked me in the eye. "You're NOT. You're not abusive, aggressive, or cruel. We want that to be very clear. You're not any of those things. It's really important you understand that."

She waited until I acknowledged her. Man, she was clever. She'd just hit on the second reason I'd never had children. I'd always been told that I'm just like my father, and I feared that meant I'd be abusive as well. Between him and my bipolar mother, it just seemed safer not to reproduce.

"Good. Do you have any questions?" she asked.

"Umm . . . not really. Although my father's the one who physically abused us, I don't dwell on that very much because he's Serbian, and that's what Serbs do. Plus, it wasn't really bad until they joined the church and they—"

"—gave them permission."

"Exactly! They gave them permission. *Spare the rod, spoil the child*. I understand my parents' generation was heavy handed, but then they joined the church, which not only gave them permission but fully encouraged corporal punishment. In the beginning, I could actually see the hurt on my father's face when he punished us. I could forgive him because he spent the rest of his life regretting it. But her . . . she *enjoyed* it. She *created* it. She used to lie to make the beatings happen."

The Rumor Game suddenly popped into my head. It was one of my mother's favorite games. She enjoyed pitting my sisters and I against each other by telling us lies. She'd tell Sidney I'd said something bad about her, then Sidney would get mad, and I wouldn't know why. She'd break my toys and blame Sienna, and then I'd yell at her.

This led to loud arguments, a lot of hitting, kicking, punching . . . and then she'd turn around and punish us for fighting. My mother LOVED this game. When we were really bad, she told my father, and he'd whip us with his belt. He was part of her game, too.

She did this for many years, and my sisters and I spent a lot of time being mad at each other, even as adults, over things none of us were even guilty of. My mother realized early on that she had the power not only to boss us around, but to manipulate us, creating discord that only grew with time. She never wanted us to be close. We were much easier to manipulate when she kept us apart. Separation and isolation—the first step in every narcissist's handbook.

"Yes, she loved to manipulate," said Luna, bringing me back to the present. "She fed off it."

"Yes, she did," I said bitterly. "She still does."

"Your mother is a slave to entities. They control her."

I was about to take a sip of tea, and I nearly spilled it. "Wait a minute . . . *what?* Entities are real?"

"Of course they are! In everything there must be balance, so if there's light in the world, there's also darkness."

Holy crap. There were so many thoughts in my head I didn't know where to begin. This changed everything. Or, rather, it *confirmed* everything, like my childhood nightmares and my deepest, darkest fears.

"Trying to release these entities is what I do, but it's not easy. Once they're gone, that human needs to work on releasing the sound and smell for a good gestation period. It can be six to nine months trying to keep them at bay, but usually they can't. The human can't, so not only do the originals come back, they bring more. Tribes. Hundreds of entities would have controlled your mother, and they love nothing more than *death*." She delivered this word like a blow. "You're lucky you weren't beaten to death. It's what they wanted."

I snorted. "They tried. Believe me, they tried."

We were both quiet for a moment, and then she spoke again.

"So the question is: are you intended to write about this story and your experiences with sociopathic, bipolar, mentally ill, narcissistic, psychopathic people? The answer is yes. You need to share your story, Sage. When somebody has such a profound experience—and this is a *profound* experience—it means that others are having it, too, and they need to hear about it."

She takes a sip of her tea, then chuckles. "It's a great story. Has anyone ever told you to write a book before?"

"All the time, but I thought it would be about my travels not my childhood." Good Lord. How was I supposed to write about a childhood I couldn't even remember?

"You have two years to write the book, and it starts October 1st. Then you need to find a good editor, and eventually you'll publish. You *are* a writer, Sage, and by writing your story, you'll find healing. This is how you break the pattern, and your book will help others do the same."

Jeez, I thought. *No pressure.*

"I was thinking of taking a vacation to either Bali or Thailand this winter. Maybe I can do some writing while I'm there," I said, thinking out loud.

"Bali," she said. "You're going to Bali."

Two

1983

My parents were extremely strict, even when we were young, and they firmly believed that children should be seen and not heard. Empty threats didn't exist in my family, either. Every threat was carried out *to the fullest*. It was the seventies, after all. When your parents said, "You're going to sit in the car if you can't behave," they weren't kidding. You sat in the car.

Soon, we were silenced with a LOOK. If you got that look from my mother, it meant a backhand, a wooden spoon, or a plastic brush was headed your way. Sometimes all three. If my father gave you that look, you were in deep shit.

At that time, there were three girls in my family, and I was the middle child. Sidney was a year older than me, and Sienna was three years younger. Having three girls that began with the letter "S" was a bit confusing, especially when we got into trouble. My mother would go through the entire gamut of our names (sometimes twice) before landing on the right one, and by then, she was even angrier than when she started.

For the most part, we grew up in the greater Vancouver area—the whole area. We moved a lot. Life was pretty normal until I was ten years old. That's when my parents joined a fanatical church that not only isolated us from the rest of the world but also came with a whole list of rules. Rules that made you the "church freak" when you went out in public. Rules that were impossible to follow.

It was quite common for people to come over after church. This was a time for drinking coffee, eating dessert, and gossiping. Man, did church people love to gossip. The Bible says it's a sin, but since we weren't allowed to watch television, they needed something to keep themselves entertained.

There were a lot of contradictions like that, but whenever we pointed them out, we were told to be seen and not heard. That's how it went in our house. The church people were a bunch of hypocrites, but we were the ones going to hell.

When I was twelve, several people came over after church one night, along with the pastor and his wife. They invited a young man whom they suspected was "possessed with the Devil" so they could perform an exorcism. In our living room. With three kids in the house.

Apparently, my sisters and I were the only ones in the dark because when things first erupted, we had no idea what was going on. My mother rushed over and immediately sent Sienna to bed, saying she was too young to watch. Then she looked at Sidney and me and said, "You two sit right here and don't move. We're performing an exorcism, so you better pray *really* hard, and don't stop praying for *one second* because when the demons leave that man, they'll be looking for someone else to go into, and children are an easy target."

As you can imagine, we were terrified. We'd never seen an exorcism before. I'm not even sure we thought they were real. Wasn't it enough that we were scared to death of going to hell, and now they were inviting the Devil into our home? Why weren't they doing this at church?

We watched as everyone put their hands on the young man and started to pray. He didn't like that, so he tried to get away, but they wouldn't let him go. The pastor kept shouting as he ordered the demons to leave his body. They prayed while the man groaned and struggled, until eventually he ended up on the kitchen floor with everyone holding him down.

He got angry, and then he started foaming at the mouth, just like it says in the Bible. I kid you not, there was white foam dripping down the sides of his face. Sidney and I were petrified, but just like a car crash, we couldn't look away.

The man growled and thrashed as everyone prayed, and then he started yelling at them in several different voices. Voices that weren't human. Voices that made my skin crawl. The more violent he became, the harder they prayed. The pastor was at the center of it all.

The man started swearing and calling them names, so they prayed harder. I was glued to the spot, wishing I was anywhere but there. At some point, the pastor asked the demon, "What is thy name?" and the man started laughing. A sick, evil laugh that echoed off the walls.

"I am Legion," he growled, "and we are many!"

Oh shit. Even I knew that scripture. It referred to the worst kind of possession possible. There could be thousands of demons in that man! I knew I'd never forget his laughter, the look on his face, or the sound of those voices as long as I lived. It was seared into my memory.

This went on for quite some time, and at one point, the man on the floor threw one of the other men across the kitchen and into the ceiling with the flick of his arm. It's like he was possessed with superhuman strength. We watched him go flying in the air, hit the ceiling, then land on the floor with a thud.

Luckily, he wasn't hurt. In fact, he got up and scrambled right back over, where he prayed even harder. Sidney and I were huddled in the corner, watching as this horrific spectacle unfolded. Everyone else had their eyes closed, since they were praying, but we saw everything. Every . . . last . . . tiny . . . detail.

We had no idea what to do. This couldn't possibly be real, yet there we were, watching *The Exorcist* play out in our kitchen. There was a palpable evil in the air, and we all felt it. It went on for ages, this battle between good and evil, and then . . . it was over. The "good guys" had won. The group was elated. The man was saved!

They decided to celebrate while Sidney and I were sent to bed. We had nightmares for weeks. Actually, I had nightmares for the next thirty-five years because nobody could ever tell me that what I saw that day wasn't real.

Over the years, I desperately tried to come up with explanations for what I saw that night. He was on PCP. He'd made those voices himself. The drugs had made him foam at the mouth and possess superhuman strength . . . yup, I told myself all kinds of things, yet deep down inside, I knew it was true. I knew that demons were real, and I was profoundly afraid of them.

Shortly after that, my mother had a mid-life crisis and decided she wanted to have another baby. When she told my father, he hit the roof.

"Absolutely not! We're on welfare, and we can't even afford the kids we have."

But my mother always got her way. She simply went off the pill and pretended the pregnancy was an accident. She told everyone at church it was her "miracle baby" and basked in their attention. Dad wasn't happy, though. He didn't like being manipulated.

The three of us weren't impressed, either. Sidney wanted to know where the baby was supposed to sleep (since Sienna and I already shared a room), and Sienna was worried that she'd no longer be the baby of the family. Personally, I thought my mother was too old to have a baby, but in truth, she was only thirty-five. She ignored our concerns because, as she put it, "This isn't about you." It was never about us.

"The three of you were mistakes, but not this one. This is a precious gift from God," she told us. "I never wanted *any* of you, and it looks like I was right. You're ungrateful little brats, and I'm done with you. I can't help that the three of you were born in sin, but *this . . .*" she said, caressing her belly, "will be my *perfect little church baby.*"

Believe it or not, this barely got a reaction from us, other than an eye roll. We were used to her insults. I don't think a day went by where she didn't call me fat.

"So I guess the only thing we're good for is cleaning the house," said Sidney after my mother left the room.

"Even me?" asked Sienna, wide-eyed.

"Sorry, kid." I ruffled her hair. "You're not the baby anymore."

Christmas was bleak that year. The only presents under the tree came from the welfare office, and Dad was so embarrassed. We pretended it didn't matter because we could see how awful he felt, and we never kicked a man when he was down. It wasn't our way. Besides, that was my mother's job.

On New Year's Eve, my mother went into labor, and just like that, we had another sister. My father joked he'd never see the bathroom again. As it was, we were four females fighting over the world's smallest loo.

When they brought Bailey home from the hospital, my mother went to her room and didn't come out for a week. She was consumed by depression and cried every day. We'd take turns holding the baby, changing her diaper, dressing her, and putting her to sleep. I particularly remember the diapers because we couldn't afford the disposable ones. Dipping the poopy diapers in the toilet was enough to make me gag, but we weren't allowed to complain.

Eventually, Mom went back to church and loved showing off her *perfect little church baby* . . . but the minute she got home, she'd hand her over and go to her room. She was barely functioning, and we couldn't understand what was wrong with her.

We still had to go to school every day, do our paper routes, babysit for people in the church, keep the house clean, and learn how to take care of a new baby on top of going to church four times a week. It was a lot to handle. Let's just say my grades were *not* amazing and hadn't been for a long time. Dad was hoping the depression would ease off eventually, but it never did, so this became our new normal.

The good news is that Dad finally got a job. He worked a lot of overtime to catch up on the bills, and although he'd never admit it, I think he wanted to escape my mother. If he thought her mood swings were bad before, these days they were in serious overdrive. She was either in her bedroom crying or on a rampage no one was safe from.

It was heartbreaking listening to my mother cry, and although I didn't understand it at the time, I felt sorry for her. I could feel her pain as if it were my own, and all I wanted to do was help her. She was so sad . . . so broken . . . and I didn't know why. Sidney mocked me for trying to comfort our mother, saying she didn't deserve our sympathy, but I couldn't help it. I wasn't hard like Sidney, and I couldn't stand by and do nothing. She was suffering, and I needed to make it better.

After bringing my mother dinner or a cup of tea, then holding her while she cried, she'd go right back to belittling me and calling me names. It was very confusing and only made me hate her even more, because every time she lured me in with her crying, she'd turn around and lash out once again.

This is when we understood that something was truly wrong with our mother. It was obvious she suffered from depression, but she was also cruel. Sidney, who was thirteen and much wiser than me, was convinced she was schizophrenic, which explained why she'd do something one minute, then the next minute she had no idea what you were talking about (and she'd call you a liar). It was the elephant in the room my father loved to ignore.

When Bailey was two, Dad was offered the position of "onboard host" with VIA Rail, and he jumped at the opportunity to get out of the baggage department. The new position meant he'd be traveling a lot, which was great news.

That same year, Sidney and I asked if we could go back to public school. In fact, we begged all summer long, refusing to back down until we got our way. Sidney was sixteen, and I was fifteen, and we were determined not to spend another year at the oppressive church school. Since our sponsor fell through and Dad didn't want to accept any more handouts, he finally gave in to our demands. Sienna wasn't so lucky. My parents decided it would be worth it to pay for her education, so she had to stay at the church school a little longer.

I enjoyed the new school, and although I wasn't very popular, I still managed to make a few friends. We weren't allowed to take gym class (it was against our religion) or do any extracurricular activities like choir, drama, or sports, but it was still a win. To be honest, I didn't even know most of those activities existed. That's what happens when you live in a bubble.

As for Sidney, she secretly started dating an older man (he was twenty-two, and she was sixteen), and then she started sneaking out of the house. Dad was always away, and Mom lost interest in us after Bailey was born, so when we said we had a lot of homework, she'd let us skip church, and Sidney would sneak out.

When Dad *was* home, he started spending a lot of time with the youth group at church, and the young men *loved* him. In fact, everyone loved my father, old and young alike. He's the kind of man you desperately wanted to please, and if he praised something you did (which was almost never), it was the best feeling in the world. He was charismatic, charming, and smart, but most of all, he had *presence.* That's not something you can learn. You either have it or you don't.

As soon as he entered the room, everyone noticed. If he spoke, everyone listened. If he didn't speak, everyone still listened. Robert DeNiro has that kind of presence. So does Al Pacino. My father was no different, and because of it, the pastor decided he'd make a great preacher one day. He wanted him to have his own church so he could help spread the word of God.

As for the young men, they saw him as a mentor and went on and on about how lucky we were to have him as a father. That's the thing about Dad. He was part awesome, part monster. It's strange, because I remember it was around that time that Dad suddenly wanted to hug us all the time, and we had no idea why, nor did we want him touching us.

Perhaps it was because he loved his job and was finally happy, but while he was living his best life, we were stuck at home with our mother, who continued to remind us on a daily basis what a waste of space we were and how we'd never amount to anything. She drilled this mantra into our heads for so long, it became programming. Programming that would have a profound effect on my relationships as I got older.

Mother also noticed Dad's sudden effort to get closer to his girls, and she didn't like it. She wanted his attention all to herself, so she flicked the switch, put away the depression, and went back to playing games. She devised new ways of making him choose between us and her, except now that we were teenagers, her games were far more deadly.

She was always looking for a fight, and if she didn't get one, she created one. Then she'd use her favorite line. "Wait 'til your father gets home. He'll beat you senseless." Sometimes it felt like being taunted by a six-year-old with power. She used that threat to terrorize and dominate us for years, but it was starting to grow old, and although we knew it was true—he *would* beat us—we also knew he wouldn't be home for a week, and that made us bold.

I have no idea what lies my mother told him when he got home, but he *never* doubted her, and he *never* asked us to explain ourselves. He'd simply take off his belt and do his "duty" as the head of the house and a man of God. Punishment was the only language he knew, the only thing he'd been taught, and my mother used that as a weapon to trap us in her twisted little game.

I've always been a keen observer of human behavior, and I was starting to understand just how messed up our situation was, so when my father came home from one of his trips and started beating me—then took it too far, like he usually did—I looked at my mother to see if she'd stop him.

There she was, on the other side of the room—arms folded across her chest, leaning against the wall, *smiling.* When she saw me look at her, she flashed her smug little smile, lifted one shoulder in a shrug and mouthed, *see what I can do?* She took pleasure in watching my father beat me, and she wanted me to know it.

I'll never forget that look as long as I live, but what really got me was what I saw in her eyes. Something dark and scary was lurking behind them. That was the moment I understood that my mother wasn't just mean—she was *evil.* I knew right then and there, in the deepest part of my soul, that we weren't loved by these people and that they might actually kill us one day.

Something inside of me changed, and I vowed that the next time he came after me or my sisters, I'd stand up to him. My parents, the people who were supposed to protect us, were nothing but bullies, and I was tired of it. My sisters and I were so traumatized by years of physical, mental, and emotional abuse that I knew I had to stop them. I was the only one who could. I was the strongest, and more importantly . . . I had nothing left to lose.

Three

October 2019

"Do you really believe in all that crap?" Sidney asked, her skepticism clearly showing. "I know you're into all that spiritual stuff, but I don't get it. It sounds too much like *church* to me."

It had been two months since my meeting with Luna, and I'd invited my sister over so she could tell me everything she remembered about our childhood. She warned me to be careful what I wished for, but I wanted to hear it from her point of view, since she's the oldest and remembers it best.

We were sitting in the living room of my one-bedroom apartment. Sidney was on the loveseat, and I was in my papadum chair. My apartment is small, which is typical of downtown Vancouver, but it's beautifully decorated with art from all over the world. My home is my sanctuary, and it's a very peaceful place. As for my art, it's the story of my life, reminding me of all the beautiful places I've been.

Sidney and I were smoking a fatty as per usual—only this time, I paired it with a bottle of wine. I knew this conversation would be difficult for my sister, who still bitterly resented our parents. In fact, for years she refused to talk about them at all. The only reason she was doing it now was that we'd recently rekindled our relationship, and she knew it was important to me.

"Oh yes, there's no doubt Luna's gifted," I said.

"Well, if I'm being honest, what she says about the entities in Mom makes sense. For the longest time, I was convinced she was schizophrenic, so it doesn't surprise me that something's controlling her. Actually, do you remember when they did that exorcism in our house in Surrey?"

I shuddered. "It's kind of hard to forget, as are the nightmares that followed. What I don't understand is why we were there in the first place."

"Because Mom *forced* us to be there. She sent Sienna to bed but told us we had to watch and we'd better pray real hard and not stop for one second or the demons might leave that man and come straight into us."

"She actually said that? What kind of person says that to their kids?" I shook my head in disbelief.

"She said children were an easy target, but I always wondered if they went into *her* that night. I mean if what Luna says is true, she was already full of them."

"Holy crap. I never thought of that, but you're probably right. Her own demons would have welcomed them with open arms." I rolled my eyes. "No wonder I have nightmares. We lived our own up-close-and-personal version of *The Exorcist,* not to mention the daily threats of going to hell and burning for all eternity. How were we supposed to come back from that? Man, they really fucked us up."

"That they did."

We were both quiet for a minute, and then something occurred to me. "How old were we when that happened?"

"I was thirteen, so you were twelve."

"Oh my God! So that's what Luna was talking about when she said all she could hear was 'I don't want to be here' over and over again."

"That makes sense. Neither of us should have been there."

"I know we always hated them, but I don't think I ever fully understood how bad it was until now. Hearing it as an adult and imagining someone saying that to a kid . . . it's messed up."

"Exactly. It wasn't until I had my own kids that I understood the severity of their actions. Why do you think I stopped talking to them for so many years?" She picked up the bottle of wine and poured herself another glass. "You know, Mom had Bailey shortly after that, then she went through postpartum depression. She'd lock herself in her room, and we had to take care of the baby."

"I remember. I always thought it was the hormones that kicked the mood swings into high gear, but if the entities went into her, adding to the ones she already had . . ."

"Yup, it all fits."

"You know, I swear I saw them in Mom's eyes one time while Dad was beating me. I saw evil there, I just didn't realize it was so *literal*." I shuddered as I remembered the look on my mother's face.

"Oh I saw it many times. That evil look in her eyes."

"You did?"

"Of course I did. I was the one begging her to make Dad stop beating you, but she'd just smile and say you deserved it."

"Really? I never noticed, although I guess I was a little preoccupied at the time."

We both laughed. My sisters and I have a dark sense of humor that few people understand. We're able to joke about things like demons, death, and childhood abuse because that's how we survived. I believe they call it gallows humor.

"Why do you think I grew up with so many issues?" she asked.

"I don't know. To be honest, I always wondered why I was able to let it go while you were the one who held on to it all these years. Of course I only remember the broad strokes, while you remember the details. Until recently, I thought that was a good thing."

"Yes, but I'm the oldest, and it was my job to protect you. You're my little sister, yet no matter what I did, I couldn't protect you from them. Do you have any idea how that made me feel? To be the one who had to *watch?*"

I had never thought of it like that. All these years and all the guilt she'd been carrying on my behalf. That must have been such a weight on her shoulders. No wonder she wasn't able to forgive them. Even now, I could feel her anger.

"Sidney, I'm the one who pushed Dad by mouthing off. You know that, right? I could have pretended to cry like Sienna, and he probably would have stopped, but I *chose* to fight back. That's not your fault. It was worse for me because I made it worse. I never blamed you for that, and you need to stop blaming yourself."

"Yes, but I'm the one who rebelled. I'm the one who snuck out and pissed them off, while you were the one who took the beatings. They were *my* beatings."

"Did it ever occur to you that I took the beatings because I'm the strongest and I knew I could handle it? And I'm fairly certain I did my fair share of pissing them off."

Sidney laughed. "I'll never forget the time you told Dad to go ahead and break your arm so you could show everyone at church what a monster he was. That took balls."

"Oh man, he was so mad I thought he'd kill me!" I said, laughing.

"So did I," she said seriously. "So when are you going to Bali?" she asked, suddenly changing the subject.

"In January. I decided to treat myself, so I booked a wellness tour, then I rented a condo for three weeks.

"And are you really going to write this book?"

"I think so. I kind of feel like I have to."

"And you're going to write about our family?" she said, scowling.

"Well, I can't tell my story without talking about childhood so . . . yes."

"What if I'm not OK with that? I understand *you're* OK with it, but what about the rest of us?"

She was right. In fact, the thought of betraying my parents and everyone else I'd have to write about gave me a fair amount of anxiety, not to mention guilt. After all, I'm pretty private myself, and I wasn't sure how I felt about telling my secrets to the world.

FOUR

1986

Sidney was pretty and popular with the boys, but I was the complete opposite. At fifteen, I was funny and had a great personality, but deep down inside, I always felt like the ugly duckling living in her shadow.

Unlike my sisters, I have curly hair, but since we weren't allowed to cut it and no one ever showed me how to take care of it, I usually ended up with a lot of frizz, not to mention five years' worth of dead ends. It didn't help that I wore thick glasses and desperately needed braces, nor that my mother had brainwashed me into thinking I was fat.

When I learned that Sidney had been secretly trimming her hair for years, I wanted to do it too. The only problem was that I had no idea what I was doing, so instead of trimming a few hairs here and there, I accidentally gave myself a thick layer of bangs. And then I couldn't fix it.

When my mother saw my hair, she went ballistic. She waved the scissors in my face as she screamed at me. I had my hands up, trying to protect myself, when Sidney and one of the church ladies came home. They ran to my room to see what all the commotion was about and quickly put two and two together. Sidney told my mother to put the scissors down before she poked my eyes out, but she wasn't listening. She was in a blind rage.

"I should cut it all off and teach you a lesson!" she screamed at me.

I must have been feeling bold that day because I gathered my waist-length hair in my hand and held it right under her nose. "I *dare* you," I said.

My mother stopped screaming, narrowed her eyes, and in one quick motion . . . cut it off. I couldn't believe it. I was obviously baiting her, but in her rage, she didn't stop to think it through. There was a collective gasp as my mother realized what she'd done and worse, that she couldn't take it back. We were all standing there with our mouths hanging open, not sure what to do.

My mother threw the scissors on the dresser and stormed off in a huff, furious that she'd been thwarted. Even worse, there was a witness. One who liked to gossip. She knew we were about to be the center of attention at church, and not in a good way. She also knew she couldn't twist the story and blame everything on me.

After she left, I looked in the mirror. My hair was now shoulder-length and very uneven. I looked down at the ponytail in my hand and Sidney started laughing.

"Dude! I can NOT believe you just did that!"

"I know," I said, still shaking. "I can't believe she actually fell for it." I looked in the mirror at my lopsided hair. "Can you fix it, please? I look stupid."

"With pleasure!"

I was still shaking, but I was proud of myself for standing up to my mother, even though I knew I'd catch shit when my father got home. He'd never let this act of defiance go unpunished. The problem wasn't that I'd defied them; they knew how to deal with that. It was that it couldn't be hidden, and now it was all anyone at church talked about. Mostly, they judged me for being a sinner and a terrible daughter, but that wasn't the point. I'd publicly embarrassed my parents, and that was unacceptable. In our family, you did not air your dirty laundry in public.

The beatings usually started the same way. One of my parents would yell at us; we'd inevitably "backtalk" them, and the fight would escalate from there. My father would come at us in a blind rage, knocking us to the floor, picking us up, and knocking us down again as we do-si-doed down the narrow, mold-infested hallway leading to the back of the house where Sienna and I shared a room.

Once we'd landed on the bed, the belt would come off (if it wasn't off already), and the real beating began. Sienna was the smart one. She'd cry and yell, "No, Daddy!" which was usually enough to make him stop, but Sidney and I were harder to break. Crying wasn't our thing, yet that's exactly what Dad was looking for. He wanted our submission, except now that we were teenagers, we had no intention of giving it to him. The irony is that we inherited that stubbornness from him.

So there we were, doing our usual dance down the hallway, and I don't know what came over me, but I suddenly stopped resisting, stood up, looked my father straight in the eye and said, "You can beat me all you want, but you will NEVER break me."

Oh, man. All the air left the room and time stood absolutely still. At first, Dad looked shocked. He'd never been challenged like that before. Then his face contorted into a mask of rage as he lunged straight for me. I'd never seen him so mad, but I was mad too, and since I was just like him, I knew exactly how to poke that bear.

I was tired of living in fear, and I knew if we weren't afraid of him, he'd no longer have power over us. Of course, for all my bravado, he still had the upper hand.

Sidney watched this scene in horror, powerless to help, as my father hit me over and over again. She screamed at him to stop, and then she grabbed my mother, begging her to intervene. Mother only wrinkled her nose in response.

"Why on earth would I do *that?* She deserves whatever she gets."

"He's going to kill her!"

"And how is that my problem?"

Desperate, Sidney ran upstairs and banged on our neighbors' door. She begged them to help, but they refused, saying they didn't want to get involved. You can't imagine what that does to a person. When you finally find the courage to ask for help and the door is slammed in your face. Everything inside of you dies.

We often talked about going to the police and even threatened our parents, but they told us to go right ahead. My father was a respected man of God, and we were nothing but rebellious teenagers. No one would ever believe us over them.

That didn't stop Sidney, though. The next day she went to the church school (the one we attended for five years) and told our teacher, but she didn't want to get involved, either.

"Why don't you pray on it, Sidney? Your father's a man of God. It can't be *that* bad."

Next, she went to see the pastor. We generally avoided him, but she was desperate. She cried and begged him to help us, but he didn't believe her.

"Sidney, the Bible says *spare the rod, spoil the child.* Your dad is just doing his job. It's God's will that he disciplines you when you're bad. Perhaps you should go home and pray for forgiveness for disobeying your parents in the first place and try to do better next time."

That broke Sidney. She knew then and there that no one was coming to save us. Not now, not ever. No one even cared. Not our parents, not our grandparents, not the church, and certainly not God. Sienna was so traumatized she started talking in her sleep, while Sidney completely shut down.

It was time to take matters into my own hands. I needed to protect my sisters, and the best way to do that was to keep the attention on me. It was easy enough. Whenever Dad got mad, all I had to do was open my mouth and poke the bear, and he'd forget all about them.

Over the next few months, the beatings became more brutal and more frequent, but I wasn't finished. After a lifetime of being silenced, I had finally found my voice, and there was no stopping me. So I took the beatings because I knew I could handle it. In fact, with each beating I became stronger, until I was no longer afraid of him. He could still hurt me physically, but he couldn't break my spirit or my will.

My father did *not* like this new attitude, and he was determined to break me, so during one of our fights, as we did our little dance down the hallway, he picked up the first thing he saw and smacked me with it. It was a hammer, and although it hurt like hell, it also infuriated me.

I ran to my room, and he came charging after me. Sienna screamed, Sidney yelled at him to stop, and Mom did her little clap of glee. He hit me again, and I tried to get away, but there was nowhere to go. I was cornered, so I did the only thing I could. I sat up, threw my shoulders back, and shouted, "DO IT! Do it and make sure you break something this time so I can *finally* show the people at church what a MONSTER you are."

My father was so stunned by my outburst that he froze with the hammer mid-air.

"DO IT!!" I screamed.

That snapped him out of it. He looked at the hammer as if seeing it for the first time, then he looked at me and saw the sheer hatred in my eyes. He dropped the weapon and stormed out with my mother on his heels. I collapsed on the bed as relief flooded my body. My sisters looked shell-shocked. I'm pretty sure I did, too.

"Are you OK?" asked Sienna, tears streaming down her face.

"I'm OK," I said shakily. "A little bruised, but he didn't break anything."

"Holy shit," said Sidney, "I really thought he was going to kill you this time."

"Yah . . . me, too." I said, still shaking.

We both let out a nervous laugh as she sat down on the bed. We were all quiet for a minute, and then Sidney turned to me and raised her hand.

"High five, dude," she said seriously. "That took *balls.*"

It wasn't long before Sidney ran away from home. She couldn't take it anymore.

I think having to watch the abuse and feeling powerless to stop it was worse than receiving it. I'm not saying any of this was my fault, but let's face it, taunting my father only made it worse, and that was my choice. It was my way of fighting back, and while that made me stronger, it had the opposite effect on Sidney.

When we had yet another fight with our parents, who then forced us to go to church so we could listen to a preacher we hated, spew lies about a God we no longer believed in, she reached her limit. My parents went out after church one night, and that's when Sidney made her move. She threw some clothes in a backpack, then came to my room to say goodbye.

"Please don't go," I said desperately. "Don't leave me here by myself."

"I'm sorry, Sage, but I can't do this anymore. If I stay any longer . . ." She didn't finish, and she didn't have to.

"It's OK," I said. I tried to smile, but inside I was dying. The only ally I'd ever known was leaving, and she was never coming back.

"Please don't tell them where I am. No matter how much they ask. If they find me and bring me back, they'll kill me. I can't come back here, Sage. Promise you won't tell."

"I promise."

She hugged me and Sienna tightly, and then she snuck out her bedroom window for the last time.

⁓⁓

My parents interrogated me for weeks, threatening me with everything they had, even though they knew I'd never betray my sister. My mother was so angry she circled the date that Sidney left on the calendar. In big bold letters she wrote *my day of freedom!*

Then she gave all of Sidney's things away before she could come back and get them. As for my father, he laid down the law. I was to come home right after school, there'd be no more skipping church to do homework, and from now on, we were to sit together as a family, whether we liked it or not. It was unbearable, and what made it even worse was seeing how Bailey reacted.

She was only three and didn't understand what was happening. All she knew was that her big sister was gone. She cried for weeks and laid on the couch for months, staring into the void without saying a word. She was in a deep depression, and it was heartbreaking to watch.

As for me, my life was a complete nightmare. Every day, I went to school and listened to Sidney rant about how my parents deserved to suffer. Then I went home and listened to my parents rant about how Sidney was nothing but a sinner. I was getting it from both sides, every day, until I was mentally and emotionally exhausted.

Of course, the good people at church didn't disappoint, either. They were having a field day with this one. For months, I listened to them gossip about my sister. This was a huge scandal, and they milked it for all it was worth. Never for a second did it occur to anyone that Sidney was the victim in all this.

Instead, they judged her. They called her a backslider and a whore while sympathizing with my parents for all of the terrible things she'd put them through. I sat stone-faced through every service, ignoring their stares and their vicious gossip, building a wall around my heart and reinforcing it with my hatred, waiting until it was my turn to leave.

That day came about six months later. I was halfway through the twelfth grade when one of my friends became pregnant. She asked me to be her coach, but the Lamaze classes were on Tuesday nights when we had church. When I asked my mother's permission to skip church, she refused. She didn't want me hanging out with a girl who was obviously "a slut."

I tried reasoning with her, pointing out that it was the Christian thing to do, but she only reminded me that we weren't supposed to fraternize with people outside the church.

"She's a sinner, and we don't associate with people like that!" she said, piously.

"Wasn't it Jesus who protected Mary Magdalene when everyone tried to stone her? Didn't he say, 'Let he who is without sin cast the first stone?' I'm pretty sure the Bible teaches us to be kind to those in need, not to reject them."

My mother did not like that. She kept throwing out condemnation, and

I kept rebutting her with scripture. All those years on the Bible study team were finally paying off. I had memorized entire books of the Bible, and I could out-scripture her any day. Realizing she couldn't win this argument, she changed tactics.

"If you walk out that door on Tuesday night, don't ever come back."

I tilted my head to the side and thought about it for a second. "Deal."

"Hmph! We'll see about that."

When my father got home, he marched straight to my room to confront me. We were arguing and getting wound up, so I knew the beating was coming, but I wasn't in the mood. Besides, I was tired. Old and tired. My father was in the middle of a rant when I looked him in the eye and quietly said, "God, I really hate you."

It was such a simple thing to say and something I'd been feeling for so long, but it was the first time I'd ever said it out loud. It knocked the wind right out of him. He stepped back as if I'd slapped him. He searched my eyes, and what he saw there wasn't anger or a desire to hurt him. It was resignation and truth.

I saw the hurt in his eyes when he realized I meant it. I think he finally saw things clearly that day, and deep down he knew he'd lost his children. My very proud father hung his head as he walked out of my bedroom, a defeated man. I breathed a sigh of relief as I watched him go. It was finally over.

I waited until the weekend to leave. Sidney and her boyfriend came to pick me up. Just before I left, my father called me into the living room and pleaded with me to stay until I graduated from high school. It was too late for that, but I didn't want to be cruel, either. I saw how much Sidney's departure hurt my family, and I didn't want to inflict any more pain.

That's the problem with being an empath. No matter how awful my parents were, I knew that underneath it all, they were suffering too, because I felt it. I felt *everything,* and I was drowning under the weight of it.

"Dad, we both know I can't stay here anymore," I said quietly.

I watched as his shoulders slumped. He knew it, too.

Bailey started crying. "Now I'm losing *all* my sisters!" she wailed.

I knelt down and took her in my arms. "Listen, munchkin. Just because we don't live here anymore doesn't mean we don't love you. I'll always love you."

"That's not true. Sidney left, and now I never see her anymore!" Fresh tears pooled in her eyes, and I thought my heart would break.

"Where will you go?" asked my father.

"I'll be staying with Sidney and her boyfriend at his mother's place. She has an extra bedroom, and she's only charging me a hundred dollars a month. I'll stay there until I graduate, and then I'll find my own place."

My father looked so defeated, but he smiled anyway. "Thank you for telling me that and for letting me know where Sidney is."

I could still hear Bailey crying as I closed the door.

FIVE

September 1994

It was my first day of college, and I was incredibly nervous. The sun was shining; the birds were singing, and my stomach was doing flip flops. I think going to college is harder when you're older. I'd graduated high school just five years prior, yet I felt positively ancient as I walked into my first class and saw a bunch of kids straight out of high school. Even worse, they were all experienced drama majors.

As I stood to the side observing the group, someone came over to say hello. At first I thought she was the teacher, and then I realized she was another student. I breathed a sigh of relief because she was a few years older than me. Her name was Trinity, and unlike me, she didn't look nervous at all.

After high school, I'd realized I had no idea what I wanted to be when I grew up, so I decided to put off college. I'd been sharing an apartment with Sidney and her boyfriend for six months before they'd rudely kicked me out. I imagine it's because he tried to kiss me on my eighteenth birthday and then he needed me gone before I could tell my sister. Sidney and I had barely spoken since. In fact, she barely spoke to any of us. Once she left home, she never looked back.

Shortly after that, I moved to Italy for a little over a year. I was offered a job as a nanny, and I jumped at the opportunity. I worked for an extremely wealthy family who treated me terribly, yet for some reason I stayed. Probably because adversity is all I've ever known, and besides, I'm not a quitter. Gen X never quits.

Despite working for the family from hell, I loved my time in Italy. It was my first trip overseas, and I met some amazing people while I was there. The experiences I gained taught me a lot about the world and my place in it. It also ignited a passion for traveling, and I promised myself that one day, I'd see the entire world.

Somehow, I've managed to take a vacation every year since then, although it was always on a budget and was often a simple road trip. My friends couldn't understand how a waitress could afford these vacations, but I've been working since I was eight, and I know how to save money. I had to work two jobs in high school just so I could survive, and with the help of a student loan, my part-time waitressing job would get me through college.

It was actually my colleagues who first convinced me to audition for the two-year theater program. I resisted at first because I've never acted before, but they reminded me how much I love the theater and how good I am at impersonating people. I can sing, dance, and I'm great with accents. They made a strong argument. I figured it couldn't hurt to apply, except the auditions were taking place while I was on vacation in England and Scotland. Luckily, one of the teachers let me audition a week early, and now, here I was.

I remember walking into the green room after class on that first morning and feeling so intimidated by all the pretty young girls. They giggled as they flirted with the boys in some weird first-day-of-school mating ritual that made me want to gag. I wasn't interested in romance because I had far too many responsibilities, and I couldn't afford the distraction . . . and then I saw him. Jamie Montgomery—a second-year student who was quietly observing the scene from the back of the room.

When I first laid eyes on him, my heart actually stopped beating. He was positively the hottest man I'd ever seen. He ticked all my boxes: tall, dark, handsome, mysterious, smothering eyes, and when he smiled and two giant dimples appeared . . . that was the end of me. I was smitten.

I stood there staring at him like an idiot. And then my Greek God did something—I don't know—he flicked his hair or something. Whatever it was, it was subtle, but it was arrogant. He was hot, and he knew it. And just like that, I was over it. I'd never liked arrogant people. Besides, he was too young for me, and his eyes were currently on the blonde hippie in the center of the room. In fact, everyone's eyes were on Heather, and she loved the attention.

The theater program was intense, and although I'd taken out a student loan, I still had to work to cover my living expenses, which meant I didn't have a lot of time to socialize outside of school. We had long days and lots of homework, and I couldn't understand how the other students found time to party. Then again, they had years of experience, while I was desperately trying to catch up.

My younger sister Sienna and I were currently sharing an apartment, and she was a big help when it came to running my lines or reciting a monologue. We lost touch after I left home, but I went to see her just before school started, and when I saw the crowd she was hanging out with, I asked if she wanted to move in with me instead. I was pleased when she said yes because her friends looked like trouble, and I was pretty sure she was waiting for someone to rescue her. We found an apartment close to the college, and so far everything was going well.

The acting program had two teachers, Charlene and Tom, who each treated me differently. Tom was encouraging and told me my age was actually an advantage because I had life experiences that couldn't be faked. It's hard to tap into emotions like pain, anger, and fear when you've never felt them before. I knew these emotions all too well.

Tom was an older gentleman in his late fifties who was kind, gentle, and patient. He never made me feel like I didn't belong—unlike Charlene, the senior teacher. She was a nice lady, but she clearly didn't think I could act, so she critiqued me extra hard, which embarrassed me in front of the other students. On the outside, I was a tough cookie, but on the inside, I was extremely insecure. My mother's voice was always in my head, telling me I wasn't good enough.

When you're in a theater program, you get to know each other very well. Not only did we spend twelve hours a day together, but we spent most of those hours critiquing each other. Sometimes the teacher critiqued us in front of the class; sometimes we were in pairs critiquing each other, and sometimes it was a free-for-all, with the entire class weighing in on your performance.

As you can imagine, it can be a little overwhelming, which is why we had a strict rule: keep it constructive or keep it to yourself. There's a big difference between critiquing and criticizing. The teachers reminded us to be sensitive. "Know when to stop" was their favorite mantra.

For the most part, the critiques didn't bother me because I knew I had the most to learn, and if I took my ego out of the equation, they were a valuable tool. Besides, I'd been criticized my entire life. It was the only way my parents knew how to communicate.

At the end of the first semester, when Charlene gave us our final movement project, I was determined to impress her. For months we'd been learning how to *be a cloud* or *act like a triangle*, but this was different, and I knew I could create something amazing.

We were instructed to take an experience from our lives and turn it into a movement piece. I loved this assignment. It reminded me of dancing, and for once I felt like I had the upper hand. I worked on this project day and night, and I was really proud of it. The music I chose was a haunting instrumental from *Interview With The Vampire*. It was full of intrigue, its pace changing as it unfolded. It was perfect for what I had in mind.

Through movement, I told the story of a little girl who wanted to be a ballerina. It started off light, playful, and full of innocence. Then the music changed. It became dark and threatening. The child suddenly entered a terrifying new world, fighting off demons until finally freeing herself and coming out the other side, no longer a child. It was personal, honest, and powerful, and it left me feeling vulnerable and exposed. It was everything Charlene loved.

On performance day, we gathered in the classroom and sat in the bleachers at the back of the room. We were excited, and everyone chatted amiably. Although the performances were only five minutes long, they were a huge part of our grade, so a lot was riding on this. Our classroom was quite large, so we dimmed the lights at the far end, creating a kind of stage at the front of the room.

Everyone did a great job, and Charlene was very proud. I was the last one to perform, and I poured my heart into my performance, moving through my childhood nightmares, leaving everything on the stage. It was the best thing I ever did, and when it was over, the room was completely silent. You could hear a pin drop.

At first, I was worried when nobody clapped. Had I bombed? Then I looked up and saw a few tears in my classmates' eyes. I gave a sigh of relief and allowed myself a little smile. I was proud of myself . . . until Charlene gave her critique. She ripped my performance apart. My emotions were still raw, yet there she was criticizing me in front of everyone *again*. She seemed to forget every rule about knowing when to stop, and for the first time, I thought she was being unfair. Her critique felt personal.

I was devastated, humiliated, and angry. She was so hard on me that the other students started shifting in their seats uncomfortably, yet I refused to flinch. I looked her straight in the eye and gave nothing away. When she finished I simply asked, "Anything else?"

"Well . . . yes," she said, and continued critiquing me until Trinity interrupted and said it was enough. She looked surprised by that.

"Is it *enough,* Sage?" she challenged me.

"Not at all. Please continue," I said sarcastically, and she did. I was so angry I was shaking. It was all I could do to hold back the tears. I had started off my day so excited, and now all I wanted to do was hide. I bolted from the room as soon as the class was over. I would not give her the satisfaction of seeing me cry.

When I emerged from the bathroom, some of my classmates were waiting for me. Trinity gave me a hug, and Heather asked if I was OK. I was embarrassed that I'd let Charlene get to me the way she did. As actors, we needed to be tough. Rejection is a huge part of the job.

"Sage, your movement piece was so beautiful!" said Trinity.

"Thank you, but you don't have to say that. It obviously wasn't."

"Are you kidding? I bawled my eyes out. It was so moving! Everybody thought so."

"Thanks. I worked really hard on it."

"I know you did, and it showed! I was *furious* with Charlene for what she said to you. She would never have spoken to anyone else like that. She gave everyone high praise today except *you!* And it's not the first time, either."

I was stunned, and touched. "Thanks, Trinity. I really needed to hear that."

"We were mortified by the way she kept going on and on. I mean, we all know Charlene's reputation, but that doesn't make it right."

"What reputation?" I asked, confused.

"Every year, Charlene chooses one student who's her favorite and one . . . who's not. Mark is obviously her favorite, and you are the one she picks on."

"I see," I said, processing this information. "That explains a lot, but how do you know this?"

"She's done it for years, but she took it too far this time, so I went up to her after class and told her off."

"You didn't! What did she say?"

"Get this. Apparently, she's pissed off that Pam let you into the program even though you didn't go through the full audition process. She said it wasn't fair, and if it had been up to her, you would never have gotten in."

"She might have a point."

"No, she doesn't. She's just mad that she didn't get to approve of you herself. Pam's the one who fought for you. She said even though you lacked experience, she saw a raw talent, and it was their job to mold you into something great. Pam overruled Charlene right before she quit, and now Charlene's holding a grudge."

"I see. How am I the last one to know this?"

"Because you never hang out with us after school," she said, punching me in the arm.

Things really changed for me that day. Not between Charlene and me, but with the other students. After four months, I finally realized they weren't judging me for not being good enough. They actually had my back. So I let down my guard, and we became friends, especially Trinity and me.

Charlene continued to be harder on me than the other students, but I refused to let it get to me. The way I saw it, her critiques were hard, but they were honest, and by having a magnifying glass held up to my every move, I was getting better.

It would have been easy to ignore her, but I wasn't built that way. Adversity only made me stronger, so I took every criticism and learned from it. I was glad I wasn't her favorite because he could do no wrong, and he'd probably end up being the exact same actor he'd been when the program began. The girls were angry that Charlene picked on me, but I saw the value in it. Because of her, I was a better actor.

SIX

March 1982

When I was little, I wanted to be a ballerina more than anything in the world. I know a lot of girls say this, but I *really* wanted to be a ballerina. My mother enrolled us in all kinds of classes hoping that one day we'd become rich and famous and support her for the rest of her life. My sisters and I took tap, jazz, ballet, piano, gymnastics, and swimming lessons. We were busy children.

My dancing career started when I was three years old. Sidney took ballet, and my mom and I used to watch from the back of the class. How I envied those girls, prancing around in their pink tutus and satin slippers. I wanted to be just like them.

Sidney would practice her lessons when we got home, but she wasn't very good, so I'd have to show her how to do it. This amused my mother (not so much my sister) until one day she realized I knew what I was doing. The next time we went to class, she pulled the teacher aside and asked if I could join.

"She's a little young, don't you think?" asked the teacher.

"True, but you should see her dance. She's learned everything you've taught so far, and she's really good. Could you let her participate in one class to see if you agree? She's been begging me for weeks!"

The teacher took one look at my big, brown, pleading eyes and relented.

I was ecstatic and ran over to join the other girls. When the class was over, the teacher approached my mother.

"You're right. She's a natural. If you lie about her age on the application next semester, I'll look the other way. In the meantime, keep bringing her to class."

And so it began—my life as a dancer.

I loved all my dance classes, but ballet was my favorite. By the time I was ten, I was the youngest person in my class. I was proud of this fact, and so was my mother. She really went to bat for me, and now here I was, her little *prima donna*.

I had several teachers over the years, but the one I remember most was this old-school Russian lady who never smiled. She used to walk around the studio with a long wooden ruler, smacking it methodically against her palm, eagle eyes watching, daring us to make a mistake.

Whack! on your butt if you weren't standing straight. Tap, tap, tap, if your arms weren't high enough. She was strict, and she expected nothing less than perfection.

This probably scared the crap out of the rest of the class, but my mother beat us with wooden spoons on a regular basis, so it felt just like home to me. I don't know how many years I was with that teacher, but I was the only student who never got smacked, because I (hair flip) was perfect. If she said "first position!" I stood in first position. If she said "plié," I did a perfect plié. When she said "jump!" I leapt across the room. Ballet made sense to me.

My favorite part always came at the end. The teacher would put on a piece of music and instruct us to dance however we wanted. Most of the girls were intimidated by this sudden lack of structure, but not me. I'd close my eyes, listen to the rhythm of the music . . . and soar.

One weekend in April, when I was ten years old, my teacher pulled my mother aside.

"Mrs. Petrovic, I'd like to talk to you about Sage."

"Why? Has she done something wrong?" my mother asked sternly, mentally locating the wooden spoon.

"Oh no, it's nothing like that! It's a pleasure having Sage in my class. She's an *exceptional* dancer. In fact, that's what I wanted to talk to you about. The Russian Ballet is coming to town next week. They're auditioning children for *The Nutcracker*, and I think Sage should go. She has an excellent chance of landing a part, and this would be a huge opportunity for her. She'd get to learn from the best."

My mother raised an eyebrow. "Isn't she a little young to be traipsing around the world with a Russian ballet company?"

"Not at all. Children do it all the time."

"And you honestly think she's good enough?"

"Listen, Sage has a gift. I'm convinced she has the skills to be a professional ballerina. She's the youngest person in her class, yet she puts the other students to shame. Next year, she's getting her pointe shoes, and she's only ten! You should be proud of her. Every teacher dreams of having a student like her in their lifetime. Mrs. Petrovic, I'm not giving you false hope here. I'm telling you that Sage is the real deal. You must audition her for the Russian ballet."

I was bursting with excitement when I heard the news. The *Russian Ballet?* There's no higher goal for a ballerina! Even Sidney was happy for me.

"Way to go, sis. I always knew you had it in you. Maybe one day you'll make enough money to get us out of here."

I pictured myself on the stage in a pink tutu, dancing in front of the whole world. I just knew I'd get the part. It was my destiny. I'd rehearsed every day since I was three years old, and this was my chance to shine. I was going to be a famous ballerina. I could feel it in my bones.

That weekend, my parents threw a dinner party and everybody got drunk. After the guests left, my parents had a fight, and Mom locked Dad out of the house. He pounded on the door, but she wouldn't let him in. He started yelling, but she ignored him. Eventually, he broke down the door, stormed upstairs, and the fight continued. I was oblivious as I laid in my bed dreaming about *The Nutcracker.*

The next morning, they called a repairman and told us it was an accident, except Sidney had heard the whole thing and knew they were lying. She was sure divorce was imminent, and we worried that we'd get stuck with our mother if that happened. She was known for holding a grudge.

I was sitting at the kitchen table, dreaming about the ballet, when somebody knocked on the door. It was the church people, so I went and got my mother. They'd been knocking on our door every Saturday for years, trying to convince my parents to go church. My sisters and I had been attending Sunday school for two years, and we really liked it. So did my parents because the church was neither Catholic nor Orthodox and they thought it was a good compromise. They also loved getting rid of us for a couple of hours every Sunday morning.

My mother was at the door for a long time, and when she came back, she told my father about the Easter play and said she wanted to go. When we overheard their conversation, we *begged* them to come and see the play. Not because we were religious but because we wanted to collect the prize for bringing them. Our teacher promised us a prize if we brought our parents that year.

We couldn't believe it when they actually said yes. We'd been asking them to come to Sunday school for almost two years, and they'd always said no. Little did we know that this was a day we'd regret for the rest of our lives.

The next morning, we dressed in our Sunday best and went to church as a family. The classes were separated by age, so while we ended up in the basement with the rest of the kids, our parents were ushered into the main hall.

What we didn't expect that day, what we couldn't have possibly known, was how much our parents would love church. We kind of expected it to be a one-time thing. You know, so we could get the prize, which ended up being a chocolate bar.

The church people were quick to welcome my parents and made a big fuss over them, which made them feel very special. They were moved by the play, the songs, the sermon, and as they watched Jesus die on the cross . . . that was it. They were converted right then and there.

It was the answer to all their problems, exactly what they were looking for. They talked about it all the way home, and we couldn't believe it when they said we were going back that night. Twice in one day?

It was quite a big church, with high vaulted ceilings, red carpets, row after row of pews, a massive pipe organ behind the pulpit, and beautiful stained-glass windows. There were at least two hundred people in attendance, and I noticed all the women were wearing skirts or dresses, and they all had long hair.

Some of them wore hats, but most of them wore lace doilies on their heads. They were completely devoid of makeup, jewelry, or any kind of fashion sense for that matter. It felt like we had walked into an episode of *The Twilight Zone*. Funny that I never noticed that before. Probably because I was surrounded by my friends. Now that they were gone, church suddenly felt weird, and it made me uneasy.

The evening service was different from what we were used to. As we sat with our parents, we were surprised by the attention they received. Everyone kept hugging them and calling them "Brother" and "Sister," as if they'd known them for years. Sidney and I watched with a fair amount of trepidation. Sunday school was one thing, but this was different.

The service began with prayers and music. There was even a choir. They were clapping and jumping while they sang, and as I looked around, I noticed people had their eyes closed and their arms raised in the air. When the singing was over, we bowed our heads while the pastor prayed, and then he started his sermon.

He was loud and kept shouting as he preached, but the congregation loved it. They shouted back at him with words like "Amen!" "Preach it Brother!" and "Hallelujah Jesus!" When the sermon was over, they started praying again. I leaned over and whispered to Sidney.

"Holy cow, these people pray a LOT."

"It's even worse than Sunday school," she whispered back.

We were hoping this meant the service was over, but things were just getting started. Everyone was praying, shouting, and crying. Then people started dancing in the aisles and falling on the floor. I'd never seen anything like it. The woman in front of me started "speaking in tongues," then everyone around her joined in. How did they all know this strange language?

The pastor came over and started talking to our parents while people gathered around. He asked if they were ready to let Jesus into their hearts, and my parents said yes. He started praying, as he put his hands on their heads. He was shouting at God to forgive their sins while pushing their foreheads like he was trying to shake the sins right out of them. My parents were crying and praying right along with everyone else.

Sienna, Sidney, and I were dumbfounded, and something told us things would never be the same after this. We were right. It happened the following Tuesday when we went to church *again.* The sermon wasn't nearly as exciting as the last one, but my parents didn't seem to mind. They were hanging onto every word. When the service was over, the pastor called them into his office, and they stayed there for almost an hour. We couldn't imagine what was taking so long, but we were about to find out.

My parents were sitting in the front seat while the three of us sat in the back on the drive home. My father, who was in a really good mood, started to speak.

"Listen girls, now that we're Christians, we'll be making a lot of changes around here."

I looked at Sidney. "We're Christians?" I whispered. She rolled her eyes.

"First of all, we'll be going to church a lot more often. Tuesday night is Bible study. Friday is youth service. Saturday is prayer service, and there are two services on Sunday. We'll be attending all of them from now on."

"You've *got* to be kidding," said Sidney, ever the lippy one.

"I assure you I'm quite serious. And that's not all. The pastor has given us a list of rules, and I expect you to follow them."

"That's right," said my mother. "And step one is getting rid of our television."

"What?" the three of us shouted in unison. Were they crazy?

"Why?" I asked.

"Because it's a *sin*, and since these rules come straight from the Bible, I don't want to hear any complaining," my mother snapped. I never once saw my parents read the Bible, yet suddenly they were experts.

"And that's not all. Tomorrow we need to go through your clothes and give away everything that's inappropriate. Girls are to look like girls, so you can't wear pants or shorts anymore. From now on you're only allowed to wear skirts that go below your knees, shirts with a high collar, and your sleeves need to be below your elbows."

Sidney exploded. This was too much for her. "You can't be serious!"

"Silence!" bellowed my father. "You will obey the commandments of God, and you will *like* it. We all have to make changes, so stop whining. Alcohol is no longer permitted nor is swearing or wearing makeup or jewelry, and women are not allowed to cut their hair."

Not allowed to cut our hair? Gross. Is that why all those women had long hair? I looked at my mother's stylish red hair. *It's not going to look like that for long*, I thought. And I couldn't imagine a world where my parents didn't drink. They loved drinking, especially an expensive bottle of wine.

"We're going to look like freaks!" Sidney complained.

"I don't care," said my father. Easy for him to say. Most of the rules were designed to make *women* look like freaks, while the only rule for men was that they had to be clean-shaven. Woopty-freaking-do.

"What about swimming?" I asked, thinking about our lessons.

"You'll have to go in your clothes from now on."

"That's impossible!"

"Then I guess there's no more swimming."

"What about when we play sports or ride a bike?"

"You'll have to do it in a skirt."

As I tried to wrap my brain around these new rules, my mother continued, "You also have to get rid of your heathen music because we're only allowed to listen to Christian music from now on. Oh, and one more thing: There will be no more dancing, so you're dropping all of your classes."

"WHAT?" I practically leapt out of my seat. I couldn't imagine a world without dancing. "But I have my audition with the Russian Ballet next week!"

My mother smirked. "You're not going. Dancing is a *sin*. It says so in the Bible."

"But I *love* dancing!" I wailed. "I've been doing it my whole life! It's my dream to be a ballerina! You know this!" I'd thought it was her dream, too. What was happening? Would they really take dancing away from me?

"Oh, please. You're ten," said my mother. "What do you know about dreams? Do you think it was my dream to get stuck raising kids? Hardly. I wanted to be a model, yet here we are."

"But Mom . . ." I said as tears pooled in my eyes.

My mother whipped around in her seat. "Do you want to spend all eternity in Hell?"

I reeled back in shock. "What? No."

"That's *exactly* where you'll go if you don't obey me! The Bible says RESPECT your parents and OBEY them. If you don't obey me, you'll spend all eternity burning in the fiery pits of Hell. Try imagining that," she said as she glared at me. "It's the worst pain imaginable, and it *never* ends. They have a special place for disobedient children, too."

Sienna whimpered beside me. She was only seven, and my mother was scaring her. Heck, she was scaring me, yet this was only the beginning. Fear was about to become our whole life.

"They were dancing at the church tonight," said Sidney, ever the defiant one.

"That's different. They were dancing for God."

"Maybe Sage could dance for God."

"Don't get cute," my father warned. "This isn't a joke."

It most certainly wasn't. I had nightmares that night about spending eternity in Hell. I was petrified. We all were. In an instant, our lives were turned upside down, and in place of music, dancing, and laughter, we now had darkness, fire, and brimstone. Not to mention rules that were impossible to follow.

That was the day my sisters and I stopped being children. It was no longer allowed, just like everything else. And there were more rules too; no sex before marriage, no drugs, no homosexuality, no talking back to our parents, and no friends outside of the church. My parents were completely brainwashed, and it was all our fault. We had sold our souls for a bar of chocolate.

Things got even worse when we went back to school. My parents called the principal and told him that due to our religious beliefs, we were no longer allowed to wear shorts in gym class. The principal said it wouldn't be safe to do sports in a skirt, so they took us out of gym class altogether.

It was bad enough that we were suddenly wearing odd clothing, but missing a class drew attention, and soon the entire school was talking about it. Just like that, we were no longer the cool kids but the "church freaks" that everybody made fun of.

It was even worse for Sidney. She was eleven, and the kids in middle school were cruel. They bullied her and made fun of her new clothes. She went from being super popular to not having any friends at all, and every day she came home crying.

My parents ended up pulling her out of school two months early. As for me, I had to quit the soccer team, the last of my activities from my old life. We went from being the most active children in the world to nothing. No activities . . . no dancing . . . no friends . . . no television.

My mother said we'd better stop eating now that we weren't exercising. "I wouldn't want you girls getting fat! Lord knows you weren't blessed with my figure." Ruining our lives wasn't enough for my mother. She had to mock us, too. This was nothing but another game to her—only this time, my father was in on it.

A few weeks later, Dad came home and told us he was starting a new carpet cleaning business. He'd quit his maitre d' job at the restaurant.

"But Dad, you love that job," said Sidney.

"I can no longer work in a place where people drink alcohol," he said piously.

A few weeks later, the stock market crashed and so did the economy. It got so bad my parents had to declare bankruptcy. First they took our car, then they took our townhouse. I remember the day they came to our home and took everything of value. I can't tell you what it felt like having strangers walk into our house and take whatever they wanted. Sidney cried when they took the piano, and my mother cried when they took the gold clock my father had given her on their wedding day.

We had nothing left by the end of the day. We lost our friends, our school, the house, the car, Dad's job, ballet, our freedom, our youth, and now our possessions. In just a few short months, our lives completely changed.

In September, the brainwashing got even worse when we were forced to attend the two-classroom school run by the church. And with that, our separation and isolation was complete.

SEVEN

January 1995

During the Christmas break, Sienna and I took a cruise to the Caribbean. When we got back, I got braces on my teeth, something we couldn't afford when I was younger. You didn't see a lot of adults with braces in those days, but as an entertainer, I knew nice teeth were important. I talked to my teacher Tom before making the decision, and he agreed.

"Look at it this way, Sage. By the time you start auditioning for roles, you'll be ready. It's a smart move, and it shows you're committed."

"Thanks, Tom. You always say the right thing. You're like the super nice dad I never had."

"You never had a dad?"

"I did, but he wasn't nice."

When school started up again, there was a fair amount of drama going on (pun intended). Apparently, Jamie (who had a girlfriend outside the program) was having an affair with Heather (who had a boyfriend inside the program), and now everyone knew about it because Heather's boyfriend had found out, and he was furious.

I shook my head when I heard the news. Rookie mistake. Never shit where you eat, as the saying goes. I was in the bathroom when I overheard the girls talking about it. Heather was holding court while everyone else listened.

"The asshole has a girlfriend, and he *cheated* on her! Can you believe it?"

"Umm . . . I'm sorry, but don't you have a boyfriend?" I asked as I washed my hands.

"Yes, but that's different. We were drunk, and he seduced me."

"Honey, you're not a child, and it takes two to tango. The way I see it, you both cheated."

She made a pouty face. "Why are you taking his side?"

"I'm not. All I'm saying is I fail to see how it's his fault, when you're both to blame."

Apparently, I was the only one who understood this concept, because by the end of the day everybody hated Jamie, except me.

When I passed him in the hall a few days later, looking dejected, I decided to check in on him. I knew what it felt like to be on the outs, and I thought everyone was being unfair. Heather talked non-stop about what a scumbag he was, and both classes had turned against him. He was painted as the villain in this tragic tale.

"Hi," I said as I sat down. "Whatcha doing out here all by yourself?"

"In case you haven't heard, I'm persona non grata around here."

"Ah yes . . . Heather. She's being quite a bitch about the whole thing, isn't she?"

"What? You mean you don't hate me like everybody else?"

"No. I don't condone what you did, but like I told Heather, it takes two to tango."

He studied me for a minute, confused by my words. "I thought you were her friend."

"I am her friend, but that doesn't mean she's right. It's fairly obvious she's only trying to destroy you in order to take the heat off herself. And it seems to be working."

"Hunh. I never thought of it like that. That's rather perceptive of you."

"Yeah, perception is kind of my thing. Unless it's my own crap. Then I'm clueless."

He laughed, and it was good to see him smile. It brought out his dimples, which were positively adorable. I could see why the girls threw themselves at him, especially when he showed his vulnerable side, like now.

"Don't let her get to you, Jamie. She can call you all the names she wants. It doesn't make it true."

"Thank you, Sage. I really needed to hear that. You're a good person."

"I know," I said, grinning and tossing my hair. Much to my delight, he burst out laughing. I liked talking to Jamie. He was like a lost puppy looking for a friend. A really handsome puppy.

As we got up to leave, he turned to look at me. "Why haven't we ever talked before?"

"Because you were too busy chasing tail to notice me?"

"Ha! Are you always this honest?"

"Yes. My sisters call it a character flaw."

"Well, I like it. It's refreshing." He was quiet for a beat. "I'm kind of a jerk, aren't I?"

I shrugged. "You're not a jerk, you're just arrogant."

From that day forward, Jamie and I were the best of friends. We were an odd pair, but it didn't matter. We made each other laugh, and he was fascinated by my stories about Italy, London, Scotland, and New York. I was only twenty-six, but I had already lived a lifetime, and he looked up to me. In fact, he started asking my opinion on a variety of subjects, especially when it came to girls.

It was nice having someone to share my stories with, and there was almost a reverence on his face when I spoke. Maybe because I was three years older than him. Whatever it was, I liked having the attention of such a handsome young man. It was an ego boost that I sorely needed, and I was sad that he'd be graduating soon.

People wondered if Jamie and I were sleeping together, but it wasn't like that. He was too young for me, far too cocky, and he was a cheater, so our relationship could never be romantic, yet I loved having him as a friend, and I knew he felt the same way.

Every semester, the theater department put on two plays. Tom directed one, and Charlene directed the other. The first semester I wasn't cast in either show, so I ended up being Charlene's assistant, and I actually enjoyed it. Since I'd never been in a play before, I found it educational to see it from the directors' perspective. In fact, I think I learned far more than I would have if I had been on the stage.

The second semester, I had a small part in Tom's play, and by the third semester, I was given a part in Charlene's. *Ten Lost Years* is a series of monologues about The Great Depression. It's the most boring play I've ever seen, but at least I got a part. My family came to see it, as did Jamie, and when it was over, Sienna said, "Well that's two hours of my life I'm never getting back," which pretty much summed it up.

Sienna was invaluable while I was in college. Not only did she help me run my lines, but when I had jaw surgery as part of the whole braces-as-an-adult experience, she nursed me back to health. The surgery was awful. It felt like someone had taken a hammer to my face, probably because they had. For six weeks my jaw was wired shut, which made acting and eating difficult. Sienna went above and beyond to help me out. I never could have done it without her.

For the final semester, the teachers hired professional directors to help prepare us for the real world. We auditioned for both shows, and for once I had a chance of getting cast without Charlene interfering. The show I wanted most was *Steel Magnolias.* The cast consisted of six women who were all strong, fabulous characters.

Although my heart was set on playing M'Lynn, I didn't get the part. I got cast as Truvy instead and ended up falling in love with her bubbly, witty character. From the very first reading, we were excited about the play. There was comedy, tragedy, southern accents, big hair, and lifelong friendships all rolled into one brilliantly written script. And since all the scenes took place in Truvy's Hair Salon, I was in practically every one of them.

We were brimming with excitement on opening night. My friends and family were in the audience, as were the teachers, directors, and the local press. Not only was it opening night, but this was our final performance before we graduated, making it a bittersweet experience.

I was surprised that my parents came since I was fairly certain the church didn't allow them to see plays. Bailey, who was now eleven, called to say they'd be there. I hadn't seen much of them since leaving home seven years ago. They called every couple of months and dropped by a few times a year, but mostly, I avoided them.

Sometimes we'd spend Christmas together, and Bailey would be so excited to see her sisters, whom she missed dearly. I generally had to bite my tongue at these gatherings because my mother was still my mother, whereas my father was just happy to have his girls together again. Yup, that was us. One big happy family.

Sidney still wanted nothing to do with my parents, so she never came. She and her boyfriend got married when she was twenty, and they had two beautiful children. Since her husband didn't work, she had to hold down two jobs just to support them. I still didn't see her very often, but every once in a while, she'd ask me to babysit. I wouldn't say we were close, but at least we weren't fighting anymore.

The play went off beautifully, and it was music to my ears when the audience laughed and cried in all the right places. They even gave us a standing ovation. What a beautiful sight that was! Jamie and Sienna were waiting in the vestibule when it was over.

"Oh, my God. That was *so* much better than the last piece of crap you made me watch," Sienna said as I laughed. She ran the lines with me so many times she probably knew them by heart. She's also not big on compliments, so that was pretty expressive for her.

"Well done, Sage. You were really great tonight," said Jamie as he hugged me.

When Charlene saw us, she rushed over with a big smile on her face. She gave me a hug, which surprised me. "Listen, I just want to say that that was the best show Douglas College has ever put on, and you were positively *magnificent* as Truvy. I laughed and cried throughout the entire performance. I've never been so proud," she said, sincerely.

I didn't know what to say. After two years of nothing but hard critiques from this woman, I had finally earned her praise. I beamed from ear to ear.

"Thank you, Charlene. That means a lot coming from you."

"You're welcome. You earned it. I mean it. You were perfect tonight."

Trinity was standing nearby, and she turned to listen. After Charlene left, she looked at me and raised her eyebrows. "Did Charlene just say you were amazing?"

"Yup," I said, still grinning.

"Wow. It's about time!"

"And . . . my work here is done," I said, taking an elaborate bow.

EIGHT

After graduation, Sienna and I moved to an apartment in the west end of Vancouver, and Jamie became a permanent fixture in our lives. I worked two jobs that summer in order to pay off my student loans, but in my free time, we'd go to the beach, play volleyball, rollerblade, or walk the seawall around Stanley Park—anything that kept me outdoors and in touch with nature.

That's what I love about this city. There's no need to have a car because whenever I need to escape, the ocean and forest are right there. It was a good thing, too, because I had neither a car nor a driver's license, which sounds odd, but it never really interested me.

In the winter when it turned cold and rainy, which is typical of Vancouver, we'd throw great big dinner parties, go clubbing with my gay friends (who drooled over Jamie and berated me for not sleeping with him), or we'd simply stay inside and cuddle while watching movies.

Although I wasn't in love with Jamie (once a cheater, always a cheater), I absolutely adored him, and I was devastated when he told me he was moving to Australia for an entire year. The irony is that the only reason he was going was because of me. After listening to my travel stories for the past two years, he was ready to make his own. He asked if I wanted to go with him, but the travel visa was for people under twenty-five, and I was already twenty-six. I'd miss him like crazy; that was for sure.

It was the middle of October, and we were carving pumpkins when Jamie asked if he could bring a girl the next time he came over. He had never asked that before, so I figured she must be special.

"Listen, she's really out there. She's one of these New Age people and comes off a little flaky at first, but the more I listen to her, the more she makes sense. She calls herself a 'white witch,' and she has these . . . gifts."

"Really?" I said dubiously.

"Yes. She's into things like astrology, numerology, and tarot cards."

"And you want to know if she's full of shit or not?"

"Exactly. You have a great bullshit detector."

"That I do. Why don't you bring her over on Friday? I'll make dinner."

"Great. I'll invite my friend Luka as well. I'd love for you to meet him before I leave. He's the Serbian one that I went to high school with."

"Oh yes, I remember you talking about him. Wait, you're not trying to set me up, I hope."

"Why not? You haven't dated anyone since I met you."

He wasn't wrong about that. In fact, I'd never dated anyone at all. I was twenty-six and I'd never been on a date. It wasn't by choice, though; it was just that men never showed any interest in me, which only furthered my belief that I wasn't pretty or desirable. Gay men loved me to death and fawned over how gorgeous I was, but straight men never did.

When I first left home, I had a series of one night stands that left me feeling used and unsatisfied, so I created rules for myself. I never slept with anyone I worked with or anyone who lived close to home. That way, if it went south (and it always did), I wouldn't have to face them.

The affairs I had on vacation were safe because they were short-lived. This way, I could still have fun without any emotions getting in the way—meaning mine. So far it seemed to be working, except deep down inside, I wanted someone to love me more than anything in the world.

The *me* I presented to the world was strong and carefree. The only thing she cared about was having a career and traveling the world. But my inner child, the one who'd never known love—she desperately wanted someone, anyone, to notice her. I wasn't about to admit that, though.

"I'm not interested in dating. Men are nothing but trouble and heartbreak, and I've had enough of both. Besides, I want a career, and dating only gets in the way."

"What about sex? Don't you miss it?"

"I don't need a boyfriend to have sex. Why do you think I take a vacation twice a year? Besides, when was the last time you saw someone hit on me? I'm not exactly popular with men, in case you haven't noticed."

"That's because they're afraid of you. You're so confident and independent. You know exactly what you want, and you make no apologies. It's a little intimidating, you know."

I scoffed. "It amazes me that men are both attracted to and afraid of confident women. No matter what I do, I can't win. The way I see it, I'm not the problem. Men are."

He laughed. "True that. Anyways, I'm not setting you up, and if I was, it wouldn't be with him. He sleeps around a lot."

"Ha!" I snorted.

He was one to talk. Jamie slept with everything that walked, and he didn't even have to try. Girls practically threw themselves at him. It was disgusting. He had no idea what it felt like to be ignored by the opposite sex. Whatever girl he wanted, he got her.

When Friday rolled around, Jamie and Lilith were the first to arrive, and I have to say I found her quite fascinating. Jamie was right. She was definitely out there, yet it was impossible not to fall under her spell. When I greeted them at the door, she threw her arms around me like we were the best of friends, and then she strolled into my apartment like she owned the place. She was dressed in jeans and a flowery top that suited her petite figure. She oozed confidence, and I liked that about her.

She had a bubbly, animated personality, and although she said some strange woo-woo things that didn't always make sense, she made no apology for her beliefs, and I admired her for that. She loved to talk and dominated the conversation, but not in a bad way. It's more like we were hanging off her every word because she was so out there.

I never met anyone with "gifts" before, and until that moment I'm not sure I believed in them, but after spending an hour with Lilith, I knew she wasn't making it up. For so long, I'd been bitter about church and tended to avoid any conversation about religion, but that night, I learned the difference between *Christianity* and *spirituality*.

When Luka arrived and I opened the door, something unusual happened. The moment I saw him, I felt a jolt of electricity right in my chest. The impact was so strong I actually took a step back. It's hard to explain, but something about him was so familiar.

He was incredibly handsome and well dressed, which is something I've always appreciated in a man. Whereas Jamie was wearing jeans and a white t-shirt (his usual garb), Luka was dressed in black pants and a stylish shirt. He was approximately five foot eight, with thick, dark, wavy hair, olive skin, and the most sensuous lips I'd ever seen.

"This is going to sound strange, but have we met before?" he asked, as he removed his shoes. Even his voice was beautiful.

"I was just thinking the same thing. You seem so familiar."

After dinner, we sat in the living room smoking pot and drinking wine. Sienna had just come home, and she and I were sitting on the futon while Jamie and Luka sat on the floor. Lilith was in the armchair next to me. We were having a wonderful time, and I was so pleased that Jamie had arranged this little get together. We laughed and joked like we'd known each other for years.

"I don't believe for one second that men and women can be friends," said Luka. "Sex always gets in the way. At some point, you're bound to sleep together. It's just the way it is."

"That's nonsense," I said, "I have lots of male friends. In fact, I have more male friends than females, and none of us are sleeping together."

"That's because most of them are gay," said Jamie.

I punched him in the arm. "Hey, whose side are you on? You and I are practically inseparable, and we've never slept together."

Sienna gave me a sideways look. She, too, wondered how we could be friends and not sleep together, especially when we got along so well.

"You know, he might be right," said Lilith. "Even when you're friends, one person is often in love with the other one. Not always, but often."

"I told you so," said Luka.

I turned to look at Jamie. "Jamie, are you secretly in love with me?" I asked very seriously.

"No, I am not," he said, equally serious.

"Well thank God, because that would be awkward with your girlfriend sitting right there." I whispered that last bit with my hand in front of my mouth, and everyone burst out laughing. I picked up the wine bottle and filled everyone's glass, and then I turned to look at Luka.

"So, Luka, tell me about yourself. Do you have any brothers or sisters?"

He nodded towards Lilith. "Let's hear what she has to say. I'm curious to see these 'gifts' of yours in action."

Lilith grinned. She wasn't afraid of a challenge, and after several bottles of wine, we were all a little looser in the tongue.

"OK . . . let's see. You have an older brother, and you really look up to him. You're a Taurus, and you love the outdoors. You're also incredibly private and hate drama, especially when it comes to women. You love beauty and value nice things. That's the Taurus in you."

We all turned to look at Luka to see if this was true. His face gave nothing away.

"Jamie could have told you those things. Tell me something he doesn't know."

All eyes shifted back to Lilith. We were enjoying this.

She tilted her head to the side as she studied him. "You're a bit of a player. You plan to sleep with as many women as possible before getting married and having kids, and she must be Serbian, like you." She squinted her eyes. "When you were younger, your brother told you to sow your wild oats as often as possible. That way, you'll be sure to get it out of your system before settling down."

She wagged her finger. "Your brother has strong opinions about women, and you listen to him. He's the one who told you that men and women can't be friends and that we aren't to be trusted because we always have an agenda."

Jamie burst out laughing. "That sounds like Zoran."

"Your brother sounds like an ass," Sienna mumbled, and I smiled because I was thinking the same thing. Luka looked amused and *very* surprised.

"Your father cheated on your mother, and you vowed that you'd never do that to your wife. You never date anyone for long, and as soon as they start having feelings, you dump them and move on to the next one. You're honest about it, though. You tell them not to fall in love with you."

"OK, I think that's enough," said Luka holding up his hands, and everyone laughed.

"What does your crystal ball say about me?" I asked. This party trick was very entertaining. I'd never seen anything like it.

Lilith turned to look at me. "You are strong and independent. You love to travel and are deeply connected to Mother Nature. Very free spirited. You don't like commitment, and you're the complete opposite of him." She threw a thumb at Luka. "You don't want to get married *or* have children. If I had to guess, I'd say you're a Sagittarius."

Wow. I was impressed. She'd nailed it.

"You don't want children?" asked Luka.

"Hell no. They're loud, messy, demanding, and expensive. Besides, marriage and children have never interested me. I want an acting career and the freedom to travel without anyone holding me back."

Jamie grinned. He'd heard it all before, and he admired the fact that I knew what I wanted. Shortly after that, Luka left, and when I got back to the living room Lilith was grinning like the Cheshire Cat.

"What?" I asked. I looked at Jamie, and he was grinning, too. "What?" I repeated.

"The chemistry between you and Luka is off the charts!" said Lilith.

"You think so?"

"Absolutely. And it makes perfect sense. Tell me, did you feel anything when you first met him?"

"Actually . . . yes. When I opened the door, it was like a jolt. Like he was familiar somehow."

She giggled. "He felt it, too, and no wonder! You're soulmates!"

"Soulmates? You mean soulmates are real?"

"Of course they are! That's why you recognized each other. You've known each other for many lifetimes."

I frowned. All of this was new to me, but it certainly explained what happened when I'd first seen him. The familiarity. I'd never believed in reincarnation before, but I was starting to think there was something to it.

"That's not all," said Lilith, interrupting my thoughts, "I'm afraid I have bad news. Your relationships never last. You keep hurting each other in every lifetime."

"Well, that sounds ominous."

"Yeah. What's worse is that it's your turn to pay."

After they left, I was lying in bed thinking about what Lilith had said. I was incredibly attracted to Luka, there was no doubt about that. And I was intrigued by the idea of having a soulmate. I just hoped she was wrong about the whole karma thing. The last thing I needed was more heartache. *Maybe this will be the lifetime where we get it right and end the karma,* I thought as I drifted off to sleep.

Lilith and Luka came over all the time after Jamie left for Australia. He told them to look after me, and that's exactly what they did. He was super protective, even when he wasn't there. I can't explain what happened that winter, but something strange was going on. The three of us would sit in my living room for hours on end, laughing and talking, drinking and smoking pot. Sometimes we made plans to go clubbing, but we never seemed to get there. We were having too much fun in our own little bubble.

It wasn't long before I fell madly in love with Luka. In fact, I'm pretty sure it happened that first night. He was handsome, funny, elegant, and I could talk to him about anything, but it was more than that. Much like my father, he exuded presence, and without saying a word, he commanded attention.

He was strong, smart, grounded, and manly, yet he had a softer side that appreciated art, music, expensive wine, and the finer things in life. I liked that about him because I was the same. I was just as comfortable in an elegant dress and high heels as I was camping. He's the first boy I ever met who was just like me, and I was intrigued.

It wasn't lost on me that I was falling for a man who was just like my father. Even the way he valued his privacy reminded me of my dad. Still, the idea that Luka was my soulmate felt like a fairytale. Even knowing he'd break my heart didn't stop me. I mean, maybe Lilith was wrong. Maybe it would work out.

Every time we talked, she insisted that he was in love with me, except he was confused. When he saw my last name on a letter during his second visit and realized I was Serbian, he was surprised and pleased, and then he remembered that I didn't want children, so he slammed the door shut.

If he was so in love with me, I wondered why he never made a move. Then one night I got my answer. Luka and I were sitting on the couch, chatting until the wee hours of the morning. When he started to yawn, I suggested he spend the night. We had been drinking, and I didn't want him driving.

"Come on. Let's go upstairs. You can crash with me," I said as I blew out the candles.

A look of complete panic came over his face. "I can't do that."

"Why not? It's not like I'm going to jump you. I promise you're quite safe."

"It's not you I'm worried about," he said seriously.

"I see. You mean you don't think you can keep your hands to yourself?" I teased. He nodded vigorously. Oh, my God. He was serious. "Would that . . . really be such a bad thing?"

"Yes."

"Ouch."

"It's not like that. I'm really attracted to you, Sage, but I cannot sleep with you. Even though I really, really want to."

I was confused. "Why not? We're both consenting adults, and in case you haven't noticed, I like you, too."

"That's the problem. Jamie will kill me if I touch you. He made it very clear that you're off limits. Plus, you're not that kind of girl."

I raised an eyebrow. "OK, wow. Where do I even start with that? First of all, Jamie's not my keeper, and although I adore him for being protective, I'm pretty sure I can make my own decisions. Second, I'm not *what* kind of girl? You don't actually think I'm a virgin, do you?" I was trying to make light of the situation, but he wasn't having it.

"Listen, Sage, I don't usually say this to girls, but you're different, so here it is. There are two types of women in this world: the ones you *fuck* and the ones you *marry.* You are most definitely the second one."

I frowned. "That's the most ridiculous thing I've ever heard."

"Say what you will, but it's true. That's how men think."

"Well I have no intention of getting married, so this is awkward. Are you telling me I'm never getting laid again because men think I'm a *good girl?*"

"Yup."

"Luka you're being ridiculous. Come to bed."

"I can't. I'll sleep on the couch."

I sighed. "Suit yourself. I'm not gonna force you to sleep with me."

And so he did. Most men would have caved, but Luka meant every word he said.

NINE

1996

Two months after Jamie left, I received my first letter, and I tore it open.

My dearest Sage, how I wish you were here, sharing in this wonderful experience with me. I've met so many people, and I'm learning a lot about life, but none of it compares to how much I miss you. Every day I walk the beach thinking about you, my beautiful diamond Sage.

> *I'm currently living in Byron Bay and believe it or not, I found a job at a local youth hostel run by Hare Krishnas. I'm now a vegetarian and have been dating a girl from Germany since I got here. I'm excited because she's planning on coming back to Vancouver when I leave. Wouldn't that be nice? I miss you, old friend. Please write back and tell me everything. Are you still hanging out with Luka and Lilith?*

It was exciting reading his letter so I wrote him back right away, filling him in on everything that had happened since he'd left.

Dear Jamie, I'm so happy for you! You sound like you're having a wonderful time. I wish I could be there too, instead of here in the rain . . . but in the meantime, thanks for introducing me to Luka and Lilith. They're doing a great job of keeping me company while you're away. We spend a lot of time together and I'm learning a lot from Lilith. You were right, she's amazing. As for Luka, I'm crazy about him! I miss you, too, and omg. Hare Krishnas? I'm dying!

Luka usually came over once or twice a week, but I saw Lilith more often. In fact, we were becoming great friends. Her tarot readings were so accurate it blew my mind, and when she gave me an astrology book, I obsessed over it for weeks. Any doubts I'd had about her abilities were long gone, and I couldn't get enough of her teachings. It was so different from the way I'd been raised. The church offered nothing but fear and condemnation, but her messages were full of love and light. It was like night and day.

One rainy afternoon, we were sitting at the table drinking tea, when she suddenly said "Give me your hands. I want to read your palms."

I was intrigued, so I raised my hands, and she moved a little closer so she could get a better look.

"Your left hand is your past and your right hand is your future," she said cheerfully. "Let's start with your past." She grasped my left hand and bent over my palm, tracing one of the lines with her finger. All of a sudden, her face darkened, and I watched several emotions play out. Tears slid down her cheeks. I was mesmerized until she suddenly closed my fingers and pushed my hand away.

"I can't read this," she said sadly. "It's too painful." When our eyes met, I saw sympathy and understanding. She leaned in to embrace me. "You don't remember," she said. "It's probably for the best."

I was surprised by her reaction, but once again she proved she wasn't faking it. I *didn't* remember my childhood, and I was impressed that she knew that. Wanting to change the subject, she asked about Luka instead.

"I don't understand, Lilith. You keep telling me he's in love with me, but it doesn't feel like it. He looks at me with such admiration, and he flirts with me all the time, yet he doesn't make a move, and I fear he never will. He's so damn stubborn."

"He's confused. There's a lot of pressure from his family to get married and have kids. He wants you, but he respects you and he doesn't want to get in the way of your career. Plus, his code of conduct is really strong. Warped, but strong. He sees women as either a Madonna or a whore. For him, it's very black and white."

Oh yes, he made that clear the night he slept over. "It's doing my head in," I said miserably.

"I know. Be patient. Soulmate relationships are challenging."

In December, Sienna and I went on a cruise, and when we got back, everything was different. The three of us got together and had a great time as usual, but something was off. I couldn't put my finger on it, but I could feel it. Luka seemed normal, but Lilith was acting weird.

She dropped by a week later, and once again she wasn't quite herself. It felt like she was nervous or something. After an hour, I couldn't stand it anymore, so I confronted her. She wasn't the only one who could read people. Something was up.

"Lilith, what's going on? Something happened while I was away, I can tell. Did Luka start dating someone? Is he in love with someone else? You have to tell me."

"We're sleeping together!" she blurted out loudly and then clamped a hand over her mouth.

I completely froze. It's like my brain couldn't register what she was saying. Lilith, of all people. The person who literally read my thoughts and knew better than anyone how much I loved him. She'd been stoking that fire for months, telling me to hold on, that he was in love with me, too.

"Oh God, please say something!" she wailed, "I'm so sorry! We were on ecstasy, and it just happened."

I still couldn't speak, but my face said it all as I tried to process this incredible betrayal. I thought about Luka and how happy he was to see me when I got home, flirting as usual, all the while being completely content with his lies. It had happened right under my nose, and I'd had no idea. I felt like such a fool.

"How long?" I asked.

Fresh tears sprang to her eyes. "The past three weeks, but it didn't mean anything. It was just sex. You were gone, and we went clubbing, and then we started hanging out. I swear it won't happen again. The only reason I didn't tell you is that he made me promise, but the guilt has been killing me. You're my friend, and I had to tell you." She reached out to touch me, but I pulled away.

"I think you should leave now," I said calmly. "I need to be alone."

"Please don't hate me. And don't hate him, either. He really is in love with you, Sage."

"Stop. Please stop."

After she left, I went to my room and cried. I was so humiliated, and for a week, I ignored both her and Luka's calls. I knew I had to face them eventually, but first I had to sort through my emotions. After a week, Lilith stopped calling and simply dropped by. She came over every day, begging me to forgive her, and I did. I was still angry, but I didn't want to lose her. I still had so much to learn, and she was the only one who could teach me.

Our trio was definitely over, though. Luka yelled at Lilith for telling me about their affair, and now he wasn't speaking to her. He called me every day that week, leaving messages and begging me to call him back. On the seventh day, I finally picked up. He told me he was sorry for hurting me, but he didn't understand why I was so upset when we weren't even dating.

"It's not like I cheated on you," he said.

"I know that."

"You do?"

"Of course I do. I'm not a child. You don't owe me anything, and you're free to sleep with whomever you like, but that doesn't mean it didn't hurt. You say you're attracted to me and the only reason you can't touch me is because

Jamie told you not to, but then you go and fuck his girlfriend. Surely you can see why that's confusing. Not to mention insulting."

He sighed. I'd hit home. Jamie was his best friend, and although he and Lilith weren't together anymore, he'd still broken the friend code by sleeping with her.

"I know, you're right. I fucked up. I'm so sorry. Are you going to tell him?"

"Of course not. I'm not five. Telling him is your job."

"Wow. This isn't how I expected this conversation to go at all. Most girls would have freaked out, but you're different. So what happens now? Can we still be friends? A bunch of us are going out on Friday. Will you come if I pick you up?"

I did go out on Friday, but it was a mistake. Luka showed up with one of the girls I went to college with, and I was surprised, but then again, she went to high school with him and Jamie, so they all knew each other. We danced all night, and I tried to have a good time, but my emotions were all over the place.

At some point, Amy and I went to the bathroom, and when she asked what was going on in my life, I told her. All of it. Once I started I couldn't stop, even though I sensed it was making her uncomfortable. We were friends back in college and talked about boys all the time, so I couldn't understand her reaction or why she wasn't giving me any advice. I immediately regretted it and begged her to forget everything I said, but she didn't.

The next morning, Luka called and yelled at me for spilling his secrets when I knew how much he valued his privacy.

"You're just as bad as Lilith! Why can't girls keep their mouths shut?"

"I'm sorry. I don't know what came over me."

"You're sorry? Sorry doesn't cut it. Why on earth were you telling those things to my friend? Who the hell do you think you are?"

I was shocked by the hatred in his voice, but I was also pissed off.

"Excuse me, but Amy is my friend, too, and last night I needed someone to talk to. The timing wasn't great but—"

"You know what? I don't care. I'm done with you. You're dead to me, Sage."

I gasped. Did he really just say that? He knew my parents had heard those exact same words when they got married and again when my sisters and I were born. He knew how much saying that would hurt me. My temper flared as my voice lowered to a deadly calm.

"How *dare* you speak to me that way. Fuck you, Luka. Don't ever call me again."

And then I slammed down the phone. My karma had been paid in full.

As for Lilith, she moved to Mexico a few weeks later, and then it was over. Even though this technically wasn't a breakup, I mourned the loss of my friends for a long time, especially Luka. I played it over and over again, wondering if I could've done something different.

Over the next six months, my life went through some major changes. I joined a gym, started volunteering at a hospice, and I auditioned for a play. I was ecstatic when I got the part. It was just what I needed to pull me out of my winter blues.

I was still working at the restaurant I'd been at for the last seven years, and now that it was spring, my friends and I started going out again. I even made a new friend. She was my co-worker, Heather's roommate, and we hit it off immediately. Vivien was funny, and I absolutely adored her, so the three of us started hanging out.

When the play was over, I threw myself into a second project—becoming a jazz singer. I had never listened to jazz before, but I loved that era. When Sienna and I saw a trio on the cruise ship, it gave me an idea. I figured this was a wonderful way to see the world while doing something I loved, so I attacked it the same way I attack everything—full on.

I rehearsed with a pianist for months, and we were just about to make a demo reel when the lease on my apartment expired. The owner wanted to move in, so Sienna and I had to move out. She figured I'd be working on ships soon, so she found herself another roommate, leaving me homeless.

Luckily, a friend from work offered me her couch until I could figure out what I was doing. Five minutes later, everything fell apart. My new boss and

I bumped heads on several occassions until eventually we had a blow-out that led to my termination. At the same time, the agent got back to us about the cruise ships, saying he thought I was too young, and suggested that I do some local gigs first. I approached three different restaurants to see if they'd hire me, and they all said yes, but the pay was lousy, and I was beginning to panic.

When I heard about a man who did past-life readings, I decided to check him out. He knew I was broke, so he offered to do it in exchange for a photo session, which was fine by me. He wanted to practice his photography skills, and I needed head shots, so it was a fair trade.

"Close your eyes and breathe deeply," he said, as I laid on the floor in his living room. "Now, picture a door to your past. Can you see it?"

"No," I said. "I've never been good at visualizing. Is this the only way to see my past?"

"Not at all. With your permission, I can jump in and tell you what I see."

"Yes, please."

"OK, close your eyes . . . breathe . . . good. So it looks like we're going to the lifetime before this one. We're in Africa, and you're a man. There's something wrong with your foot, so you can't go hunting with the rest of the men. Instead, you look after the women and elders while the men go hunting. You play several instruments. You like singing. In fact, music seems to be a theme in all your lifetimes. You've always been a musician."

That made me smile. Maybe there was hope for me yet. As he spoke, I suddenly remembered what Lilith said about people reappearing in our lives, and I was curious to see what this guy had to say. "May I ask a question? Is there someone named Luka in my past life?"

"There's an entity here that you call Luka, but she's a woman. You had an affair with her and broke her heart. You had affairs with several women in the tribe, but this woman . . . she loved you and never got over it. She spent the rest of her life pining over you."

Woah. Considering he didn't know anything about me, this was amazing.

"What about a girl named Lilith?" I asked.

"Yes, there's an entity here you call Lilith. Oh! She's powerful. She's the healer of the tribe, a witch doctor if you will. Interesting—she's been a witch in *all* her lifetimes. The three of you are very connected. You've had many lives together."

This was incredible. I mean, you can't possibly make this stuff up.

"Is there anything else you'd like to know?" he asked.

"Yes, but it's not about that lifetime. It's about this one." I told him what had recently happened between the three of us and asked how I could stop the karma from repeating itself or if that was even possible.

"Oh yes. It's very simple. All you have to do is forgive him."

"That's it? Just . . . *forgive* him?"

He laughed. "Yes. You're the one who got hurt, so you're the one who has to forgive. But you have to *really* forgive, then let it go. Don't hold onto it, or you'll take it into your next life."

TEN

I was ecstatic when Jamie finally came home. I had missed him so much while he was gone. He came over to my friend's place, and we stayed up all night talking about Byron Bay, his trip to Fiji, and the girl he was dating. In turn, I told him about my new jazz project and how I'd quit my job to become a real artist, which is why I was currently residing on someone else's couch.

I'd made a lot of sacrifices lately, except it was taking way longer than I anticipated, so not only was I flat broke, but the girl I was staying with—well, let's just say I'd worn out my welcome.

"I'm so proud of you, Sage. I know things are tough right now, but it'll be worth it in the end."

"I hope so. I'm broke and homeless, and I have to say, I don't enjoy either."

"Hey, a poor, starving artist is a real thing."

"True that!" We both laughed, and my heart melted when I saw his dimples. I really had missed him, and I was glad he was back.

"So . . . now that we've talked about everything else, are you ready to talk about Luka?"

I was a little startled by the sudden change of subject. "What do you mean?"

"Give me credit, Sage. I *know* you. Besides, for three months, he was all you talked about and then nothing, and not a word since. So tell me, what did he do?"

I sighed. I should have known that ignoring the elephant in the room wouldn't be easy. "Honestly, Jamie, it doesn't matter anymore. It was nine months ago, and all is forgiven."

"If all is forgiven, then why can't you tell me?"

"Because I'm not that girl, and you know it. I have no intention of coming between you and your friend, so please leave it alone."

"All right. If that's what you want, I'll drop it."

He did drop it, but the next day he went to a party, and Luka was there. He hadn't told his friends he was home yet, and when Luka saw him, he panicked. He asked Jamie if he'd seen me yet, and when Jamie said yes, he asked if he could tell his side of the story before Jamie got mad at him. When he finished, he asked if his story matched mine, and that's when Jamie told him that I had refused to talk about it.

"You should have seen the look on his face, Sage. All he said was 'Fuck. I'm *such* an ass. I really messed up, brother,' to which I replied, 'Yes, yes you did.'"

"Good. I'm glad that's settled, then. Now you know what happened and we can all move on." As far as I was concerned, that was the end of the conversation.

"He wants to see you," Jamie said quietly.

"What? Absolutely not!"

"He wants to apologize. He asked for your number."

"Did you give it to him?"

"No, I told him I had to ask you first."

"Well, the answer is no. Please tell him his apology isn't necessary."

"Seriously?"

"Yes, seriously. Leave it alone, Jamie." I did NOT want to see Luka again.

He put his hands up. "OK, I will. Sorry."

But he didn't leave it alone. The next time I saw him, he brought it up again. "You know what? I'll just invite you out for coffee, and he'll be there, and then you'll *have* to talk to him."

This time I lost it. I knew he was joking, but this wasn't a joke to me. I'd had my heart broken several times over the years, crushes that led to one-night stands and a lot of tears and self-recrimination about how undesirable I was—something someone as hot as Jamie could never understand. But Luka? He was different. He was the first boy I'd ever *truly* loved, and it took me a long time to get over him.

"Don't you dare," I hissed. "Let me be really clear here, Jamie. If you do that, I'll consider it an act of betrayal, and I'll never speak to you again. Do you understand me?"

"Holy cow. You're serious, but—"

"No *but*! Listen, I never told you my side of the story, but Luka really hurt me, and it took me a *long time* to get over it. Now that I have, I don't need you bringing it up again. LET. IT. GO. Please. I'm begging you, Jamie. I don't want to talk about this again. OK?"

"OK. Sorry. Wow. I've never seen you lose your temper before."

"You still haven't. Believe me, you'll know when I do."

So imagine my surprise when the phone rang a few days later and it was *him*.

"Hello?" I said cheerfully and ignorantly as I answered the phone.

"Sage."

It was one word. One word was all it took. I gasped as fear gripped my entire body. Fear and betrayal. I started to hang up, but he spoke again, desperation in his voice.

"*Wait!* Please don't hang up. I know you don't want to talk to me, but I only need two minutes. Please."

I sighed. "Fine. You have two minutes."

"Thank you. Listen, I owe you an apology, and I know it should have come a long time ago, but I had a lot of growing up to do. I always felt sick about the way I treated you and that last conversation . . . I never should have said what I said."

"No, you shouldn't have," I said coldly.

"I'd really like to go for coffee so I can apologize in person. I owe you that. Will you come out with me so I can do this properly? Please? I have to make this right."

"Why? Why do you even care?"

"Because you're a good person, and I was an ass. I owe you this."

Suddenly the words from my past life reading echoed in my head. *The only way to release the karma is to forgive. Really forgive.* "Damn it," I said out loud.

By the time he got there, my rage had subsided, and I was resigned to what I knew had to happen. I had to forgive him. I had to be the bigger person. I always had to be the bigger person.

When I opened the door, he stepped closer so he could give me a hug, but I stepped back. I wasn't ready for that just yet. Instead, he smiled as he gave me the once over.

"Hey, you got your braces off! You look amazing," he said sincerely.

"Thanks," I mumbled.

We made small talk on the way to the restaurant but didn't get into it until after we sat down. I let him take the lead, since this was his idea. Once again, he apologized (quite sincerely, I might add), and then he explained.

"Listen, this isn't an excuse, but I was doing a lot of drugs back then, mainly ecstasy, and I made a lot of bad decisions that hurt the people I love. Once I slowed down, I realized what I'd done to you, and I would have called, but after the way things ended . . ."

We were both quiet as we remembered that last phone call.

"Thanks for telling me that. And I'm sorry for breaking your trust by talking to Amy that night at the club. I knew you valued your privacy, and I never meant to betray you. I was hurt and desperately needed someone to talk to. I never thought she'd tell you. That was never my intention."

"Well, can you blame her? I was sleeping with her and Lilith at the same time, and then you basically told her I thought she was a slut and not the marrying kind."

"Wait a minute. You were sleeping with her? Oh my God. It all makes sense now. No wonder you were so mad."

"You didn't know I was sleeping with her?"

"Of course not."

"Hold on. So you didn't say those things to break us up? Oh my God. All this time, I thought it was intentional, but you were totally innocent. That makes this so much worse."

He reached across the table and took both my hands as he looked me in the eyes. "I'm so sorry, Sage. I was such a jerk. Can you ever forgive me?"

I smiled. God, I missed him. His smile, his magnetism, his sensuality, the way he looked at me as if I were the only person in the room . . . all of it. And I could tell he missed me, too. Why else would he have orchestrated this meeting? To clear his conscience? To apologize? He could have done that over the phone.

"I'm sorry, too, Luka. And thank you for making me come here tonight. It's nice to finally know the truth."

We talked for hours as we sat in that cafe. Luka was like no one I'd ever known, and being with him was so easy. I caught him up on my life, and he caught me up on his. He told me about his job with at-risk youth and how much he loved it. He told me how he taught them survival skills by taking them camping and hiking on the weekends. I admired him for that. I, too, loved the outdoors and camped as often as I could. Nature is my happy place.

It was like no time had passed at all, but that's how it is with the people we truly connect with, isn't it? We made a promise to forget the past and start over as friends—just friends. When I told him about my first gig, he asked if he could come. I said yes, and that was it. Just like that, Luka and Jamie were back in my life.

ELEVEN

The next morning, Jamie called, and I let him have it. "Don't think I'm not mad at you for betraying me. Seriously, Jamie. How could you do that? Even after I threatened to hate you and never speak to you again. You know I don't say those things lightly. Were you really willing to throw away our friendship over this?"

"I know you're mad, and I'm sorry. I just wanted all of us to be friends again. Besides, I'm kind of responsible for what happened, since I introduced you in the first place."

"That doesn't excuse your actions," I said firmly.

"I know, but it all worked out in the end, right?"

It did, but I wasn't willing to concede just yet. I needed him to understand that I didn't take betrayal lightly.

"Don't ever do that again, Jamie. I'm not kidding. I won't forgive you a second time."

"I won't. I promise. But . . . how did it go?"

"After I got over the initial shock, we had a really nice talk. He apologized and explained what really happened last year."

"Good, and you forgave him?"

"I did, and the truth is, I'm glad we're friends again. I missed him. I missed both of you. Actually, he's coming to my gig on Saturday."

"He is?" Jamie sounded surprised, and then he went quiet for a moment. I felt his energy shift, even over the phone. "Are you still in love with him?" he asked quietly.

"Don't be ridiculous. Been there, done that, and I don't care to repeat it."

"Good, because I'm not sure how I feel about that."

"What's that supposed to mean?"

"Nothing. I'm just being protective."

Even though I was insanely nervous, my first gig went pretty well, considering I had no idea what I was doing. About a dozen friends showed up to the little café in Whiterock where I was doing my gig, and I was grateful for their support. The stage was in the corner of the room, and there were about a dozen patrons eating dinner, plus the long table where my friends sat, cheering me on.

Jamie beamed the entire time, and Luka couldn't keep his eyes off me. It's like they were starstruck seeing me on that stage. To be fair, I was dressed like a fifties movie star (finger waves and all), and I looked pretty amazing, if I do say so myself.

Afterwards, we were having drinks when I caught Luka staring at me from across the table. It's like he was seeing me for the first time. Jamie noticed it, too, and he didn't look happy. In fact, as the evening wore on, he became more and more withdrawn, and then he became grumpy. After everything he'd done to throw us back together, I don't think he actually enjoyed sharing my attention with another man.

Shortly after my second gig, my friend's grandfather died, and her family asked me to babysit his house for six months while they decided what to do with it. That was six months rent-free, with my only expense being the electricity bill. I couldn't believe it. The best part is that it was just around the corner from Heather and Vivien, so we started hanging out even more.

And then Luka started dropping by on a regular basis after I moved. In fact, he's the one who moved me. We became very close very quickly, but it was different this time. We developed a wonderful friendship, instead of the insane intensity that surrounded us the first time. We both understood that our friendship came first, and we didn't want anything to jeopardize that. He was very clear about not wanting a relationship, and neither of us wanted to repeat what happened the last time.

Several weeks later, the boys came over and brought their friend Jasper, who was also at my jazz gig. Vivian and Heather were there, too. I loved having these amazing people in my life. The past year had been tough in many ways, but I was breathing a lot easier these days, especially now that I had a job.

The gig on the cruise ship fell through (as did my aspirations of becoming a jazz singer), but I'd recently been hired by a dinner theater company, and I loved the new job. I got to sing, dance, and act, and I even got paid. I was finally a professional actor, and because of all that dancing, I was in the best shape of my life. Things were really looking up.

We were all having a great time when Luka suddenly brought out his guitar. I hadn't even known he could play. How could he have kept that from me when he knew I was a singer? Not only did he play, he sang, too, and he was *wonderful*. This time, it was my turn to stare. How did I not know he was a musician?

He sang a song that he and Jasper wrote in high school, and I was gobsmacked. It was amazing. *He* was amazing. Why wasn't he performing in clubs? After singing his song, he asked if I would sing one, so I sang a Tracy Chapman number while he played the guitar.

I think I fell in love with him all over again that night. Despite how hard I tried to keep my feelings at bay, I lost the battle the minute he picked up that guitar. Actually, I'm not sure I ever stopped loving him.

The only person who wasn't having a good time was Jamie. He was in a foul mood and kept snapping at everyone. I didn't know what was going on with him, but ever since he'd returned from Australia, he was moody and judgemental.

He constantly criticized me: first because I wasn't a vegetarian (neither was he until he met the Hare Krishnas), then it's because I wasn't as *enlightened* as he was, and then it was something else. I didn't know what had gotten into him, but I didn't like the new Jamie. When we were alone, it wasn't too bad, but as soon as we were in a group, he turned moody again. For months, I held onto the hope that he'd snap out of it, but as time wore on, he only got worse. As Sienna so delicately put it, he'd become a sanctimonious ass.

When Jamie wasn't being hyper critical, he was feeling sorry for himself, and I'm not sure which was worse. I'm not a big fan of self-pity. It reminded me of my mother, and I saw it as a weakness. Lately, he was using the death of his own mother (who'd died when he was five) to garner pity. I heard the story when we first met, and I gave him plenty of sympathy over the years, but these days it seemed to be his excuse for everything that was wrong in his life.

He was such a Debbie Downer that we secretly hoped he'd be busy every time we made plans. Preachy and sulky seemed to be his only state of mind these days, and I didn't like either one. I missed the old Jamie, and I often wondered what had happened in Australia to make him turn out like this.

After everyone left, Vivian rounded on me. "What the heck was that? I don't care what you say—Luka is in love with you."

"No, he's not. Every time we go clubbing, he brings a different girl. Believe me, he's not interested. He's very clear about that."

I told her about the first time we met and what he said about the two types of women: those you sleep with and those you marry. "Essentially he has a Madonna/whore complex."

"You can't be serious. Men don't actually think like that, do they?"

"You know, I wouldn't be too sure about that. Men have some pretty messed-up ideas when it comes to women and sex. When I lived in Italy, all the men had mistresses. They told me it was out of respect for their wives. The way they see it, their wives are sacred.

They make *love* to their wives. They *procreate* with their wives. But they do everything else with their mistress. They were positively mortified by the idea of their wives giving head. They were shocked that anyone could allow the same mouth that kisses their children to do something so dirty. That's what their mistresses are for." I rolled my eyes.

"So what . . . the wife's stuck with missionary position while the mistress has all the fun?"

"Yup. Pretty much. Don't marry an Italian—or half of Europe, for that matter."

"Wow, and men think *we're* the complicated ones. That aside, Luka's in love with you, Sage. He can deny it all he wants, but you should see the way he looks at you. He couldn't hide it if he tried."

This was déjà vu. I'd been here before, but do you think I learned? Of course not.

"You really think so?" I said like a lovestruck teenager.

"You'd have to be blind not to see it. The sparks coming off you two are crazy, especially when you sang together! It was so beautiful, and he couldn't keep his eyes off you. His face was pure adoration."

I lived in that fantasy for a moment, and then reality kicked in. "That may be, but he'll never act on it."

"Why not?"

"Because he knows I don't want to get married or have kids, and dating me isn't an option in his mind. It's just that cut and dry."

"But you're in love with him. Don't deny it. I know you."

My face fell. "I know I am. And the truth is, I'd do anything for him, even get married and have kids. But don't tell him that. I want him to love me for me, not for my baby-making abilities."

"So what are you going to do? Are you hoping one day he'll get tired of those other girls and realize that the person he's been looking for has been right here all along?"

That's exactly what I was doing. "Oh, God. Does that make me pathetic?"

"No. I get it. If you tell him how you feel and he doesn't reciprocate, you'll lose him as a friend. It's too bad, though. You guys are great together."

TWELVE

One night, a year or so later, Luka asked if I'd like to try ecstasy. I had tried plenty of drugs in my life but never ecstasy, so I said yes. I was surprised when he said he wanted to do it at his place because he usually went clubbing with whatever flavor-of-the-month he was dating when he dropped E. I didn't mind, though. I liked being alone with him, and we ended up having an exceptional evening. All your senses become heightened, and I could see why it was Luka's drug of choice, especially since he was such a sexually active guy.

We talked about our upcoming trip to Jamaica and how excited we were to camp on the beach for ten days. We both loved the outdoors and camped quite often in the summer. My father recently got hired with the airline and offered me two free tickets, so I asked Vivien if she wanted to go, but she couldn't afford it. Then I asked Luka, and in all honesty, I hadn't expected him to say yes. I thought for sure it was crossing the line, but he didn't even hesitate, so we planned a trip around Christmas, when my show would be finished for the season.

Luka picked up his guitar, and we sang some songs, just like we always did, and then he played several new songs he was working on. They didn't have lyrics yet, but they were catchy tunes. I asked him once why he didn't perform in clubs, but he had no interest in that. He loved music, but it was only a hobby, which was too bad because we made a great duo, and I could picture us performing together.

Somewhere around midnight, I was rubbing my neck when Luka offered to give me a massage. I had received massages from Luka before (plenty, actually), and while touch is often a sensual experience, this was a *whole other level*. Touch is where ecstasy excels. In fact, I was starting to understand why he'd been so flirtatious when we'd first met two years ago, back when we were hanging out with Lilith. All that time, I'd thought he was in love with me, but in reality, he'd been in love with everything and it had nothing to do with me.

When he finished his massage, I offered to return the favor, but he declined, and I didn't push it. I never pushed it. I was always cognizant of his many rules and invisible lines when it came to me. It wasn't long before he changed his mind, though. After all, I give great massages.

When I finished, it was close to two in the morning, and I was tired, so I went to bed. I usually slept in Luka's bed when I stayed over. Remembering what had happened when we'd first met, I was shocked the first time he suggested it. After all, he had a two-bedroom condo, and I could have slept in the spare room.

I think he liked having me close by, even though nothing ever happened. His brother told him he was playing with fire and he should stop hanging out with me, but Luka had never known a girl like me, and he couldn't stay away. It had been over a year since we'd rekindled our friendship, and I saw him several times a week. It wasn't uncommon for me to sleep over, especially since my job was just around the corner from his condo.

Luka said he needed a minute, so I left him on the floor. I didn't need to ask why, and I'm not gonna lie, I was glad that I still had the power to turn him on. That's one thing he couldn't hide, how much he was attracted to me. I don't know what time it was when he finally came to bed, but I was fast asleep and didn't hear him come in.

I did, however, wake up when I felt him wrap his arms around me. We slept together all the time, but we never cuddled. That was against the rules.

His embrace felt nice, and I was about to go back to sleep when he suddenly kissed my neck. Still half asleep, I smiled to myself in the dark. I figured he'd stop any second and fall asleep except . . . he didn't.

He started drawing circles on my back and arms . . . gently caressing my skin . . . taking his time. I murmured something about how nice it felt, and then his hands traveled south, and my eyes flew open. He definitely had my attention now. I was wide awake, wondering what the heck he was doing. We'd never even kissed before, let alone what he was doing with his hands.

I didn't want to have sex with Luka just because we were high, so I started to protest, believe it or not. "Luka, what are you doing?" I whispered in the dark. Why I was whispering I don't know, since it was just the two of us.

"Shhhh. It's OK. Just relax. I *want* you. You've been driving me crazy all night."

"Are you sure . . ." I started to say but was cut short when he kissed me. It was incredibly passionate, and that was the end of my protesting. I'd been waiting for him to come to his senses for a long time. *I deserve this*, I decided. *We both do.* Maybe our karma was over, and this was our reward. Maybe this was our happily ever after, and we'd finally get to be together.

When we finished, he took a moment to catch his breath, and then he slowly lifted his gaze until his eyes met mine. I smiled, but he didn't. In fact, he looked genuinely shocked, as if he was seeing me for the first time.

"Oh my God . . . *no!*" he said.

"No?" I repeated, incredulous. This is not what I was expecting him to say.

"Not you," he said, shaking his head. "Oh my God, not YOU."

And then he rolled off me and turned away as if not looking at me would make it *not me.* I was stunned, hurt, furious, humiliated. The entire gamut of emotions was running through my mind as tears sprang to my eyes. He hadn't even given me time to enjoy the aftermath of sex before ruining it.

I laid there for a second, not sure what to do, but as I desperately tried to understand what was happening, the bastard started snoring. I couldn't believe it. I sat up and stared at his back in utter shock. There's no way I could sleep now, and I wasn't about to be treated like a whore, either. I was so mad I got out of bed and went to the living room, where I sat on the floor and fumed. Then I cried.

I cried because every man I'd ever slept with made me feel this way, and I couldn't understand how men could be so cruel. Cruel like my parents. Cruel like the church. Cruel like having my dream of becoming a ballerina ripped away from me. Life had handed me nothing *but* cruelty, and I was tired of it. As I laid there, crying on the floor, I half expected him to check on me, but he never did. And why is that? Because Prince Charming is a big, fat, fucking lie, that's why.

I wanted to go home, except there weren't any buses at this hour, and I didn't want to call Vivian in the middle of the night. Instead, I laid there crying and shaking (it was really cold) wondering how he could do this to me. Would I never learn?

When he came into the living room the next morning and saw me lying on the floor, he looked surprised, and then he looked disgusted. I knew what he was thinking, that this was typical girl behavior, and he didn't have the patience for it. He didn't even look guilty for what he'd said to me. He probably didn't even remember.

"Did you sleep here all night?" he asked, coldly.

I kept my eyes down as I nodded my head.

"Listen, I have to go to work, but feel free to stay as long as you like. We should probably talk when I get back. Last night . . . we shouldn't have done ecstasy. It was a mistake."

I didn't answer, and he didn't push it. In fact, he walked out the door without another word. My Madonna image was tarnished, and I'm not sure he knew how to deal with that. Sure, he'd dated a lot of women, but I was the only one he played house with. I was the one who cooked meals with him, spent weekends with him, went skinny dipping in the lake with him, camped with him. Except now he saw me as the whore, and it was all his fault.

The second he closed the door, I leapt into action. I didn't care what time it was. I called Vivian and begged her to come get me. She arrived a half hour later and took me to her place, where I cried and cried and cried.

I didn't answer the phone when he called a few days later. I mean, come on. He waited a few days to call me? In girl time, that's like . . . *weeks.* I knew what he was doing. He was giving me time to cool off, but I wasn't having it. When I continued to ignore his calls, Jamie called me instead.

"Hey," he said when I picked up. "It's me. How are you?" His voice was sympathetic.

"He told you, didn't he?"

"Yeah. He's kind of freaking out. Do you want to talk about it?"

"Actually, yes. I could use your advice."

"I'll be over in an hour."

When he got there, I told him everything because that's what we did—or, at least, that's what we used to do. He listened without judgment and gave me advice from the male perspective. He told me how much pressure Luka was under to get married, and how much his brother disliked me because he could tell that Luka had feelings for me. His whole family was worried about our upcoming vacation, and they constantly nagged him about it.

Jamie and I talked for hours, just like we used to, and I felt so much better after he left. It was nice having the old Jamie back, even if it didn't last very long. I hadn't seen a lot of him since he'd moved in with his latest girlfriend, but he seemed happy, and I was happy for him.

Luka called again, and this time I answered. I couldn't avoid him forever. He said he was coming over so we could talk. As I waited for him to arrive, I wondered if this was the end. I suspected it was. I prepared myself for the worst, steeling my emotions so I wouldn't cry, and then he surprised me. We were sitting cross legged on the floor, facing each other, when he began.

"We never should have crossed that line," he said, and he actually looked sad, like he, too, expected this to be the end.

"Then why did you?" I asked.

"Hey, we're both to blame here."

"No, actually, we're not. This one's on you."

"What do you mean? We both tempted fate by doing ecstasy and then that massage . . . I mean, what did we think would happen? My brother's right. We were playing with fire. Men and women can't be friends. Sex always gets in the way."

"Sorry, Luka, but you don't get to do that this time. We've managed to be friends for well over a year, and we never even kissed before now, so that's bullshit. "

OK, so I was secretly in love with him, and maybe his brother was right. But he didn't know that, and I was seriously pissed off. Calm, but pissed off.

"Yah but—"

"No! No buts. *You* decided to break the rules. It was *your* idea to do ecstasy. It was *your* idea to do it at your house, alone. It was *your* idea to exchange massages, even though you knew it was asking for trouble."

"You agreed to it, though," he pointed out.

"Yes, I did. I'm not ruled by my penis like you are. I'm capable of doing ALL those things and still resisting the urge to have sex. In fact, I was sound asleep when you made a move on me. I didn't do that. *You* did. Hell, I even asked if you were sure, and you shushed me."

"It was the ecstasy! I came into my room, and there was a beautiful girl in my bed—"

"I don't care, and oh my God, could you be any more insulting? You only had sex with me because I was in your bed? Wow. You hurt me, Luka, and you need to own it."

He wasn't ready to own it. He still wanted to lay blame.

"You see? It's just like I said from the beginning. I knew we couldn't have sex without you getting emotional."

"Fuck you, Luka. I'm not emotional because we had sex. I'm emotional because you treated me like a whore. You looked at me like you thought you were having sex with someone else, and when you realized it was me . . . I'll never forget the look on your face as long as I live. "

He stared at me for a minute, and I'm pretty sure he wanted to challenge me, but then he crumbled. He knew I was right.

"I'm sorry, Sage. You're right. I never should have touched you. Sex always complicates things, and I don't want to lose you. I really value our friendship. I've never met a girl like you. You love dancing, music, camping, hiking. You're not afraid of anything, and we have so much in common."

"You don't have to lose me. When are you going to learn that I'm not that person?"

He studied my face for a minute before he answered. "Man, you are constantly surprising me. You really aren't like other girls. You're amazing." We were both quiet for a beat. "So, where do we go from here?" he asked.

"You need to sort your shit out, Luka. Have sex with me. Don't have sex with me. I don't care. But don't ever treat me like a whore again."

He hugged me then. "I'm so glad we worked this out. I actually thought this would be the end of us."

Two weeks later, he made a move again, only this time it was very deliberate. I wasn't expecting it, but he obviously couldn't stay away from me. He'd tasted the forbidden fruit, and now he wanted more. At least he acted like a gentleman this time, and the next, but I could feel his internal battle every time we had sex. He *liked* making love to me, and that worried him.

With those other girls, it was just sex, but it was more than that with me. We were soulmates, and that connected us on a deeper level. As Vivien pointed out, he kept saying he wanted to keep it casual, yet his actions spoke louder than words. In those moments, I truly believed he was in love with me, but his brother was always in his ear telling him that he needed a traditional Serbian wife who'd stay at home and raise the kids. Not someone like me, who wanted a career and would never be submissive.

A few weeks later, Luka sat me down and said he didn't want to have sex anymore because the guilt was killing him. I was tired of the emotional roller coaster, so I agreed. I needed him to figure this out on his own, except the next time the gang went dancing at our favorite Latino nightclub, Luka brought a girl with him. She was a much older woman, and I wasn't sure what he was trying to prove.

Vivian said he was trying to forget me and to be patient, but my patience had run out. So, a few days later, when I saw an advertisement looking for girls to work at a hostess bar in Japan, I gave them a call. I had always wanted to see Japan but could never afford it, so this seemed like a perfect opportunity. The contract was for three months, and it included airfare and a place to live.

Going overseas was exactly what I needed, so I accepted the job and agreed to start as soon as I returned from Jamaica. When I told Sienna that I was moving to Japan, she asked if she could come with me. When I told Luka, he freaked out. So did Jamie. In fact, everybody freaked out, especially my father. They were convinced it was a scam to kidnap me and put me into a prostitution ring. *Good*, I thought. *Luka should be worried. Maybe he'll stop taking me for granted. Maybe he'll realize I won't wait for him forever.*

I worked like crazy that December. It was the busy season, and we had a full house every night. I welcomed the distraction, but the downside was that with all that free time on his hands, Luka started partying again. His new fling lived across the border in Washington, so he spent his weekends at her place (instead of with me), and then she started staying at his place. Maybe he really liked her; maybe she was a firecracker in bed, or maybe he was trying to get my image out of his head, but he dated this woman a lot longer than he dated the others.

I didn't see a lot of him that month, and even when I spent the night, he asked me to sleep in the spare room. He didn't want to be alone with me anymore. It was doing my head in, and Jamie wasn't much better. He was angry that I hadn't asked him to come to Jamaica, and he pouted every time we spoke. I told him he was being childish, considering he was living with his girlfriend, but he still pouted.

I realized that if it was up to Jamie and Luka, they'd sleep with every woman on the planet while keeping me in a glass box. They both adored me, yet they put me so high on a pedestal that they couldn't reach me. It was irritating, which is why I needed to get away for a while. I wasn't their plaything, and frankly, I was tired of them toying with my emotions.

Thirteen

December 1998

Since Luka and I planned to camp in Jamaica, we had a lot of gear to take with us. When we got to the airport, we checked in and waited for our flight. I'd never flown standby before, and I grossly underestimated how difficult it was to get from Vancouver to Toronto the week before Christmas.

There was a flight every couple of hours, but as we sat there watching plane after plane leave without us, I started to worry. And while I worried, Luka slept. All day. He'd partied the night before, and now he was exhausted and withdrawn. Actually, it felt like he didn't even want to be there, while I was really looking forward to being alone with him again, especially since I was leaving for Japan as soon as we got back.

By midnight, we were *still* at the airport. I was freaking out, but he didn't seem to care, which stressed me out even more. We finally spoke to an agent, and she said, "Honestly, your chances of getting out of here are nil. It's Christmas, the busiest time of the year. "

I asked if we could fly somewhere else, anywhere with a beach, and she said the flight to Maui wasn't sold out yet. I think she saw how upset I was, because she booked us seats and told us we didn't have to bother with standby anymore. I wanted to kiss her.

When we arrived in Maui, we waited for our backpacks, but they never came. We filled out the paperwork and found out our bags were in Jamaica. This was not going well. Since it was already dark, we decided to stay at a youth hostel, figuring we could make a plan from there. The people were really nice and gave us lots of tips about the island. They even told us where we could camp if we still wanted to.

In the morning, we sat down to talk. Luka was in a better mood, and I was less exhausted now that I had slept. We really had our hearts set on camping, so we decided to buy some camping gear instead of spending a fortune on a hotel. We also decided to rent a car for three days in order to get the lay of the land, and then we planned to hitchhike for the rest of our vacation.

When we saw a place called Good Karma Car Rentals, we rented an old clunker, and when the song *My Piece of Shit Car* came over the radio, we turned up the volume and sang at the top of our lungs. Next we picked up a tarp, a sleeping bag, string, fishing line, a knife, a pot, and two forks at the local Kmart. That was it for camping gear.

I also grabbed a swimsuit, a pair of shorts, and a tank top, and that was it for clothes. We stocked up on water, fruit, and rice, and then we were done. We didn't even buy a tent. We figured it was warm enough to sleep outside, and if it rained, we had the tarp. The airline had given us those tiny pillows and a couple of toothbrushes, so I grabbed some toothpaste, toilet paper, and a bar of soap. This was definitely an adventure.

We had a blast driving around the island and even picked up a couple of hitchhikers one afternoon. We figured that would be us in a few days, so why not pay it forward? We met some nice people who showed us all the secret spots on the island, places only the locals knew about. We swam in waterfalls; went cliff diving and drove to the summit of the volcano where our "piece of shit car" died. We abandoned the car, called the rental company to let them know where it was, and hitched a ride down the mountain with a park ranger.

Before it got dark, we'd find a secluded spot on the beach and build ourselves a shelter. More precisely, Luka built a shelter while I took care of the domestic duties, like getting our bed ready, collecting firewood, and making dinner. We'd camped many times before, and both of us knew what we were doing.

One time, Luka rolled over a log to use as a headboard, and I decorated it with the long vines of purple flowers that grew along the beach. We joked about how domestic we were, and it really felt like we were playing house again, only this time on a tropical island.

During the day, people would see our shelter and they'd come over to talk to us. They'd ask if we were squatters, and when we explained that we were Canadians who'd ended up here quite by accident, they became fascinated by our story of lost luggage and last-minute itinerary changes.

Inevitably, they'd have extra sandwiches or something else they wanted to give us. We'd laugh and say we weren't poor; we *chose* to vacation this way. But the more we protested, the more they insisted. So we learned how to smile, say thank you, and enjoy the gifts we received from these kind-hearted strangers.

There's something freeing about not looking in the mirror for two weeks, and something truly magical about Maui, because every day was just like that. I'd mention I was hungry, and someone would magically appear with sandwiches. Luka would say he was thirsty, and someone would give us two bottles of water. It was crazy. Everything we needed, the Universe provided.

I was starting to understand how unimportant material things were once you let them go. We had nothing but the clothes on our backs, yet we were blissfully happy. Luka and I were of the same mind on that. We were surrounded by Mother Nature, and we were in tune with her every heartbeat. It was incredible.

Because it was winter, it got dark by five, which meant we had the beach to ourselves. Every night we'd watch the sunset, then we'd go skinny dipping under the moon. We'd light a fire, make something to eat, play the guitar (the only thing we brought on the plane) and talk. It was perfection. Every few days, we'd pack up and move to another beach, and the crazy part is we never even had to hitchhike. We'd be walking to the road, and someone would pull over to offer us a ride. That's how nice the people of Maui are.

One time, a guy in a Mercedes picked us up and gave us a bottle of champagne. We drank it lukewarm (because we neither had a cooler nor ice), but we still enjoyed it, especially since it was Christmas Eve and the moon was out. On Christmas morning, we treated ourselves to Denny's for breakfast. It was the only time we stepped foot in a restaurant, and believe it or not, it was really good.

When we got back to the beach, Luka spent ages working on an ankle bracelet made of tiny white flowers and fishing line. He knew how much I loved flowers and often referred to me as his *Flower Child*. It was the perfect Christmas present, and I was touched. I'd never felt so close to anyone in my life, and I wanted to stay there forever. Now that it was just the two of us, we were at peace. No one was telling us what we should or shouldn't do.

We were together twenty-four hours a day for ten days, and not once did we get tired of each other. It was the best vacation I'd ever had, and it had a lot to do with the fact that it was so spontaneous. It was a truly spiritual and life-changing experience. We trusted that the Universe would provide for us, and it did.

I knew Luka and I were still in the "friend zone," but on the second morning, while we were lying in bed, he made a move, and it was really nice, but then he didn't touch me for a week. I figured he was still working on his never-ending internal battle, but still, I was frustrated, and time was running out. So, for the first time in my life, I decided to take action.

It was early in the morning, and after psyching myself up for over an hour, I finally made a move. He responded. We were right in the middle of it when we suddenly heard a noise. The sun wasn't up yet, and we thought we had the beach to ourselves, but we hadn't seen the stairs leading to a private residence above us. We only knew someone was there when we heard her cough.

I should have been embarrassed (she saw everything), but I knew I'd never see her again, and I actually thought it was funny. Luka, on the other hand, was really upset. Two hours later he still seemed upset, so I asked him what was wrong. He took both my hands and looked me in the eyes.

"Sage, you're one of the most incredible people I've ever met, but I don't think we can keep doing this. Sex makes everything so complicated; it just does, and I don't want to have sex with you anymore. I respect you way too much. It will explode if we keep doing this, and I don't want that to happen. Can you understand that?" The look of concern on his face was touching.

"Of course I can. I don't want any weirdness between us, either, so if this bothers you, it bothers me. No more sex."

His whole face changed as his body relaxed. "I'm so glad you understand. Man, you really aren't like other girls, are you?"

"Nope. I'm a Sagittarius. It's a masculine sign, and we value freedom above all else. I kind of think like a dude, really," I said, laughing. OK, maybe not always, but sometimes.

"There is *nothing* masculine about you; I promise you that. You are all sexy curves and feminine wiles. Why do you think this has been so complicated for me?"

I gave him a hug, and then I made a stern face. "No more sex for you, mister! We're just friends." He laughed, and for the rest of the vacation we kept our hands to ourselves. I may have been super cool about it on the outside, but on the inside I was dying. I was so in love with him it hurt.

Every time we'd been intimate in the past, it was just sex for him, but for me, it was sex with the man I loved. Being secretly in love with your friend really sucks. And the thing was, I really could separate sex from emotions. Just not with him.

When we got home, Luka dropped me off at my apartment, but he lingered for a few minutes, like he didn't want to leave. "This feels weird, doesn't it?" he asked.

"Yes, it does."

"I can't believe you're moving to Japan in a few days."

"I know! I really need my luggage back. I can't believe they still haven't found it."

"Listen, it's New Years Eve in a few days. Would you like to spend it with me?"

"I'd love that."

He hugged me for a long time. "Thanks for an exceptional trip, Sage. I had a really great time."

I smiled. "Me, too. Thanks for coming with me."

Vivian came over the next day and wanted to hear all the gory details. When I was finished, she looked perplexed. "So what happens now?"

"Now I'm going to Japan."

"But how could you? The two of you are so close. What if he decides you really *are* the one and then you're not here? Aren't you worried he'll find another girl while you're away?"

I rolled my eyes. "Luka's a sex machine. He'll always find another girl."

"Sage . . ."

"Of course I don't want to go! It all seems so stupid now, but what can I do? Besides, he doesn't want me, Vivian. He's made that abundantly clear on more than one occasion."

"I don't believe that for one second. Anyone who's seen you together knows you're perfect for each other."

"But *he* doesn't Vivian, and that's all that matters."

"Maybe he'll realize how much you mean to him when you disappear for three months. Absence makes the heart grow fonder, right?"

"Not in my experience, but I can always hope, and in the meantime, I have to get on with my life. I can't do this anymore. I can't keep pining over someone who doesn't want me."

I wanted to do something special for Luka, so for the next two days, I worked on a scrapbook of our trip and presented it to him on New Year's Eve. He loved it. He looked at all the pictures, and when he got to one of me bogged down like a packhorse, half dripping from the waterfall we'd just swum in, he smiled.

"This is my favorite," he said affectionately.

"This one? Really?"

"Yes. It's exactly how I think of you. Completely natural. You look beautiful."

"Thanks."

"Hey, check this out." He went to his room and came back with his sarong, the one he'd worn while we were away. "Smell this. It still smells like Maui! Every time I start missing the beach, I take a whiff of this, and it brings me back." I smelled the sarong, and he was right. It smelled like Maui.

We had a great time that night, just the two of us hanging out on New Year's Eve. We were still in the afterglow of our trip, and the zen hadn't left us yet. I slept with him in his bed—after all, we'd been sleeping together for the past two weeks, so it seemed weird not to. Nothing happened, of course, and in the morning he drove me home.

"Do you really have to go?" he asked once we got there.

"Yes, I do. Sienna's already there. She left a few weeks ago."

"I don't want you to go. I still don't think it's safe."

"It's only for three months. It'll go quickly, you'll see. Besides, I'm sure you'll be chasing skirt by tomorrow and you'll forget all about me."

"Will you write?"

"Of course I will."

He paused for a second. "Are you coming back?"

"Of course I am!"

"Good. Make sure you stay alert at all times. I'm still not comfortable with you running off to Japan. What if something bad happens to you?"

"I'm a big girl, Luka. I can take care of myself."

"Have you heard from Sienna yet?"

"Yes, she called yesterday. She sounds like she's having the time of her life. She said the club is super cool and it's a big party every night. The apartment is tiny, but she's arranged for us to share a room, so that's good."

"OK, that makes me feel better. Please call me when you arrive?"

"I will," I said. And with that, I was gone.

Fourteen

Whenever things get tough, or we feel cornered or frightened, humans tend to go into *fight or flight* mode. I generally choose *flight* myself. There was the flight to Italy, the flight to New York, and now the flight to Japan. My life had a habit of blowing up, and whenever it did, I ran. Especially if it had to do with the opposite sex. I liked to call it *traveling*, but my sisters always called it *running away*.

Sienna and I were in Japan for two and a half months, and it was putting a strain on our relationship. I hated everything about the club and the girls we worked with, but she loved it and resented the fact that I was so unhappy.

After my trip to Maui, it was such a shock to be surrounded by cut-throat people who only cared about money and material things. It weighed heavily on my spirit, and I constantly complained, which is why we fought. Eventually, I found my footing, and we met some nice people, which made a huge difference. We started exploring the area, and I even started having fun, although I still hated the job.

"Moshi moshi," I said cheerfully as I answered the phone.

"Is that really how you answer the phone in Japan?" said a familiar voice, one I hadn't heard in two and a half months.

"Luka! Oh my God, is that really you?"

He laughed, and it was music to my ears. How strange to hear his voice while I was still in this place. It brought back a flood of emotions. I hadn't heard from him since I'd left, which felt like a lifetime ago.

"How are things in Japan?"

"Good. I mean the job's *meh*, but everything else is good. I can't believe you're calling me. This will cost you a fortune."

"I won't keep you long. I just want to know when you're coming home."

"Oh! Um . . . I haven't decided yet. Technically, I'm finished in three weeks, but I'm thinking about doing another contract. I might go to Bali for a month, then I was thinking of trying out a different club. Something in Tokyo, perhaps."

"What? No! You can't do that!"

"Um . . . OK. Although I'm fairly certain you're not the boss of me," I said, laughing.

"I'd really like you to come home, Sage. Now. Not later."

I didn't answer for a minute. These were the words I'd longed to hear for so long, but I wasn't sure I trusted them. Luka had been stringing me along for years, even if that wasn't his intention. If he really wanted me to come home, I knew I'd go, but after everything we'd been through, I wasn't about to make it easy. I left for a reason, and I wasn't ready to go back.

"Before you answer, just listen. I've been doing a lot of thinking lately, and I have a proposition for you. Please come home so we can talk. We really miss you."

"A proposition? What kind of proposition?"

"Something that's been on my mind lately, but I'd prefer to talk about it face to face."

Could it be? Had my absence made his heart grow fonder? What else could he possibly be talking about? Hesitantly I said, "OK . . . wait a minute. Who's *we?*"

"Jamie's here, and he wants to talk to you, but before I go, promise you'll think about it?"

"Sure," I said non-committedly.

"Scratch that. Don't think about it, just get back here. This is where you belong. I'm going to pass you over to Jamie now. It was good to hear your voice, Sage. I'll see you soon."

A new voice came on the line. "Hello?"

"Jamie! Oh my gosh, two of you in one day. How are you?"

"Sage, my sweet Sage, how I've missed you. I'm not very good, to tell you the truth, so Luka thought it might help if I talked to my dearest friend."

"Oh no! What's going on?"

"I don't want to talk about it now, but I'll write and tell you everything. I just needed to hear your voice for a minute."

"Oh, Jamie, I'm sorry you're sad. I wish I could give you a hug."

"I'd like nothing more. Are you coming home soon?"

"Well, like I told Luka, my contract's up in three weeks, and I'm trying to decide whether or not to do another one."

"Don't! I need you. *We* need you. Come home, OK?"

"Awww . . . I miss you guys too. I really do."

"So you'll come home?" he said, hopefully.

I thought about it for a minute, but who was I kidding? Of course I was going home.

"How could I possibly resist you two? Yes, I'll come home, if that's what you want."

"Thank God," he said on an exhale. "I can't wait to see you. Listen, I'd better go. I'll write soon."

After I hung up, I sat down. Luka had a proposition? What did that mean? The more I thought about it, the more I foolishly convinced myself that this was the part where the boy asks the girl to come home, then falls on his knees, begging her to forgive him for taking so long to get his head out of his ass. Girls and their bloody fairy tales.

"What was that all about?" asked Sienna.

"Luka wants me to come home. He said he has a proposition."

"What kind of proposition?"

"He didn't say. He was rather elusive about it. He wants to talk face to face."

"Maybe he'll finally get his head out of his ass and admit he's in love with you."

I laughed. Great minds think alike.

"Were you really planning to do another contract?"

"I was thinking about it. I wanted to see if another club would be different."

"And you're avoiding Luka."

"Yah, pretty much."

Jamie's letter arrived a week later. It was fifteen pages long. He loved writing.

> *March 19th, 1999: My Dearest Sage, as I sit down to write you, I do so from a bench in English Bay. I know how much you love the ocean, and I wanted to be here, in our favorite spot, while I tell you my story. My very foundation has been pulled from beneath me. I'm sure Luka already told you and said not to admit it. It's been and continues to be hard to share my Diamond Sage with anyone else. At times, it even feels like I've lost you to him. I'm jealous of the way you two have your music to share. I don't know if I can handle much more of it. I know that's my problem, so I'll just write . . .*

I sighed when I finished the letter. Yes, Jamie had gone through something terrible with his girlfriend, and I felt bad for him, but I was frustrated, too. Once again, he was feeling sorry for himself. It reminded me so much of my mother. And if he was so concerned about losing me, why had he treated me so terribly for the past year and a half? I never *chose* Luka over him. I didn't even realize I *had* to choose. He did that all on his own.

Also concerning was what he wrote about not wanting to share me with Luka. Is that what was going on? Was he still telling Luka to stay away from me? I couldn't imagine what the two of them talked about while I was gone, but it couldn't be good.

What I really wanted was a letter from Luka, but it never came. Part of me dared to dream that things would be different when I got back. I tried not to put too much hope into it, but hope was all I had. I was still in love with him. I couldn't help it. The heart wants what the heart wants, even when your head tells you to run.

I was in a weird headspace when I got home, and apparently I wasn't alone. I was staying with Vivian and Heather until I could get myself situated, and I immediately noticed some tension between the girls, even though they were ignoring it. Still, it was there under the surface, making me nervous. This wasn't an unusual experience for me. Every time I moved away, I lost friends, especially those I was closest to. It was a high price to pay for my neverending wanderlust.

Heather had a new boyfriend, so she wasn't around much, but Vivian was definitely off. When I asked, she told me it was nothing. I knew she was lying, and I couldn't understand why she was shutting me out. I had missed her so much while I was away, and I looked forward to catching up. Japan was lonely, even though I was surrounded by people. The entire time I was there, I longed for the peace I'd felt in Maui, the same peace I'd been searching for my entire life.

Something must have happened while I was away, but neither girl admitted it. I wondered if it was because Heather found a boyfriend at the same time that I left. Had Vivian felt abandoned by us? Like I said, it wouldn't be the first time I lost friends because of my travels. It happened when I moved to Italy and to a lesser degree when I moved to New York. Whatever it was, it felt like a foreshadowing of things to come.

I called my job at the theater to let them know I was back and ready to return to work. Imagine my surprise when they had no idea what I was talking about. I had arranged a leave of absence before flying out, but my boss didn't remember and told me she was sorry, but she couldn't fire the girl who had replaced me. Once again, I was jobless, homeless, and starting from scratch.

When Jasper and I went to Luka's place the following Friday, I learned that his proposition had nothing to do with being in love with me. What he wanted, was for the three of us to collaborate on a music project. He was finally ready to record his songs, but he needed Jasper to write the lyrics and for me to sing the harmonies. This was something I'd fantasized about for ages but not what I was expecting. I was really disappointed.

When I got home, Vivian was waiting. "Well? What did he say? What's this mysterious proposition?"

"He wants me and Jasper to help him write songs. He's ready to take his music to the next level."

"That's amazing! It's about time he does something with that voice of his. Oh my God. You two should form a band! You're so good together."

"I know. I'm really excited about it. We already wrote a song and it's *good*, Vivian. It's really good. Jasper's a genius, and Luka's voice . . . well, you already know."

"What about the two of you? How did that go?"

"I don't know, to be honest. He was happy to see me, but it was weird. Everything was the same, yet different, like he's taken a step back. It was subtle, but it was there, like he's trying to keep his distance."

"Maybe he needs a minute to process. You've been gone for three months. A lot could have happened while you were away."

Is that what Vivian was doing? Keeping her distance so she could process?

About a month later, Vivian and I were in the backyard smoking a joint. Heather had given her notice, so I asked Vivian if we should move in together, but she said she wanted her own place. I was disappointed, but there wasn't much I could do. Sienna said the same thing when we got back from Japan, and I was surprised, until I realized she was still mad at me.

Things between Luka and I hadn't improved, either, and I didn't know what to do. It felt like I was losing him and everyone else, and the more they pulled away, the tighter I tried to hold on. Sienna was mad at me; Heather was busy with her new boyfriend; Jamie was busy with work; Luka was holding me at arm's length, and Vivian had replaced our circle of friends with new friends. It suddenly felt like I didn't have friends anymore, just acquaintances.

Luka rarely stopped by, and we didn't go out anymore unless it was with the gang. He said he was busy planning a trip to Serbia in a couple of months, but I knew he was still seeing that older woman. We still had our weekly music sessions, but Jasper was the one who picked me up and drove me home. It's like Luka didn't want to be alone with me anymore.

"Sage, you can't keep doing this. I think it's time you tell Luka how you feel," said Vivian as she passed me the joint.

"He knows how I feel."

"No, I'm not sure he does. Men are pretty dense, and you've never actually told him the truth. I think it's time to put your cards on the table. Tell him you're in love with him, and tell him you're willing to give him what he wants. Marriage and kids. That's always been the problem. Tell him so you don't end up living with regret, and if he doesn't feel the same way, at least you'll know."

She was right. It was time to confess my feelings once and for all, so I asked Luka if he could come over so we could talk. I paced for hours before he got there. I had no idea what I was supposed to say, and I was nervous as hell. When he arrived, we sat down in the living room, and Vivian excused herself so we could have some privacy.

"What's up? he asked after she left.

I nervously bit my lip, and he gave me a quizzical look. I stood up, pacing the floor once again as I tried to gather my nerve.

"Sage, you're freaking me out. What's going on?"

"I'm in love with you," I blurted out, and then I immediately wanted to take it back when I saw the look of anger on his face.

"What?" he practically exploded.

"I'm in love with you, and I've been in love with you since the first day we met." I said nervously, but he started shaking his head.

"No," he said. "No, no no."

I should have stopped talking, but once I started I couldn't stop. I needed him to understand how I felt and I knew I'd only get one shot at it. "I know I said I don't want to get married or have children, but I'm crazy about you, and I would happily give you those things."

"Why are you doing this?" he demanded angrily as he stood up. "This goes against everything we've ever talked about. You know the rules! We can't be friends if you have feelings for me. No wonder it's been so complicated lately." Tears came to my eyes, and he looked at me in disgust, his voice cold. "My brother was right. And all this time I thought you were different."

"I am different! Just because I fell in love with you, it doesn't change who I am."

He looked like he wanted to run. He looked like a caged animal. He shook his head and blew out a frustrated breath. "And we just started making music together. This ruins everything. How can we be friends now that I know this?"

I wanted to die of humiliation and rejection, but instead I begged him to pretend I hadn't said anything. "This changes nothing, except I can finally move on with my life now that I know the truth," I said desperately.

He looked at me like I was insane. He wasn't buying it.

"Luka, I've been in love with you this entire time, and you had no idea, so obviously I'm capable of keeping my feelings in check. Please don't throw away our friendship over this. Let's forget this conversation ever happened and go back to how it was. I'll deal with my feelings on my own."

I knew he was torn. I could see it on his face. He'd never been good at hiding his feelings. He no longer trusted me, but since he wanted to finish his songs, he agreed. He was angry when he left, and I cried because it was finally over. Luka didn't love me, and he never would.

We still got together once a week, and the sessions were fun, but I never saw him outside of those sessions. When I look back on it now, it's amazing how willing I was to accept any scrap of attention Luka was willing to give me. I was so desperate for love that I not only allowed this type of behavior, I gravitated towards it.

I guess it's not surprising that I was attracted to unrequited love. It was all I'd ever known. All my family ever showed me. Love was confusing to me. I still didn't understand it. Mentally, I was mature beyond my years, but emotionally, I was still that twelve-year-old girl wondering why her parents didn't love her.

At the end of the month, Heather and Vivian had a huge fight about money, and I was caught in the middle. I tried to stay out of it, but I obviously made the wrong choice because after we all moved out, they ghosted me, and I felt the loss of their friendship very deeply. I desperately tried to repair the damage, but they wouldn't even take my calls. Once again, I was all alone and starting from scratch.

FIFTEEN

In June, I met someone new, and it was quite unexpected—especially *where* we met. Wreck Beach isn't just a destination; it's a way of life. In the early seventies, a group of hippies made it their home, and they've been going there ever since. You have to walk down five hundred stairs through a redwood forest just to get there, but it's worth it. At the bottom is a wide sandy beach with the forest in the background and the mountains in the forefront. It's positively gorgeous.

Most people can't imagine taking their clothes off in public, but somehow, this place made it easy. Of course, in 1999, nobody had smartphones, and the locals kept a close watch for any looky-loos, so it felt safe. In fact, it was kind of a community of sorts. I imagine it's quite different today, but back then, it had a real bohemian vibe, making it a fun place to visit. Luka and I used to go there all the time.

Now, there's a lot more illegal activity going on than just nudity. You can buy weed, mushrooms, edibles, cold drinks, food, portraits, massages . . . whatever floats your boat. It's that kind of a place.

It was cloudy when my friend and I arrived, so we sat on a log and chatted while enjoying the view. It wasn't long before Sammy the pizza guy came over. He'd been selling pizza on this beach for over a decade, and he wanted to introduce himself. He was a nice man, and we ended up chatting for quite a while.

Eventually, my friend decided to get a massage, then Sammy saw someone he knew, so I laid down and closed my eyes. When Sammy returned, he wasn't alone. He was talking to someone with an incredibly charming French accent. I was intrigued, and the more I listened, the more I wanted to turn around, except I couldn't do that without being obvious.

Eventually, my curiosity got the best of me. I simply *had* to know what he looked like, so I sat up, turned my head . . . and gasped. A gorgeous, naked Greek god was staring back at me. "Holy crap balls," I said before I could stop myself. He was *stunning*, and I was momentarily blinded by his perfect teeth and megawatt smile.

Mr. Adonis had smooth, sun-kissed skin and the most amazing body I'd ever seen. He had long legs and muscular thighs. His torso formed a perfect V, and everything (and I do mean everything) was picture perfect. He was at least six feet tall and had hazel eyes, light brown hair, and a naturally athletic body.

I'd never seen anyone like him, and when our eyes met, there was an amused look on his face, like he knew exactly what I was thinking because it's what every female on the planet was thinking. He was gorgeous, and he knew it, but he also knew how to be gracious, which was an interesting contradiction.

To say he was charming, sexy, and magnetic was an understatement. His stare was so intense I found myself blushing under his gaze. I'm not easily intimidated, but this guy was so hot (Jason Mamoa hot) that I found myself *all kinds* of intimidated.

Sammy made the introductions, and we shook hands. My friend's face was still buried in the sand, and since I really wanted her to behold this beautiful specimen of a man, I kicked her in the foot. She didn't move, so I kicked her again, but she was down for the count.

Christian (said with a sexy French accent) had just moved to Vancouver from Montreal. He had a lot of energy and was extremely animated when he talked. His hand gestures reminded me of the boys, and that's when it hit me. He was gay. Of course he was gay. The perfectly coiffed hair, the manicured hands and feet, the soft-spoken accent . . . it all added up.

After a few minutes, he said he had to go, then Sammy took off, and my friend (who finally woke up from her massage coma) said she had to leave as well. I was having such a good time that I decided to stay a little longer.

At six, I was packed and ready to go when someone sat down beside me. I looked up, and I couldn't believe it. It was Christian! He smiled his megawatt smile, said hello, and opened a package of chocolate-covered mushrooms—a Wreck Beach specialty. I laughed. Luka and I used to buy them, too. They were perfect for a day at the beach.

"Would you like some? They're really good," he said, holding out his hand.

"Um . . . sure. In an hour, I'll be at home tripping out by myself, but why not?"

As we sat there, Christian and I got to know each other, but I was a little confused. It felt like he was flirting with me, but I was sure he was gay. Either way, he was fun to talk to and very intoxicating. He literally oozed sex from every pore in his body, and I was intrigued.

"A bunch of us are going camping tonight. Are you coming?" he asked.

"Camping? No. Where are you going?"

"To some hot springs around Pemberton, I think? I'm not familiar with the area. I've only been here a couple of weeks."

"I know that place! It's fantastic. The hot springs are right beside a river. You'll love it."

"You should come with us!" he said excitedly.

"Me? No, I can't."

"Why not?"

"Because I'm not prepared to go camping. All I have is a bathing suit and a sarong."

"So?"

I looked at my gorgeous new companion like he was an idiot. "You know it gets cold at night, right? I'll freeze my ass off."

Sammy spotted us and came over to where we were sitting. "Sage, you're still here. Does this mean you're camping with us?"

I laughed. "I can't."

"Why not?"

"Because I didn't bring any clothes."

"Not a problem. We're stopping at my house, and I can lend you some."

"See!" said Christian, triumphant.

"I don't have a sleeping bag, a pillow, a tent—"

"No problem. My tent sleeps six, and there's an extra sleeping bag at my place," said Sammy. They were ganging up on me, and I was running out of excuses.

"Guys, I appreciate the offer, but I was only going to the beach today, so I didn't bring any money, cigarettes, or food."

"I've got pizza," said Sammy.

"I've got cigarettes," said Christian. "It looks like you're out of excuses."

Jeez. These guys were quick. I really *was* out of excuses. Then it hit me.

"Wait . . . I can't. I'm having lunch with my sister tomorrow."

Bam! Christian handed me a phone, so I dialed Sienna's number. I guess I was caught up in their enthusiasm, which was contagious.

"Sienna? Hey, I'm thinking of going camping with some people I met on the beach, and I'm wondering if we can move our lunch to another day."

"Did you just say you're going camping with people you just met?" she asked, incredulous.

"Well . . . yes, sort of—"

"Are you fucking crazy?" she shouted. "You're not getting in a car with people you just met and letting them take you to the woods. That's how people get murdered! What the hell are you thinking?"

"Calm down. It's not just the two of them. There's like a dozen other people."

"I don't care. Tell them they can—"

"Gotta go . . . sorry about lunch . . . I'm losing you . . . bye," I said as I hung up. Yeesh. Sienna was so bossy.

As we walked up the ten million stairs (because that's what it feels like on the way up), Christian turned to me and smiled. "So, Sage . . . how old are you?" And that's when I knew he wasn't gay.

"Twenty-seven," I answered casually. "You?"

"Thirty," he said with a smile.

The four-hour drive to Pemberton is nothing short of spectacular. It's a drive I've done often, and it never gets old. On one side of the highway you have the coastal mountains, and on the other is the Pacific Ocean, dotted with hundreds of islands. Not only is it scenic, it's a little dangerous because people tend to speed. Christian was no exception.

He drove very fast, and I asked him several times to slow down. He seemed like a capable driver, but I knew he was new to the area and unfamiliar with this road. Sammy didn't seem to mind. He was passed out on the back seat despite the fact that the radio was blaring and all the windows were down.

Not only was Christian driving like a bat out of hell, but he also had only one hand on the wheel. The other one was on my thigh, which I found a bit forward, and I told him as much. He just laughed and kept his hand right where it was. He was cocky that way, and the mushrooms weren't helping. This whole scenario should have been frightening, but it wasn't. It was dangerous, but also thrilling.

I'd never met anyone like Christian before. He said exactly what he was thinking, and I found that refreshing, especially after being mind-fucked by Luka for the past two years. His energy level was off the charts, and I loved his positive outlook on life. His magnetism was so strong I couldn't have escaped it if I'd tried. I have a pretty big personality myself, but his was enormous. It was nice to meet a man who wasn't intimidated by me for once. If anything, I was a little intimidated by him.

On the drive, I learned that he was raised by a single mom and that he had an older sister and a seven-year-old son. He and his girlfriend had lived together for eight years, and their relationship ended only a few months ago. That's when he and his best friend decided to move to Vancouver. I also learned he owned a successful marketing company in Montreal, one that he'd started himself. He promoted hair salons by putting together coupons with free services.

"Who's running your business now that you're here?" I asked.

"My ex. When we broke up, we didn't want to deal with child support so we made a deal. I gave her the business and the house but took the car and ten thousand dollars so I could start over, here."

"You left her your business?"

"Absolutely. She's an amazing person and the mother of my son. I wanted to make sure they were taken care of."

"And you think you can recreate this business over here?"

"Why not? I'm an excellent salesman. That's why I left the beach today. I was signing a contract with a salon."

I was impressed. It was nice to hear someone talk about their ex that way, and I found it amazing that he gave up a successful business to make sure his family was supported. He sounded like a stand-up guy.

By the time we got to the campsite, it was late, and from the looks of it, the other campers had gone to bed. I felt bad when we descended upon them. We were many, and we were loud. Christian and I headed over to the hot springs, and when I got overheated, I perched on the side of the tub to cool off. The next thing I knew, I was lying on my back with eight faces staring down at me. Apparently I fainted, but the only thing I remember was opening my eyes and wondering who these people were and why I was naked.

"Oh my God, are you OK?" asked one of the heads.

"Take it easy, little lady," said another one. "You just fainted."

"I did?"

"Yah, man. It was crazy! One minute you were sitting on the side of the tub, and the next minute you were falling backwards!" said a third head.

I'd never fainted before. I'm guessing the heat, the mushrooms, and the lack of food are what caused it. Christian was very attentive as he walked me back to the tent, making sure I was OK. I put on some warmer clothing, and then we sat near the fire with the rest of our group, who were still naked. I laughed when I saw them all sitting there. You really had to admire their commitment to nudity.

They offered us a veggie dog and a cup of tea, which I accepted gratefully. I was feeling much better now that I had some food in my system and the mushrooms had worn off. Afterwards, I decided to go to bed, and Christian came with me. When we got to the tent, he pulled me into his arms and kissed me passionately. He was a great kisser and a little thrill ran through me.

"I've wanted to do that all day," he said, grinning.

"You have?" No one had ever said that to me before.

"Oh, yes. And now I'm going to make love to you," he said, his eyes burning with desire. He grabbed my hand and tried to pull me into the tent, but I stayed where I was. I'm not sure he was used to women saying *no* to him, because he looked confused.

I like a man who's self-assured, but not when he's so cocky he assumes you'll go to bed with him just because he asked. When men border on arrogant, I generally feel the need to knock them down a peg. The truth is that I did, in fact, want to sleep with him. I just didn't want him to take it for granted.

"That's rather presumptuous of you," I said hotly.

"What do you mean?"

"I just met you, and I'm not that kind of girl. Besides, you're a little too sure of yourself for my liking. Maybe I don't feel like *making love to you,*" I said, imitating his accent.

He grabbed me and kissed me again, calling my bluff, and this time, I laughed as he pulled me into the tent. At least I knew where I stood with this guy. Christian knew exactly what he wanted, and he went for it without apology. There were no games, no pretenses, and no false promises.

"I want to fuck you right now," he said, and somehow it sounded sexy. My whole body tingled with anticipation. He dipped me suddenly, and I laughed. Then he kissed me again as he pulled me to the ground.

"Wait!" I said, trying to catch my breath. "Do you even have a condom?"

"What? No. Does it matter?"

"Yes it *matters!* Have you never heard of AIDS? I'm sorry, but I'm not sleeping with you without protection." I was actually shocked that Enrique Suave wasn't carrying a whole *bag* of condoms. He looked positively dumbfounded. We were in the middle of nowhere, so it's not like he could go out and buy one. He stood there staring at me, and then he had an idea.

"What if I get one from one of the other guys?"

"Your plan is to ask around until you find one? Oh, great. Then everyone will know I'm easy and I put out on a first date." Which I *don't*. OK, sometimes. Like on vacation when I won't be remembered.

"Does it matter?"

"Yes it matters! I have a reputation to uphold." I didn't even know these people, but somehow my reputation was important to me.

"I'll be very subtle. I promise." And then he disappeared. I was standing in the middle of the tent wondering what I was doing. This clean cut, well-presented young man was definitely what you'd call a bad boy. It was both intimidating and exciting. I hadn't felt this alive in a long time, and I liked it. Luka and Jamie kept me on a pedestal, but Christian was different, so I decided to go with the flow, wherever that might take me.

All of a sudden, I heard someone yelling outside. "Does anybody have a condom I can borrow?"

SIXTEEN

The next morning, Christian and I were up early, and the first thing we saw were naked bodies strewn all over the place. Our crew had partied all night, and now they were passed out. I felt sorry for the unsuspecting campers who had to wake up in the middle of a hippy commune. It was funny, but I was glad we were leaving.

The drive home was very entertaining. We talked non-stop, and it must have taken half a day because we kept pulling over to have sex. We had sex in the car . . . in the forest . . . in the car again . . . I'd never done anything so outrageous, and I have to admit the danger of getting caught only added to the excitement.

It was nice to finally meet someone who found me so desirable, he couldn't even go an hour without wanting me again. My self-confidence had taken a beating for so long, and now there was this really hot guy who couldn't keep his hands off me. Damn if I didn't deserve it.

Christian told me he really liked me, but he wasn't looking for a commitment. He had just ended a relationship and wasn't ready to jump into another one. He wanted to keep seeing me, but those were his terms.

"Are you OK with that? If not, I understand."

A man who knew how to communicate. What a novelty. "Actually, I'm fabulous with that. I just got out of something intense myself, and I wouldn't mind a little fun right now."

"Wonderful! I'm glad to hear that because you are the sexiest woman I've ever met," he growled and then looked for a place to pull over.

I beamed from the compliment. Every time he looked at me, it was with such intensity it was almost overwhelming. His look was positively *primal*, and it made me feel so alive. I felt like I really *was* the sexiest woman in the world.

Sex with Christian was like nothing I'd ever experienced. Until meeting him, my encounters had all been one-night stands, and none of them were concerned with whether or not I was satisfied. I'd had plenty of partners over the years, but in reality, I was extremely inexperienced. The first time Christian asked what turned me on, I sat there like an idiot, unable to answer. Maybe Luka was right. I really *was* a good girl, except it wasn't by choice.

Christian was a wonderful lover. Under his tutelage, I blossomed sexually. He made it fun, exciting, and *normal.* I may have been a late bloomer, but I was blooming now, and I loved every minute of it. I felt empowered and sexy, and soon I started dressing in more provocative outfits because I knew it turned him on.

When the gang got together for Jasper's birthday, Christian picked out a dress that was sheer and a little too short. As we sat down for dinner, he put his arm across the back of my chair, and then he slowly ran his hand up my leg. I had to stop him before he went any further. When it came to sex, Christian had no shame, and he didn't care who was watching.

Later at the club, we danced intimately, and his expression said it all. Both Luka and Jamie looked concerned. They weren't used to seeing me with another man, let alone one who was so primal, and I'm not sure they liked it, or my outfit. Gone was the pinup girl they kept on a shelf. These days, I was the sexy vixen, and I loved that it bothered them.

We partied a lot that summer as I tried to keep up with Christian's insatiable appetite for booze, sex, and drugs. Even when we went to the movies, he brought mushrooms. Sometimes I had to say no because it was too much for me, but Christian was like the Energizer Bunny. He just kept going and going.

When my parents dropped by one afternoon, I introduced them to Christian, and they looked surprised. I still saw them several times a year, but I never talked about my personal life or boys. As far as I was concerned, it was none of their business. Christian flirted with my mother, and she ate it up, which was a little unnerving, but he also managed to charm my father, and I was impressed.

After they left, he told me they were lovely and we should have dinner with them. He was especially taken with my father, probably because his own father had died when he was young. We even talked about Sidney and how she still blamed my parents for everything that was wrong in her life. She had no intention of ever forgiving them, seeing them, or letting them meet her children.

"If your sister is miserable, it's no longer your parents' fault. It's been over ten years since she left home. If she's still unhappy, that's on her. Not them. She needs to take responsibility for her own life and her own happiness."

I'd never heard anyone explain it like that, and I was impressed with his insight. I liked that he was older than me, and that he was worldly and wise. I could tell that he understood things from a spiritual perspective. He'd traveled all over the world, and he promised that we'd travel even more once his business was up and running.

Now that I'd found Christian, I'd have done anything to keep him around. We were still casual, but in reality he'd been sleeping at my place for two months, and neither of us seemed interested in anyone else. In August, he went to Montreal to see his son and called me every day. When he got back, I noticed scratches above his eye and asked what happened.

"Sit down," he said seriously. "I have something to tell you."

"Uh oh. That can't be good."

I listened as he confessed to sleeping with his ex while he was away, and that last night when he'd called me, she had overheard our conversation. She knew about me and thought I was just a fling, but after listening to our conversation, she realized he was in love with me. An argument ensued, and that's where the scratches came from.

I tried keeping my face neutral as he told me this, although he probably saw the hurt there. He was pretty astute that way. His confession was full of information, and it took me a moment to digest it. This was his second visit to Montreal and I'd had no idea he was having sex with his ex, but we weren't in a committed relationship, so he was allowed to sleep with whomever he liked. More importantly, did he say he was in love with me?

No one had ever said that to me before, and although it was kind of a back-handed compliment . . . he *loved* me. Somebody actually loved me. I'd known for weeks that I was falling for him, but I'd kept it to myself. After confessing my love to Luka and being squashed like a bug, I promised myself I'd never do that again. He watched me closely and waited until I was ready to hear more, because there *was* more.

"So what are you saying?" I asked cautiously.

"I'm saying that until that moment, I hadn't realized I'm in love with you, but she's right. I'm in love with you, Sage, and it scares me to death, but that's not all. This morning on the plane, I was freaking out. As I told you, I'm not ready for another relationship, so when the woman beside me started flirting and wanted to join the mile-high club . . . I took her up on it."

This time, I couldn't hide my shock. Two women in twenty-four hours? I tried to pull my hands away, but he held them tighter.

"Please, Sage. Let me finish. I know this hurts, but I have to tell you every-thing. After we had sex, I felt sick to my stomach. It didn't make me happy. It made me feel empty, and I realized that you're the only woman I want. What I'm saying is, I want us to be exclusive from now on, and I'm hoping you feel the same way."

He paused, and I waited for him to continue. "Do you love me, Sage? Because I'm madly in love with you, and I don't want an open relationship anymore. I only want you."

I threw my arms around him. What can I say? None of that other stuff mattered. All that mattered was that he loved me and I loved him. For the first time in my life, somebody actually loved me. Someone actually cared about *me*. It had taken twenty-seven years, but I finally had my first boyfriend.

Burnaby 1980

Behind our elementary school was a huge forest, and we loved playing there. Today it's called *The Stoney Creek Trail System,* but back then it was simply called *The Back Yard.* It's full of massive cedar trees and shallow creeks, and whenever my sisters and I had time, we'd explore the woods with our friends.

One Saturday when I was eight, my friend and I were catching tadpoles when we suddenly heard a noise. We turned to see what it was just as a man jumped out of the bushes. We screamed at the top of our lungs, but before we could run, he grabbed my friend by the waist. They tumbled to the ground as I stood there watching, my brain trying to process what was happening . . . that we were actually in danger.

I stood there frozen as the two of them struggled, not sure what to do. The man was laughing, but his face had this weird expression on it. When my friend screamed, I realized she didn't know him and this wasn't a game. Her scream snapped me out of it, and I leapt into action, but I was no match for a full-grown man.

I knew I couldn't just stand there, but I wasn't sure what to do. He was still laughing, with this crazed look on his face, like he was daring me to do something, so I did. "I'm getting help," I told my friend, as I turned and ran towards the apartment complex, shouting at the top of my lungs. We were in the forest, on the other side of the soccer field, and I knew no one could hear me from so far away, so I *had* to get to the complex.

The first unit was a Block Parent, and as I flew across the field, I prayed someone was home. Thankfully, people were already coming towards me before I got there. As we ran to the spot where I'd left my friend, she suddenly emerged from the bushes, holding her cheek. She said the man heard me yelling, so he bit her and let her go. She looked terrified. We both were.

My mother had warned my sisters and I to be careful because several local children had gone missing recently. She always worried about serial killers, and she instilled that fear into us. In fact, it was around that time that the milk carton kids were introduced. Breakfast was a daily reminder of just how dangerous the world could be.

Several months later, I went to court. I remember driving there with my parents, swearing in, and testifying while the crazy man glared from his seat. The whole thing was very intimidating for an eight-year-old girl. As it turned out, the young man was in his early twenties and was high on drugs at the time. He said he never meant to hurt us and that he was only playing.

I have no idea what happened to him. I think he went to rehab, but I'm not sure. My parents never talked about it. Today, I would have been sent to therapy or something, but nobody considered long-term effects in those days. Burying it and forgetting it ever happened was a way of life.

I always felt guilty for running away and leaving that poor girl by herself when she was so afraid. She must have thought I was abandoning her. I'm not sure if she ever forgave me, or if she was even mad in the first place, because I never saw her again. As an adult, I know I did the right thing under the circumstances, but it haunted me as a child, and I vowed I'd never run away again.

SEVENTEEN

When Luka returned from Serbia at the end of August, he invited Jasper and I over for a jam session. He said he had good news and I was hoping it was about the music, but it wasn't. Apparently, he was walking down the street one day when he saw a girl and *knew* she was the one. He went out with her a couple of times and then he asked her to marry him. I almost fell out of my chair when he dropped that bomb. So did Jasper.

I knew I was out of the loop, but this is the last thing I'd expected. How had so much changed in such a short period of time? I always knew Luka would marry a Serbian, but not in a million years had I expected him to go there and pick one right off the street. I had so many questions, but I didn't dare ask them. I didn't want to betray how disappointed I was, and I was grateful that I no longer loved him.

"Congratulations, Luka. It's what you've always wanted," I said instead.

He went to his room to grab his guitar, and as soon as he was out of earshot, Jasper leaned over and whispered, "Is he fucking crazy? He's marrying a girl he just met? She probably just wants a visa. What a schmuck." I was glad it wasn't just me.

We spent several hours working on the songs, and then I gave Christian a call. He was supposed to pick me up, but he wasn't answering his phone. I left a message, but he didn't call back. Being alone with Luka was awkward under the circumstances, so I called again, but he still didn't answer. Luka could see my distress, and it only made it worse that it was happening in front of him, of all people.

"Has he ever done this before?" he asked while we waited.

"No, never. This is so strange." I could see his mind turning over the possibilities. I saw concern and pity, and I hated him for that. I knew he was judging me. His look said, 'I'm super happy, and I'm so sorry you aren't.'

By two in the morning, I was an absolute wreck. I'd been pacing the floor and calling for hours while every worst-case scenario ran through my mind.

"Listen, I wouldn't worry. Maybe his battery died. I'm sure there's a logical explanation for this." But I could see the look of doubt on his face, the same way I felt it in my heart. Something was wrong.

Needless to say, I didn't sleep a wink, and when the phone rang the next morning, I waited with bated breath as Luka answered it. It was Christian. Luka handed me the phone and stepped into the kitchen to give us some privacy.

"Christian, are you OK? Where are you?"

"Oh my God, Sage, I'm so sorry! Please don't worry. I'm fine. I don't know what happened last night. I went to a bar to have a drink and ended up buying coke. I should have told you this before, but I'm an addict, and last night I relapsed. I'm so ashamed."

He kept babbling, but I wasn't listening. What . . . the . . . fuck. And I thought Luka's news was shocking. I was speechless. I mean, what was I supposed to say to that?

"I know this is shocking, and I should've told you before, but I couldn't. I didn't want to lose you, and I thought I had it under control. Please, Sage . . . I'm on my way, and I'm going to tell you everything. Please don't be mad at me."

He was sobbing, and it broke my heart to hear the pain in his voice. I could feel his desperation through the phone. Luka was in the kitchen making himself busy, but he obviously heard the whole thing, and I could see the sympathy in his eyes. We may have been miles apart these days, but we used to be very close, and he knew I was in shock.

"Is everything OK?" he asked gently.

"Yes. He's on his way. He'll be here soon," I said without emotion.

"Good. Are you OK?"

I nodded, but I wasn't sure. I was glad Christian wasn't hurt, but I knew my life was about to become far more complicated. Luka looked like he wanted to hug me, but instead, he leaned on the kitchen counter, giving me space. Guys do that when they want to distance themselves from you. They take a step back instead of hugging you when you need it.

"Do you want to talk about it?" he asked.

This was a private matter between me and Christian, but under the circumstances, Luka deserved an explanation, so I told him what Christian had just said.

"He's an addict?" He couldn't hide the surprise in his voice.

"That's what he said."

"And you had no idea?"

"Not a clue. He's been with me practically 24/7 for almost three months. How is this even possible? I mean, we smoke pot and do mushrooms sometimes but nothing like this."

Luka took a moment before he answered, and I could tell he was choosing his words carefully. After all, he was far more familiar with addiction than I was. He worked closely with at-risk youth, and he'd dabbled a lot himself over the years.

"Addiction can take on many forms. Please be careful, Sage. It's a terrible disease and not one that's easy to fix. If you want my two cents, I think you should walk away."

I nodded as tears slid down my cheeks, and this time he did hug me. When Christian arrived, we hugged again, and then we said good-bye for the last time.

When I came outside, Christian hugged me fiercely. He looked tired, but I probably didn't look any better. Neither of us had gotten any sleep. We got in the car, and Christian turned to me as he explained that he was only twelve the first time he used coke. Twelve. Imagine that. He was so young!

"I was living on the streets and hanging out with very bad people. I got into trouble and ended up doing a lot of things I'm not proud of. A lot of people took advantage of me, men—"He shook his head, trying to clear the memory. "Anyways, then someone introduced me to cocaine, only we didn't snort it, we used a needle, and that was it. I was hooked."

My head was spinning. I was no stranger to drugs, but I'd never met anyone who used a needle before. It sounded so dirty. My heart went out to that poor child who never stood a chance. He didn't talk about the events that led to him leaving home when he was twelve, but I suspected it had something to do with his father, whom he never talked about except to say that he was an alcoholic and had died when Christian was young.

"Christian, I'm so sorry," I said. I could relate to childhood trauma.

"After that, I had to do even more that I'm not proud of in order to support my habit, until it became a vicious cycle. Soon, we were robbing people's houses. We got away with it for years before getting caught, and then we went to juvy. That's when I turned my life around. I got sober and joined the football team. When I got out, I went to AA meetings, and they taught me the steps to stay sober."

"Did it work?"

"It did. For many years, I kept my demons at bay, but there's no cure for what I have. I will *always* be an addict, and if I don't follow the steps and go to meetings, it will *always* end in relapse. That's what happened last night."

I was a little confused. "Why is this only coming up now? We've been together for three months. I thought addicts used all the time."

"I'm what they call a binge user. I can go months, even years, without using, but if I don't do the steps, it ends in disaster. I haven't been to a meeting since I got here, and that was a big mistake." *Because you were spending all of your time with me,* I thought.

"Did you use while you were with your ex?" I asked.

"Yes, but not often. She's very grounded, and that helped. Plus, there was my son."

"I see." This was a lot to absorb. I thought about my own childhood and I could relate to his trauma. In fact, I think telling me his deepest, darkest secrets bonded us even more, and I was touched that he shared his story with me.

He looked so vulnerable as we sat in the car. So lost, like a little boy pleading with me to understand. I wasn't sure how to help him, but what I did know was that I loved him, and I wasn't about to abandon him in his time of need. People did that to me all the time, and I hated them for it.

"So, what do we have to do to prevent this from happening again?" I asked.

"I need to go to meetings. In fact, I'd like to go to one tonight, and I was wondering if you'd come with me. It might help you understand what you're dealing with, and I could really use your support."

"Then I guess we're going to a meeting."

"Really? You don't hate me?"

"Of course not. Christian, all I ever knew was rejection until you came along. You're the only person who's ever loved me and that means something to me. I'm not giving up on you."

"But how can that be, *ma chérie?* You're so precious. So kind. You're like an angel. I'm lucky to have you in my corner."

We embraced, but I had something else to say. I pulled away and looked him in the eyes. "I want to be very clear about something. I love you, and I want to help you, but there are limits to what I'm willing to put up with. I'll give you everything I have, and I will love you fiercely, but if this continues, I *will* walk away."

"Oh, Sage . . . I was so worried. Thank you for understanding. I promise I'll do whatever it takes to stay sober. You're the most important thing in the world, and I want us to have that beautiful life I promised you."

I shouldn't have been surprised when Jamie showed up a few days later. We'd barely spoken since my return from Japan. In fact, I hardly ever saw him anymore. He was always busy, it seemed. The last time I'd seen him was at Jasper's birthday party over a month ago.

"Jamie!" I said as I opened the door. "What a nice surprise."

"I brought you something," he said as he held up a bottle of Baileys. I smiled because it's my favorite, only he wasn't smiling. *Uh oh.* Something was wrong.

As he placed the bottle on the table he said, "I thought we could have one last drink together. Then it's time to say good-bye because I never want to see you again."

My face fell as I realized this wasn't a friendly visit. Then my temper flared. "Oh, for fuck's sake, Jamie. Always with the drama. What have I done this time?"

"You know," he said, accusation dripping from his words.

"No, I don't know. All I know is that my friend went to Australia three years ago, and when he got back, I didn't recognize him anymore. What happened to you, Jamie? Why do you keep treating me like I'm the enemy when I've done nothing wrong?"

At first, he didn't answer, then he stomped his foot like a five year old and yelled, "Don't you know? I'm in love with you, and I've *been* in love with you for five years!"

"What?" I said. He'd taken me by surprise, kind of like everybody else lately. What the hell was going on? "You're in love with me?"

"Yeah," he said bitterly. "But you were too blinded by your love for Luka to notice. You kept throwing it in my face every time you talked about him. Then you started singing together. I wish I'd never introduced you. He took you away from me!"

My face turned to stone. I don't like childish tantrums. "Please tell me you're kidding. In case you've forgotten, and clearly you have, *you're* the one who threw us together in the first place. I hadn't seen Luka in months when you showed up, practically *forcing* me to forgive him. I begged you—BEGGED you—not to get involved, but you wouldn't listen. You pushed and pushed, and then you went behind my back and gave him my number, even though I *specifically* asked you not to. So don't you dare blame this on me."

He stuck his chin out in defiance. "I wanted you to be friends, not for you to fall in love with him! And you should've known how I felt about you."

"Seriously? You realize you've slept with everything that walks since the day we met. Right? On what planet does that say 'I'm in love with you?' Hell, you even brought girls to my apartment so I could *approve* of them for you."

"I was trying to get your attention!"

"Then you have a lot to learn about me, *friend,* because a different girl in your bed every night is not how you get my attention."

He was losing this argument, so he switched tactics, going from angry to pouty. "It's not my fault! My mother died when I was five, and now I have intimacy issues. None of those women even mattered. They were just killing time until you noticed me."

"Oh, for the love of God. Here we go again. Your mother died over twenty years ago. I'm sorry you lost someone important to you, but I'm not feeding your desperate need for self-pity anymore. She died when you were *five.* It's time to get over it."

"How *dare* you!" he growled as his temper flared once more.

"Someone obviously needs to say this to you, Jamie. It's time you grew the fuck up."

"Yah, well, I'm going to move away and change my name! You'll never hear from me again. How would you like that?" He lifted his chin in defiance.

Ironically, this is exactly what Luka was doing. He changed his name while he was in Serbia, choosing one that he called 'a little more adult' now that he was engaged. It felt as though I'd been in the middle of Luka and Jamie's childhood rivalry for so long, but it was time to tap out. The boys may have been friends, but under the surface, they were always competing with one another. They even slept with a lot of the same girls.

"Listen, I have enough going on without having to deal with your outrage and desperate need for attention. If you don't want to be my friend anymore, that's fine. Just know that you're choosing this, not me. I've always loved you Jamie, but I'm not *in* love with you, and I can't believe you waited until I have a boyfriend to tell me this."

He scoffed. "Oh your coke-addict-junkie boyfriend? Yeah, he's a real winner."

I stood up. "I think it's time for you to leave."

"I think so, too. Fuck you very much and have a nice life, Sage. I hope you get exactly what you deserve."

I went to the door and held it open without saying another word. First I'd lost Vivian and Heather, then Luka, and now Jamie. My friends were disappearing at an alarming rate. Thank God I still had Christian in my corner.

EIGHTEEN

Things happen between couples that no one else can possibly understand. That's the nature of intimate relationships. Nobody knows exactly what happens behind closed doors. We look at what our friends are willing to tolerate, and we wonder why they do it, but we don't know the whole story. It's easy to judge, but until you've walked a mile in someone else's shoes, you simply don't know.

Christian and I were downtown the next time he relapsed. We were at a nightclub listening to a great band, and even though I wasn't feeling well, he insisted on going to an after-hours club. Once we got there, he took my wallet so he could buy himself a drink, and when he got back, he said I was right, we should leave. I didn't think to question why he had suddenly changed his mind. I was just happy we were leaving.

When we got outside he said, "I know you're not feeling well. Why don't you wait here while I get the car." And then he was gone. I didn't even have a chance to say "You don't have to do that" before he took off, leaving me alone on a dark street. Christian did that a lot. He was extremely compulsive and usually took action before he'd even finished his sentence.

It was cold outside, and as I stood there freezing my butt off, it started to rain. I waited for fifteen minutes, and then it turned into thirty. The pain in my stomach intensified as I realized what was happening. He was doing it again, only this time he left me in a shady part of town at three in the morning. I wanted to scream. Then I remembered he had my wallet and keys. How was I supposed to get home?

I had no idea what to do, but I certainly couldn't stay on the street. Sienna lived downtown, but waking her up was really going to piss her off. It took thirty minutes to walk to her apartment, and I cried the entire time. I cried because I was heartbroken, furious, worried sick, and a hundred other emotions. It had been two months since Christian last used, and I thought we were in the clear. I had a lot to learn about addiction.

I stood in front of Sienna's building, dreading what was coming next. It was four in the morning, and I was about to wake the dragon. I pushed the buzzer and held my breath.

"This had better fucking be good to wake me up at this hour," she said when she answered the buzzer. I told her it was me, that Christian had stranded me downtown and I needed a place to stay. She muttered something under her breath and let me in.

I took the elevator to her apartment, steeling myself for her rage. When she opened the door, she took one look at my face, and instead of yelling, she asked if I was all right. I nodded, and she let me in. I sat down on her sofa, exhausted and soaking wet. She narrowed her eyes as gave me the once over, deciding what to do next.

"You look like shit," she said.

"I feel like shit."

"Hmph. I'm going back to bed. We can talk about this in the morning."

She started lecturing me as soon as she woke up. Sienna really likes to lecture, but my head was pounding, and my stomach still ached.

"So, what happened?" she asked over a cup of tea, and I gave her the broad strokes.

"Is this the first time?"

I thought about lying, but what good would that do? "No," I admitted. "It's the second time." I told her what had happened at Luka's.

She was furious. "You know you have to dump his ass, right?"

I sighed. I really needed empathy, not a lecture. "It's not that simple, Sienna."

"Yes, it is. Does he snort it?"

I hesitated. It shamed me to say the words out loud. "No. He shoots it."

"You've got to be kidding. He's nothing but a piece-of-shit junkie. Get rid of him, Sage."

"No, he's not. He's a good person. It's not his fault he has a disease."

"Well, as far as I'm concerned, he's just another junkie, and I don't ever want to see him again."

"That's a bit harsh."

"I think you should dump him, and if you don't, then I don't want to see you, either. Don't think you can start crashing here on a regular basis."

"Wow. Tell me how you really feel."

"He'll ruin your life, and frankly, I don't want to hear about it if you choose to stay because it will be your own fault."

And with that, I was dismissed. On the way home, I added Sienna to the list of people who no longer talked to me. I was hurt by her words, but I learned a valuable lesson that day, and I was far more careful with my secrets after that.

It was two days before Christian came home, and I was sick with worry. He practically collapsed when he walked through the front door. He was pale, weak, and dehydrated. He could barely stand, and I was horrified by how much weight he'd lost. He cried and cried as he begged me to forgive him. I yelled at him for ditching me and taking my money, which made him cry even more, and then I felt guilty because he looked so *broken.*

"I'm sorry, Sage. I love you so much. I never meant to hurt you," he said as tears rolled down his cheeks.

"You left me on the street! How can you do that to someone you love?"

"Love has nothing to do with it. It's not personal, Sage. I didn't mean to hurt you, and it's not me doing it. It's the drugs. This disease is like a demon in my brain."

My heart broke as I felt his pain deep inside my soul. He was right. I could walk away, but he'd have to live with this terrible disease for the rest of his life. I couldn't imagine what that felt like. The pain. The shame. The guilt. They were always with him.

"I need to go to a meeting, and I think it's time we stop smoking pot."

"If coke is your drug of choice, what does pot have to do with it?" "Drugs are all the same to an addict. When I smoke pot, my mind latches onto that feeling, except it's not the high I *really* want, so I start craving cocaine, and the call gets louder and louder until I answer it."

This was something I appreciated about Christian. He was always willing to talk about his addiction so I could understand. I figured the more I understood, the easier it would be to help him. I'm not gonna lie—I really didn't want to give up pot, but I was willing to do it for him.

That night as I laid in bed, I wondered why the Universe had finally sent me a boyfriend only to make him an addict. It was so unfair. *Please save him*, I begged. I loved him so much, and without him I'd truly be alone. My closest friends had abandoned me; I was estranged from my family; Sienna had cut me off, and even my larger circle of friends had moved on with their lives.

The next day, Christian was in a great mood, and it surprised me how quickly he could bounce back after a relapse. When I asked him about it, he told me it didn't help to be depressed because that only made it worse, triggering an endless cycle of using and depression, which made sense. Being insanely positive was one of the things I loved about him. It's what made him *him*.

In October, it started raining and didn't stop. This is normal for Vancouver, so I was used to it, but Christian struggled, and then he used, disappearing for days at a time. Things weren't going well with his business, and he was frustrated. I had to lend him money to pay the rent on his office, and then I lost my summer job, so now we were both broke. I had to go on welfare, and I wasn't happy about it, but at least we had each other.

The next time he relapsed, he disappeared for three days, and I'm not even sure I showered or got dressed the entire time he was gone. I cried the first day, and then I shut down because worrying about him . . . was making me a nervous wreck. He was gone for so long I thought for sure he was dead this time. I wasn't entirely wrong.

He got into an accident, totaled our car, and landed himself in the hospital with four broken ribs. He came home all bandaged up, barely able to walk. He collapsed in my arms, his body full of cuts and bruises, his golden skin now gray.

He was practically hysterical, he was crying so hard. He looked scared as he put his head in my lap and gripped my legs. It broke my heart to see the man I loved looking like a prisoner of war. He was such a beautiful human being, and he suffered so much.

"I really fucked up this time. I crashed the car, and there's nothing left. They had to use the jaws of life to get me out! The doctor told me if I hadn't been so high I'd be dead right now. The only thing that saved me was that I'd already overdosed, so my body was limp when it hit the steering wheel. What's happening to me, Sage? Why am I cursed with this terrible disease?"

I blinked several times but said nothing. I was thinking about abused housewives. I'd always wondered how they could stay when their husbands hurt them so badly. My father used to beat me, and I took off as soon as I could. I was just a kid, yet I knew I had to leave, and my beatings weren't even that bad.

Some of these women ended up in the hospital over and over again with broken bones and black eyes, yet they lied to protect their partners. Even though Christian didn't have a mean bone in his body and would never hit a woman, I understood that my circumstances were similar to those women. Love makes us do crazy things. So does fear.

I wanted to scream when I thought about the car. Without a car we couldn't sell coupons, which meant there wouldn't be any money coming in. It also meant he didn't have a place to use anymore. Was this rock bottom?

Things didn't really recover after that. We were in a downward spiral, and there was nothing I could do to stop it. I hoped the broken ribs would slow down his cravings, but they didn't. Nothing could do that. I was learning the hard way that Christian was an amazing liar. I'd never seen anything like it. That sweet, kind, loving man would lie straight to my face when the cravings took over. He'd literally make love to me while stealing my wallet, so I was never able to relax.

It didn't take long until he gave into his cravings. Maybe two weeks. Since he no longer had a car, he brought the drugs home instead. To my apartment. My sanctuary. As I sat on the sofa, powerless to stop him, I got my first lesson in shooting up. I watched as he gently placed the powder on the spoon, added water, lit the lighter, and held it until it bubbled. Then he sucked the poison into a syringe. I'd seen this in the movies, but seeing it firsthand was an entirely different experience.

I didn't want to watch, yet I couldn't look away. I was glued to the spot. I thought maybe I'd understand him better if I knew what he did when he disappeared. I wanted to understand why he loved this drug so much.

His body vibrated with anticipation once the needle was ready, and I realized at that moment, I was no longer looking at Christian. I was looking at the demons that controlled him. Seeing that hurt my soul in a way I can't explain. This beautiful human being, the man I loved, was no longer there.

There are two things I remember very clearly: the terrible hallucinations and the way his voice changed after the needle went in, like he had cotton under his top lip. He struggled to speak, and in order to compensate, he ended up over-articulating yet slurring his words.

I had nowhere to go since it was a studio apartment, so I sat there watching him from the corner of the couch. He picked up the tinfoil. He put it down. He unwrapped it. He re-wrapped it. He moved the cup, the pen, the water, the remote control. He couldn't stop fidgeting for even a second. Everyone thought he was out partying when he got high, but it wasn't like that. This was nothing like sniffing coke. This was hell.

He continued this behavior until it was time to shoot up again, then a calm washed over him as he performed the familiar ritual. Eventually, he used it all, and then the fidgeting became desperate. Every piece of dust looked like coke. He searched the table, the carpet, the tinfoil, the couch, my lap, repeating this over and over again. I was mesmerized and sickened at the same time. He'd been at it for three hours. He forgot I was even there, until he needed more.

"Sage. I need money."

"No way."

"But I need it," he said desperately.

"No you don't."

"Sage."

"No."

"Sage."

"I said *no*. Do you understand that we're broke? I have forty dollars, and that's it. We have nothing left. You spent it all. All of it. All your money and all mine. There's nothing left. We can't even afford to buy food."

He waited all of three seconds before starting again. "Sage."

I ignored him.

"Sage," he said a little louder. "You can't just ignore me!"

"Yes, I can." He begged and pleaded, but I ignored him. After an hour, he changed tactics, and the pleading turned to accusation. "Don't treat me like a child. I can make my own decisions! It isn't even your money; it's ours. We're a couple."

"Oh, that's rich. Especially since I'm the one who's been supporting us for the past five months."

For the next two hours, he pleaded non-stop, and like any ancient torture method, the repetition wore me down. I moved to the bed, but he stood over me, repeating my name over and over until I screamed, cried, and pleaded with him to stop. When I got up to use the bathroom, he blocked the door and wouldn't let me pass.

"Christian, I have to pee."

"Give me the money and I'll move."

"No."

"Give me the money, Sage! Can't you see I'm hurting? You're hurting me."

"Get out of my way before I pee myself."

"Not until you give me the money."

I gave him the money. We'd had this exact same argument many times before, and I was too exhausted, both physically and mentally, to argue anymore. As soon as the door closed, I started to cry. I cried for myself, for him, and for all the people battling addiction. I cried until I couldn't cry anymore, then I laid on the bed, staring into the abyss as the darkness washed over me.

There's a defining moment when you realize your life's spinning out of control and there's nothing you can do to stop it. When the pain becomes so overwhelming that the only way to stop it is to shut it off. You shut it off and function on autopilot because that's all you have left. You do whatever's required of you and nothing more. Nothing reaches you. Nothing can, because if you allow even one crack in your armor—if just one emotion works its way to the surface—the whole thing comes crashing down, and you're forced to feel your pain.

Christian loved our new life. He enjoyed using in the comfort of our home, so it became our new normal. He was in a great mood these days, but I wasn't fooled. I finally understood the depth of his addiction, and all I felt was deep despair. Christian spent weeks trying to cheer me up, but we were way past that. The darkness had already taken me.

Christian suggested I get an acting job or that I start singing again. He always bragged about how talented I was and made me sing all the time. He was my biggest fan, except I could barely get off the couch. How was I supposed to muster up the energy for an audition? Besides, these days, I preferred staying in the shadows. It was easier to hide. The last thing I wanted was to step on a stage and shine a light on my pain.

We were caught in a vicious cycle, and I finally understood the meaning of codependence. Seeing him use made me depressed, and seeing me depressed made him feel guilty, which caused him to use. His habit was no longer sporadic, and I no longer believed I could help him. He may have stopped disappearing for days at a time, but he was using several times a week and always at home.

On one occasion, he locked himself in the bathroom, and as I sat there looking at his paraphernalia, I wondered what it would be like to jab the needle into my arm. *Would it stop the pain?* I wondered. I reached across the table and picked it up. I rolled it between my fingers. The needle was empty, but I knew plunging it into my arm would kill me, and I found comfort in that thought. I'm not sure I actually would have done it, but it was comforting knowing I could. That I still had the power to choose. I don't know how long I sat there holding that needle, but eventually he came back, and when he saw me, he screamed.

"No!!!" he shouted, as he lunged for the needle. "What are you doing? What were you thinking?"

"I wanted to know what it felt like," I said in a monotone voice.

"Are you crazy? I wouldn't wish this disease on anyone in the world!" He looked pained, and then he looked around the table. "Wait. There was more coke here. Where did it go? Did you take it?"

I didn't answer. I couldn't answer. I felt absolutely nothing.

"Sage! Answer me." When I didn't, he grabbed me by the shoulders and shook me. "Did you already take some? Let me check." He looked at my arms for needle marks. "Oh, thank God. You scared me to death! What were you thinking?"

Then he remembered what was really important, that he thought there was more coke. He quickly forgot about me. "So where is it?" he asked frantically.

"I don't know. Check the bathroom."

He grabbed the needle, ran to the bathroom, and locked the door. He stayed there for the next eight hours while I sat on the floor, too numb to cry. I could feel the darkness moving in again. It was swirling all around me, dancing in and out, like it used to do when I was a child. It was familiar and comfortable, so I allowed it to consume me once more, taking comfort in the void.

We stayed like that for weeks on end. My twenty-eighth birthday came and went, and it was neither remembered nor celebrated. No one called. Not my sisters. Not my parents. Christian felt guilty that we couldn't afford to celebrate, so he used in order to assuage his guilt, and I spent my birthday alone.

Over the next few weeks, he bounced back and forth between using and worrying about me. The sight of the needle didn't even bother me anymore. I was immune to it. I knew this situation was harming me, but I didn't know how to stop it. I was so depressed I wasn't even sure how to function anymore, and I certainly wasn't capable of holding down a job.

I finally understood the full scope of his addiction, even though it took me a while to get there. He was clever, actually. He never told me the whole story at once, just in pieces, so it took months to figure out, and by then it was too late. I was blindly in love with him.

No one understood why I stayed. They were confused because I was usually a logical person, but for me it was simple. I loved Christian, and you don't abandon the people you love, especially when they ask for help. For most people, this would have been their breaking point, but I was raised by narcissists, so my threshold of pain was different from others'. When you've been beaten down for thirty years, it's hard to imagine you deserve any better.

So many people had abandoned me over the years, and I knew how painful it was. When they looked at Christian, all they saw was a junkie, but I saw the most beautiful person I'd ever known. He was kind, caring, generous, funny, sensitive, and sweet. There wasn't a mean bone in his body. He understood exactly who he was, and he never lied about it. It was the junkie who lied, not Christian.

Most people couldn't separate him from the junkie, but I could. To me he was two separate people, and inside that beautiful man was a broken child that I desperately wanted to save. The irony is that I was the one who needed to be saved.

Nineteen

When Christian first moved to Vancouver, I remember him saying, "This is the best city in the whole world. I can't believe *everybody* doesn't live here." Then the rain started and he said, "This is so depressing. How can *anyone* live here?" That pretty much sums up Vancouver.

It was December, and we were well into several months of rain. After the fiasco of my non-birthday, Christian was trying to make it up to me by making dinner. The table was set with candles, and music filled the room. He even surprised me with a bouquet of flowers, knowing how much I love them.

Over dinner, we had a serious conversation, and we decided it was time for some major changes. We couldn't carry on this way. Neither of us could. We wouldn't survive.

"Sage, I've been thinking, and I may have a solution. I think we should move to Montreal."

"Montreal? Doesn't it snow there for, like, half the year?"

"It does, but at least the sky is blue and the sun is shining."

"Fair point, but I really hate the cold."

"Just hear me out," he said. "I'm failing here. I'm failing at staying sober; I'm failing my business, and most of all I'm failing you." His eyes softened, and he suddenly looked sad.

I saw a deep sorrow in his eyes, the kind you can't fake. Sorrow and regret. This wasn't the con man who manipulated me in order to get his way. It wasn't the demons that controlled him. It was Christian. The man I fell in love with.

I couldn't imagine the kind of guilt that came with hurting the people you love the way he did. What a weight that must be. He smiled sadly, as if reading my thoughts. "I love you so much, *mon papillon,* and you don't deserve this life. You are so kind and gentle. You give so much love to everyone around you, and all I want is to protect you. I want to take care of you and be the man that you deserve."

I reached across the table and took his hand. "I want that, too."

A determined look came over his face. "This morning, I called Isabelle and asked if she'd hire me to run the office in Montreal. My office," he added. "She has a prosperous business, but it was better when I ran it, so she agreed to hire me. This way I'm guaranteed a salary, we can both have a fresh start, and I'll be closer to my son."

It made sense. There was nothing left for us here. No jobs, no friends, no money. Fight or flight. He was speaking my language. Encouraged, he continued.

"I have wonderful friends and a great support system in Montreal. I'm struggling to go to AA meetings because I haven't found one I like, but in Montreal, I know several good ones. Isabelle promised to help me lease a car and get settled, and your dad can help us with the airline tickets. There's nothing left for us here, Sage. We need a change. I need a change. What do you think, my love?"

"I think you're right. There's nothing left for us here. A change is a great idea."

"Really? So you'll come with me to Montreal?" His face looked so hopeful.

"Of course I will. I'd do anything for you."

"Thank God. Because if I stay here, I'm afraid what will happen, and I don't want to leave without you. I love you so much."

"I love you, too."

Christian was very proud, and appearances mattered to him. It was reflected in the way he dressed, the way he thought, and the way he talked. After living in poverty for so long, he decided we needed an upgrade, so he rented a one-bedroom condo in Mont Saint-Sauveur, a tiny ski village in the mountains. He'd been saying he wanted to live there for many years, so he was ecstatic when a place became available.

He was re-energized and ready for a fresh start now that he was home. He was like an excited puppy when he showed me our new condo, and it was nice to see the old Christian again. I asked if we could afford it, and he told me not to worry about it. His ex, Isabelle, had fronted the money.

Christian loved showing me around, and I loved exploring Montreal, even though it was freezing. I enjoyed playing tourist and getting to know my new home. This change of pace was exactly what we needed. He showed me the Olympic Rings, Notre-Dame Basilica, Chinatown, Mount Royal Park, and Old Montreal. We ate bagels in the Jewish quarter and explored the busy streets while holding hands. We were happy, and both of us were optimistic about our future.

His family were lovely people, and they welcomed me with open arms. His mother lived in a retirement community for active seniors, and it was obvious where Christian got his energy from. She was a firecracker who filled her days with bingo, line dancing, and social events. She was always doing something.

His sister was the quiet one in the family. She and her husband lived in a nice house with an amazing sheepdog. We drank champagne and celebrated as we rang in the new millennium. It was a historical moment, and everyone was in a good mood. Christian was so proud as he introduced me to his family. I thought it might be strange bringing home an English-speaking girlfriend, but no one cared. They all spoke perfect English, except for his ex and his son.

I felt bad for his son. We couldn't communicate, and I worried it might be hard on him. Sometimes, he'd spend the night, and we'd be left alone while Christian went to a meeting. We'd look at each other and laugh because we both had so many questions, yet we couldn't ask them. I made a show of doing charades to see if he was hungry, thirsty, or wanted to watch a movie. He was a good kid with a kind heart, so he'd smile and nod yes or no, playing right along.

It's amazing how much support Christian had among his family and friends. He surrounded himself with exceptional people, and I could see why he wanted to come back. In Vancouver, my friends were judgmental and dismissive of him, but here, he was loved. They were firm whenever he relapsed, refusing to give him money (except his mother), but they still supported him, and I learned a lot from them. I learned that it was OK to love him and that it didn't matter what anyone else thought.

For a time, we were really happy, as he went to work every day and I played the domestic goddess, but not even his support system could stop his demons from resurfacing. When someone's hell bent on self-destruction, they usually succeed.

First, he started butting heads with Isabelle on how to run the business, and then he got jealous when she went on a vacation because we couldn't afford one. He demanded more money and accused her of stealing his business from him, but she held her ground. He became frustrated and petulant because he hated it when other people had things he didn't. He could be very childish, and once he started to obsess, he didn't stop.

When he started using again, I knew we were in trouble. Thankfully, there were long periods between relapses, but eventually we fell into the same pattern. I went back to being depressed, stressed out, and lonely. We lived far from the city, and I felt extremely isolated. No one in our village spoke English, and there wasn't any public transit, so I couldn't even leave. I had no driver's license and no car, which meant no freedom. Christian may have had a great support system, but I didn't. His family was lovely, but they were *his* family, and that left me with no one to talk to.

So when my father called and asked if my youngest sister could come for a visit, I said yes. Bailey stayed for two weeks, and it was lovely spending time with her without all the family drama. She was sixteen and struggling because my parents had stopped going to church after my father had an argument with the pastor, and she was confused, having never known life without it.

I was happy and shocked to learn that after seventeen years, my parents had finally left that awful church, but I understood her confusion. For sixteen years, they beat it into her head that she'd go to hell if she sinned, and then they stopped going to church. How is that not confusing, especially for a teenage girl?

In turn, I told her about my struggles with Christian's addictions, and we commiserated over how difficult life was. I was happy she'd come to visit, and I worried about her after she left. My parents were never physically abusive with her, but my mother was still my mother, so it had to be hard.

When Christian started missing work, Isabelle kicked him out of the office and put him on contract work instead. Once again, we were so broke that we struggled to pay the rent, and once again, Christian turned to his support system to bail us out, which is probably the real reason he wanted to move to Montreal.

I actually felt sorry for his family. Christian siphoned money from them his entire life. When he made money, he was very generous, but he didn't hesitate to throw it back in your face when he was broke. I especially felt sorry for his mother. They'd get into huge fights, and I wanted to crawl under a rock when they started arguing in French. Both of them were loud and animated, their voices bouncing off the walls of her tiny apartment.

His seventy-year-old mother had a finite amount of money, and every time he took some, she would say she'd now have to die a year earlier since she wouldn't be able to support herself after it was gone. He'd point out that she had a pretty nice lifestyle while we were starving. Guilt was his favorite tool, and he used it well.

She dealt with his addiction for twenty years and was used to it, but once he started crying and begging, she'd cave because, like me, she knew he wouldn't stop until he got what he wanted. His family adored me, and I was horrified that he used the fact that I was at home without food to elicit their sympathy.

I was embarrassed that I wasn't able to provide for myself, but we lived in a French-speaking village, so I couldn't even get a job. I'd always known we couldn't outrun our problems, and here we were, right back where we started, except this time, I was isolated and completely dependent on Christian.

One afternoon, he came home and told me that Isabelle had invited me over for tea.

"Your ex wants to have tea with me. Why?"

"She thought you could use a friend. She's been in your shoes and can probably give you advice on living with an addict. Plus, she'd like to get to know the woman who's spending time with her son. You don't have to if it makes you uncomfortable."

"No, it's fine. Actually that's really nice of her, but I thought she didn't speak English. How are we supposed to communicate?"

"She speaks a little. She's just shy."

I really needed to get out of the apartment, so I agreed to go. After the boys left, Isabelle made us tea, and we sat down at the kitchen table. Her place was pretty. It was small (like ours), but it was colorful and homey.

"Thank you for coming, Sage. I know this is . . . mmm . . . a strange situation. You probably have questions about Christian, but I do not want to talk about him. First, we talk about you. How are you, Sage?"

She chose these words carefully, in her broken English and adorable accent. I blushed at her question and the way she was probing my face. I wasn't used to talking about myself. Everything had been about Christian for so long, so I wasn't sure how to answer her question. I'd been guarded for such a long time, but I could tell she saw straight through me and understood exactly what I was going through. After all, she had lived with him for seven years.

"I'm . . . struggling," was all I could manage to say.

"It must be difficult . . . to leave your home to come here. Christian is

. . . very difficult when he is using." She gave me a knowing look, and I smirked. "I think you have a lot of time alone with nothing to do. You have no car and no freedom. You have no family or friends. You are very . . . hmmm, how do you say . . . brave."

I gave a little snort that was half laughter, half sorrow. She nailed it alright. She was perceptive, and at that moment, I understood why Christian loved her. She was calm and kind, and she had a beautiful, grounded energy. Like me. She was basically an older version of myself. The old me, anyways. The me I used to be. I was trying to stay positive, but every waking moment was dedicated to worrying about Christian, so that didn't leave a lot of time to worry about myself.

Even when we were having fun I was never able to completely relax because I was always looking over my shoulder, waiting for the other shoe to drop. Every time he went out, I wondered if he was coming back. I'd lost myself in this relationship. I didn't even know who I was anymore.

"You must remember one thing, Sage, if you are to survive this situation with Christian. You need to take care of you. His energy will . . . mmm . . . consume you if you don't take care of yourself. He will *not* do that for you. No one will."

She waited for me to acknowledge her, and then she continued. "Christian is an addict. He is selfish and will never put you first. Only you can do that. If you can't, then you need to walk away. If you choose to stay, then you need to put up . . . how do you say . . . boundaries. No matter how hard he tries to manipulate you. Don't enable him."

She cocked her head, and I smiled. Yes, I understood. This was the lecture I'd needed six months ago. I was grateful it was coming now and from this lovely woman I really admired. Sometimes, the Universe works in mysterious ways.

"You must remove the drugs from your house. Never allow him to use at home. And when he comes home after a . . . mmm . . . relapse, you don't baby him! He is not a child, and you are not his mother. When he cries, you don't feel sorry for him!" She was getting animated, and it made me laugh.

"He chose to make this bed, and he must lie in it alone. Don't let him take you down with him."

OK, I *really* liked this woman.

"Find yourself a hobby or a job. Something that is only for you. Think about *you* from now on. Then you will find your power and be better able to handle Christian. You cannot save him, Sage. Do you understand?"

She was right. She was absolutely right. It wasn't going to happen overnight, but hearing these words did me a lot of good, and I appreciated how hard she worked to find the right words, especially when speaking English clearly took some effort.

"Christian is very stubborn, but he can only . . . how do you say . . . drag you down if you let him, so your part in this is your own. Remember, if you choose to stay, then *you* choose to stay, and you must own that."

I shook my head. I was speechless. If the roles were reversed, I would have given the exact same advice. I couldn't blame him for the fact that I was still there. That was on me. I needed to get my head out of my ass and take control of my life again. I still loved him, but I had no intention of letting him destroy me.

Afterwards, when we were driving back to our place, Christian asked what Isabelle and I had talked about, and I told him. Most of it, anyways. Some of it was private.

"She's right, you know. You need to stop worrying about me and start taking care of yourself. It pains me to see you so sad and to know that I'm the one causing it. Addicts are very selfish, Sage. I know this. I know what I am. But you need to be selfish, too. Do what's right for *you*." He reached across the console and took my hand.

"Quite right," I said, and then I laid down the law. If I was to own my part in this, then I needed stronger boundaries. My conversation with Isabelle had empowered me, and I finally felt like myself again. I told him he couldn't use at home anymore, and that I wouldn't take care of him after a relapse. No more hurting me and then wanting me to fix it. I was done.

Things got a lot better after that. I worked on protecting my energy;

Christian worked on his sobriety, and we spent a lot of time outdoors now that it was summer. We were happy again, and although he still slipped every once in a while, the relapses were shorter, and I didn't fall apart every time he disappeared, nor did I take care of him when he got back. Boundaries.

One afternoon in late August, we went up to Mont Royal to watch the sunset. There was a chill in the air, and I knew winter was on its way. I snuggled into Christian a little bit more.

"I can't believe summer's almost over, and it's only August."

"I know. The snow will be here soon."

"I'm not sure I can survive another winter, Christian. I can barely handle a Vancouver winter, and it doesn't even snow."

"What do you propose? I don't think I can go back to Vancouver and deal with all that rain, so where does that leave us?"

We both fell silent as we thought about our options. He was right. Both options sucked.

"I wish we could go somewhere hot for the winter. It would be nice to spend some time on the beach. I really miss the ocean." Nine months without seeing the ocean had been hard on me. I'd always lived close to the beach, and I missed it like crazy.

Christian suddenly perked up as an idea hit him. "You know, before I started my own business, I used to sell timeshare. I bet if I called some hotels, I could get a job in Puerto Vallarta."

"Really? And you're just mentioning this now?"

"I never thought about it until now."

"Oh my gosh, I've always wanted to go back to Puerto Vallarta. Heather and I went there a few years ago, and I loved it."

"Perfect! Then we have a plan, baby."

TWENTY

Puerto Vallarta

After his first day of work, Christian came home in a great mood. He was super hyper and talked my ear off as we sat by the pool, watching a thunderstorm roll in. I was glad he liked the new job because the alternative—well, there wasn't one. Getting to Puerto Vallarta had used up all our money, and now we were broke again. I was hoping he would sell something soon because while he went to work and ate a five-star breakfast every morning, I was starving.

Christian lasted about a week before he came home and told me we were leaving. He said he'd never make any money at this hotel, so he found a new job in an up-and-coming area called Nuevo Vallarta. I wasn't happy about this decision, but what did I know about timeshare? Besides, it was too late. He'd already quit.

The new property was spectacular, but really far from town, and pretty much the only thing in Nuevo Vallarta besides construction sites. We still didn't have any food, and since we couldn't afford to eat at the hotel, I was still starving.

After his first day, he came home with a big smile on his face, which was a good sign. I hoped he liked this place better than the last one.

"Hey, baby, I'm home!" he said as he kissed me. "And I have *great* news."

"You made a sale?" I asked, hopeful. Then my stomach growled. It was hopeful, too.

"Nope, but I got you a *job!* Isn't that amazing?"

What? *Oh God, please don't let it be a sales job,* I thought. I neither liked nor respected sales people, which is obviously something I hadn't shared with Christian. Sales people were bossy, pushy, and, more often than not, bullies. It was hard enough knowing I was dating a salesman; now I was worried he wanted me to *be* one. This was not "great news."

"Uh . . . doing what exactly?" I asked trepidatiously.

"Selling timeshare, of course! You get to work with *me* baby. Isn't that exciting?"

I made a face. "Christian, I have no interest in selling timeshare."

He flapped a hand at me. "You're going to *love* it, I promise. And besides, this way we double our chances of making a sale. Isn't that great?"

Well, he had me there. We needed money, and we needed it now. "Fuuuuuuuuck," was all I could say.

"Listen, I promise you'll do great at this, Sage, and you don't have to be a front-to-back like me. You'll be a liner. All you have to do is take the guests to breakfast, show them the property, and hand them over to a closer who will do the rest."

"That's it? I don't have to sell anything?"

"Nope. Your job is to get the people to relax and fall in love with the property. If there's a sale, you get a piece of the pie; if not, at least you get breakfast."

"Hm. I suppose I could do that. Is the breakfast good?" This is what it had come down to. I was starving.

He grinned. "Yup, it's a huge buffet with all the fresh fruit and bacon you could want."

I sighed. He had me at buffet. "OK. I guess I can give it a try."

"That's the spirit! You can shadow me tomorrow, and I'll show you how it's done. We start at eight. The boss is expecting you."

"Wait a minute. You accepted the job before you even asked me?"
"Of course I did. Why would you say no to such a great opportunity?"

Because I had a mind of my own perhaps? Something Christian seemed to forget. I wanted to punch him, but I kept my thoughts to myself. The last thing I wanted was to start an argument and trigger a relapse. Keeping my mouth shut was something I did a lot. I needed to keep the peace at all costs, something I'd been doing my entire life. When we were children, this was vital for our survival. It was so ingrained in me that I did it without even thinking.

Shadowing Christian was extremely educational. I'd never seen him in action before, and I was blown away by how good he was. Right from the word *hello,* he had the guests eating from the palm of his hand. First he charmed them so they let down their guard, then he masterfully manipulated them into believing they were idiots if they didn't buy a timeshare.

He had no problem bending the truth to make the sale. He was so charming as he backed them into a corner that they didn't even realize it was happening. I was impressed by his abilities, relieved we finally had a sale, and disgusted by the knowledge that he probably manipulated me the same way. Watching him do it to someone else was a wake-up call, and believe me, I learned a lot. I've met many manipulators in my time, but he was definitely the master. We're talking con artist-level mastery.

Having learned from the best, I also made a sale that week, although I neither lied nor manipulated because that's not my style. Afterwards, the closer said I was the best liner he'd ever seen, and if it was up to him I'd be his *only* liner. It was a nice compliment, but the guy had sleazy-car-salesman written all over him, and I was pretty sure he was hitting on me.

We made over two thousand dollars that week, and I couldn't believe it. The next day, I tried to open a bank account, but they wouldn't let me because I wasn't Mexican, so now I had a new problem. Where could I hide the money before Christian spent it?

When I came home from the bank, he wasn't there, and I tried not to panic, but it was hard not to. When he finally showed up, he told me he went downtown to buy me some weed so we could celebrate. I was furious. He was playing with fire, and he knew it.

"Please don't manipulate me, Christian. I'm not an idiot. And don't pretend you did this for me because we both know that's not true. We're in MEXICO. Do you have any idea how dangerous it is to buy drugs here? You're going to land us in jail!"

"But baby . . ." he said, snuggling up to me, trying to make me forget that I was angry. "I thought you'd be happy. Come on . . . I know you love your weed, and I wanted to do something nice. And don't worry so much! I was careful, and I didn't buy any coke. I swear, I'm not even craving it. You don't have anything to worry about."

Liar. Every word from his mouth was a lie. Did he honestly think I was that stupid? That I was still buying the same old lines? We argued, but there was no reasoning with him. He had already convinced himself that he was in control, just like he always did, right before he poured gasoline all over our lives.

By the end of the week, he was using. Small amounts, but he was using. He started stealing money from my purse and disappearing for hours at a time. I begged him to go to a meeting, but it was a lost cause. At least he wasn't disappearing for several days, and he still showed up for work, but I knew it wouldn't be long before he lost control. He knew it, too.

In the following weeks, we both made another sale, which was a good thing because Christian had already spent the money from the last ones. Then he surprised me one afternoon with news. He found us an apartment, and we were moving downtown—tomorrow.

When we got there, I paid the deposit plus two months' rent. Christian wasn't happy. He argued that we needed the money for other things, but I stuck to my guns. I would *not* be manipulated anymore, and I much preferred having our money tied up in rent, rather than letting him spend it on coke.

I hadn't spent a penny on myself in over a year while he spent thousands of dollars feeding his habit. I desperately needed new clothes, but all of our money went to Christian's one true love: himself. My patience had finally run out, though. I was done playing the fool.

As his cravings got stronger, his behavior became more erratic. His demons took over, and Christian disappeared. He kept me up all night begging, arguing, accusing—whatever it took to break me down. Soon, he started failing at work, and so did I. Our co-workers noticed it, and I knew they were gossiping. Sleazy closer dude asked if anything was wrong, but I said we were fine. I was used to lying.

Eventually, Christian started missing work. I made excuses for him, resenting having to lie on his behalf, but the boss was smart and knew exactly what was going on. His brother was an addict, so he understood. He pulled Christian into the office and confronted him the next time he came in. He said he'd have to go to rehab for a month, and when he got back, he'd have to reimburse the money. The boss paid for everything himself. He was a really nice guy. As for me, I was to stay in Puerto Vallarta as collateral.

Once they'd booked the airline tickets, they brought me into the office to tell me the good news. They said they'd tell everyone Christian went home for a family emergency so we could have some privacy. When the manager saw the look on my face, he stepped out for a minute so we could be alone. I rounded on Christian the second the door closed. I was enraged beyond belief.

"You're leaving me here by myself? Are you crazy? I don't even have any money because you spent it all! How am I supposed to survive while you're gone?"

"Don't worry, baby. You'll be fine. I believe in you. You have the apartment, and you still have a job. I know you'll make another sale. This is a good thing! You should be happy."

"Have you lost your fucking mind?" I practically screamed.

"Sage, I can't stay here. If I stay here, I'll die. The coke in Mexico is so strong, and I'm no good to you even if I *do* stay. I need to get clean, and there's a *really* good program in Montreal. Besides, those were his terms if I want to keep my job."

I held up my hand to stop him from saying anything else. "I can't even look at you right now. Can we please get out of here so I can go home and freak out in private?"

"Of course. Give me your hand, baby. Let's get out of here."

When we got home, I was so upset I wouldn't let him touch me, so what did my magnificent boyfriend do? He walked out the door and spent the night shooting up while I cried into my pillow. I had exactly twenty dollars to my name when he got on the plane the next morning.

Twenty-One

There's always things to get used to when you move to a new place, and what I remember most about Puerto Vallarta are the *sounds*. When you live in the city, you're used to the sound of traffic, construction, sirens. When you live near the ocean, it's the waves. When you live in Mexico, it's the dogs and, believe it or not, the *roosters* that keep you up at night.

Our apartment was on the ground floor, and right below our bedroom was a rooster, belonging to the people upstairs. Now, I'll admit I'm not exactly educated on the ins and outs of roosters, but I could have sworn they crowed only with the dawning sun. I thought they were alarm clocks for farmers, signaling that it was time to start the day, like I'd seen in cartoons as a child. For anyone who's as ignorant about roosters as I was, let me educate you. Roosters do not crow with the rising sun; they crow ALL DAY LONG. In fact, they never *stop* crowing. Not ever. Not ever, ever, ever, ever, ever.

Now I didn't really care how much noise that thing made during the day, but I *did* care how much it made at night. When you're trying to sleep and it's going off every hour on the hour, it's enough to drive you crazy. Every single hour, all night long.

I'd be almost asleep when that stupid bird would let off an incredibly loud shriek, scaring the crap out of me. I remember the first night we slept in the apartment. I must have jumped thirty feet. I thought someone had let farm animals loose in our room. I thought I was having a nightmare featuring a giant rooster. I thought Christian had finally snapped.

As I laid awake night after night, I dreamed of all the ways I could kill that stupid bird. Poison its food, strangle it and eat it for dinner, drop a rock on it—I had a lot of time to think about it. We didn't have a TV, a radio, or a computer, so there wasn't any entertainment except my own dark thoughts.

When it wasn't the rooster keeping me up, it was the dogs. For the most part, dogs and cats aren't considered pets in Mexico. Most of them live on the street, and the locals would rather run them over than domesticate them. It's heartbreaking. There were a lot of dogs, and they all looked hungry. I knew exactly how they felt. I was hungry, too.

At night, they'd bark, and as soon as one started, the others joined in, until there was a chorus of dogs barking in every corner of the city. We're talking hundreds of dogs, barking all day and all night. These were the sounds that were slowly driving me insane.

The giant cockroaches that waltzed into my apartment weren't much better. I remember the first time I saw one fly through the front window. I thought it was a bird. I hadn't even known the hideous things *could* fly. I grabbed one of my shoes, but when I got closer, I realized it wasn't big enough.

I worried that if I missed, it might get mad and fly into my face, attacking me with its hairy cockroach legs, so I grabbed one of Christian's shoes instead. I didn't even clean the guts afterwards, and believe me, it was an epic battle to kill that thing, or at least maim it long enough to scoop it into the dust bin and throw it outside. I figured Christian deserved bug guts on his shoes after everything he did. Yes, I was still pissed off.

Every day that month, I plastered a smile on my face and went to work, when all I wanted to do was curl into a ball and cry. Every afternoon, I came home after not making a sale and sat in my apartment contemplating my life. That's all I did the entire time he was gone. I went to work, and I came home. I didn't even go to the beach. I didn't have the energy.

I also didn't have any money, so all I could afford was microwave popcorn, cheap bread, and bananas. I ate those three things every day for a month. Then I'd go to bed and listen to that stupid rooster as I plotted how to kill it.

In my darker moments, I plotted Christian's demise as well, but what I was *really* plotting was my escape. I needed to make enough money so I could bolt the next time he relapsed. I couldn't do this anymore. I wanted my life back. The problem is he was aware of every cent we earned, so I could never hide it before he spent it. It was time to get creative. I just didn't know how.

Because he left in December, I once again spent my birthday alone and un-celebrated. I was twenty-nine, and this was not where I imagined I'd be at this age. I was supposed to be a star, not tied down to an addict. My love for him came at a high price. Why was it so hard to leave him?

Things were bleak because I didn't make a sale the entire time he was gone, and twenty dollars doesn't last very long, even in Mexico. I think the clients could smell my desperation, and so could the sharks. Several men started hitting on me now that Christian was gone. Old, unattractive men who thought they could prey on me.

True to his word, the boss told everyone Christian had a family emergency, but people aren't stupid. They knew what was going on. So the predators moved in, inviting me out for dinner, which I declined even though I was starving.

After I ran out of money, I was forced to give one of the sharks a massage because I needed bus fare to get to work. I knew he'd hit on me (even though I was clear that this was a *professional* arrangement), but I didn't know what else to do. I hadn't made a dime in weeks, and I was so hungry. I didn't get breakfast at work anymore because I was so far down the line that half the time I didn't see any clients, so I'd sit there all day, waiting for nothing. My blood sugars were so low I constantly felt ill, so if giving a massage was the only way to make money, so be it.

Ten minutes in, he put his hand on my thigh, and I promptly removed it, then slapped him on the back of his head. He apologized, and I carried on. This is what my life had become. Rubbing down an old fat guy so I could make fifty bucks. I really hated being poor. I also wasn't fond of desperation. I had every right to be miserable, though. I was working for free; my boyfriend was a junkie, and I was stuck in Mexico without a penny to my name.

I was contemplating these dark thoughts as I took the garbage out one evening. There was a huge pile on the corner, so I threw mine on top. I was about to walk away when I heard a noise that sounded like mewing. I listened for a second, but it stopped. I moved some bags to see if I could spot it, when I suddenly heard it again, only it was coming from *inside* the bag.

I ripped it open and there it was—a baby kitten. Someone had thrown a kitten in the trash! He was so tiny, only a few days old. He hadn't even opened his eyes yet. My heart broke when I saw it. Who could do such a horrible thing? I picked him up and took him home. I laid him on the counter and took a good look at him. He looked OK, except for the fleas, ticks, and coffee grounds.

"Sorry, little guy. You're not gonna like this but I'll be quick, I promise."

I ran him under the water, then I used tweezers to remove the bugs. The poor thing was shaking, so I wrapped him in a towel and tried to feed him. I used a baggie, cutting a hole in the corner so he could drink.

"Hey, little guy. My name's Sage. I'm gonna take care of you, OK? How would you like to live with me from now on? I'm all alone, too, and I could sure use the company." It mewed quietly, so I took that as a yes.

I brought the milk to his mouth and dripped some inside, hoping he'd understand. I was happy when he started drinking, and once he had his fill, he fell asleep in my lap as I gently stroked his head. I couldn't believe someone could be so cruel to such a tiny animal. That night, I took him to bed with me. I was his mama now, and I wouldn't let anything bad happen to him.

"What a shitty way to come into this world, little kitten. I know exactly how you feel. I wasn't wanted, either, but we've got each other now."

When Christian came home, I was happy to see him, and I couldn't believe how fantastic he looked. I, on the other hand, did not look fantastic. That month had been the longest of my life. Sometimes I wondered if Christian was even coming back, so believe me, I did a lot of soul searching while he was gone. We embraced like long-lost lovers, and then he noticed the kitten.

"Who's that? Did you get a cat while I was gone?"

"I found him a few days ago. Someone threw him in the trash, so I adopted him."

"What's his name?"

"Kitten," I said proudly.

"Kitten?"

"I couldn't think of anything else."

He laughed. "Listen, baby, I'm *starving!* What have we got to eat around here?"

He opened the fridge, but all I had was a loaf of bread and milk for the cat. "Don't you have any food, baby?" he asked, opening the cupboards, which were bare.

"No," I said deliberately, "I do not."

"Come on, let's go to that hamburger stand on the corner. I'll treat you to dinner."

I had passed by the sweet old man who owned the hamburger cart every day on my way home. When we first moved in, we ate there several times, and he made great burgers. It was super cheap, which is why he was always busy, and after the crap I'd been eating lately, that burger was the best damn thing I'd ever tasted. After dinner we headed home, hand in hand.

"So, how was Montreal? Did you see your family? What was rehab like?" I was happy to have someone to talk to after being alone for a month.

"Oh my God, it was so great! I had the *best* time," he said, flapping his hand.

"Really? I expected rehab to be . . . you know . . . hard."

"Oh, I only stayed at that place for a week, and then I went to my mother's."

I stopped walking and blinked a few times. "You did *what?"*

"I stayed with my mother and got another contract for Isabelle so I could make some money while I was there. Isn't that great?" He grinned like this was the best news in the world.

"I thought you needed to be in rehab the whole month."

"Don't be silly," he said, dismissively. "I already know the steps, and besides, I didn't like it there. It was hard, and I had to share a room. But don't worry, *mon chéri*, I feel GREAT. I feel rejuvenated after my holiday."

Holiday? My temper flared, but he was so excited he didn't even notice.

"I saw my son almost every day; I spent Christmas with my family, and I even went skiing a few times. It was so amazing! It's *exactly* what I needed. And now I'm ready to get back to work and make some money." He smiled at me. I did *not* smile back. "What? What's wrong, baby? You look mad."

I lowered my voice to a deadly calm. "You were in Montreal having the time of your *life,* were you? You enjoyed your little *vacation,* did you? You were *supposed* to be in rehab!"

"I was! Look at me. I'm doing great. I didn't use the entire time I was gone, and I'm ready to stay sober for good this time. I thought you'd be happy."

"Really? Well, while you were having *the time of your life,* I was here, eating microwave popcorn every single *fucking* night because I couldn't afford anything else. And when I really wanted to mix it up, I had a banana."

"What do you mean? Didn't you make any sales while I was gone?"

"No. I did NOT. Every single day, I showed up to a job I *hate* and was basically doing for free. Every day, I wept because I was starving and lonely while you were having the *time of your fucking life!*" By now I was shouting, and he gasped, shocked by my fury, like it had never occurred to him that I could possibly have been having anything other than a great time.

That's what irritated me the most about Christian. He made thousands of dollars in minutes, and he always had money. He didn't always keep it, but it was easy for him to make, whereas my entire life was one big struggle. Part of the reason I stayed is because I knew he could make money when he tried.

"I was sick every single day because I was starving. I even had to massage a fucking fat asshole just so I could pay for the bus. Once again, I'm the only one in this relationship who's suffering, when YOU should be suffering! This whole mess is YOUR FAULT! Yet there you were on vacation while I was here in a deep dark hole."

By now, I was screaming. I was so angry that tears were streaming down my face. Christian grabbed me and held me to him. I tried to break free, but he was a lot stronger than I was. I pounded his chest with my fists, and he held me even tighter until I finally, reluctantly, calmed down.

"I'm so sorry, Sage. I'm sorry things didn't go well. I had no idea. Shhhhh . . . it's OK. I'm here now, and everything's all right. I'll do better this time. I promise. We're going to have a wonderful life, and this will all be behind us."

I pulled away from him and wiped my eyes. "Please don't make any more promises because this is the last time I'm doing this. The next time you use, I'm walking away. And don't think I'm playing when I say that. This is not an ultimatum or an empty threat. I told you when we first met that one day I'd reach my limit, and that day has finally come. We're here."

"Don't say that—"

"I mean it, Christian. This is the last time."

"I'll tell you what. Why don't you stay home tomorrow and I'll go to work? I'll tell them you're sick. When I get back, we'll go out. We'll take a long walk and hit the supermarket so we can fill the fridge. You need to get out of this apartment, babe. You don't look so good."

"Can we get some dog food and cat food for the neighborhood animals?" I asked as I sniffed.

"Of course we can. Oh, you have such a big heart. I love you so much."

We hugged for a long time, and then he noticed his shoe, the one I'd used to kill the cockroach. "Is that my shoe? It looks like there's legs sticking out of it or something."

"I have no idea what you're talking about," I said innocently.

The next morning, Christian went to work while I cleaned the apartment. When he returned a few hours later, I was getting out of the shower.

"Hey. What are you doing home so early?" I asked.

"I have good news, baby!"

"You sold something? Please tell me you sold something."

"Are you kidding? You were right. That place sucks, so I quit. You got your wish; we don't have to go back there anymore."

I blinked a few times. I think my mouth fell open. He quit after one day? I took the bus all the way there, every single day, and he'd quit after one day?

"Christian. You owe the boss money."

He waved his hand dismissively. "No, I don't."

"Yes, you do. You promised to pay him back. That money came from his own pocket!"

"He'll just write it off. Don't worry about him. He has plenty of money."

I'm not gonna lie, I wanted to hurt him at that moment. He took money from everyone and anyone and never paid it back. He didn't even feel guilty about it. I hated having my name linked to that kind of behavior.

Christian was nothing but a con man. Now that I'd had a break from my drug of choice (him), I was seeing things a lot more clearly. I loved him more than I even loved myself, but love wasn't enough anymore. I needed to fix this, and I needed to make sure I was able to leave the next time he fell off the wagon.

Twenty-Two

While exploring the city, we stumbled upon an apartment in an old building that we immediately fell in love with. It was a two-bedroom penthouse, but the best part is that it led to a rooftop swimming pool with an incredible view of the ocean. We didn't need two bedrooms, but only a few days later, a lovely lady knocked on the door, and the next thing we knew, we had a roommate.

Marianne was a fellow Canadian in her fifties, and when she told me she loved to cook, drink margaritas, and smoke pot, I knew she was my kind of person. There was a nice Mormon family living below us, and all of us became friends. I loved having our apartment beside the pool because not only did we get to meet everyone in the building, but for the first time since we got here, it felt like we were part of a community.

The girls and I would swim in the pool and drink margaritas while the boys sat in the hammocks, talking for hours. Mr. Mormon and Christian were serious debaters, and I was happy they'd found each other, because I had no desire to talk about religion, while Christian found every debate exciting and fun.

Now that we'd found our tribe, we settled into a nice little routine that I found comforting. I finally had people to talk to, and it pleased me to no end that they never judged me or Christian, even though they knew he was a recovering addict. It was nice not having to hide the truth, even if they didn't know the whole story.

Christian got another job and came home in a great mood every day, but more importantly, he was making money. He even went to AA meetings, and I was over the moon when that happened. He made friends, and for the first time in a long time, I was hopeful. In fact, our life was kind of amazing.

Christian's an exceptional networker, and his love of talking meant he could talk to anyone, anytime. Every day he'd bring home some stray tourist, and I was happy to see most of them came from his meetings. He was finally surrounding himself with a support system, and the difference was incredible.

Marianne was a great addition to our lives, and since we both loved cooking, we started throwing big dinner parties for our friends and the random people Christian brought home. Sometimes there'd be a guitar and we'd play music late into the night. Suddenly, we had this wonderful community of people, and our lives were full of joy.

We even started exploring the area now that we had money. We took the water taxi up the coast, visiting quiet beaches like Yelapa and Playa Las Animas. We even took the bus to Guadalajara and stayed in a hotel like actual tourists. This was the life we'd always talked about. I wondered how long it would last.

I always knew this life was possible if Christian would only believe in himself. I honestly thought love could heal anything, although I clearly had no idea what I was talking about. The problem was that other people kept reinforcing that belief. With so many people normalizing his addiction, it felt like I was the one who was overreacting every time he used.

Maybe I was the one who needed to grow up and learn that relationships aren't perfect. That fairytales aren't real. That all couples have problems. So if what we had was true love, and everyone saw that it was, then I couldn't give up. I couldn't quit. I had to put in the work and make compromises because that's what society had taught me.

When Christian used again, I was seized with panic, but then he contacted his sponsor, who dragged him to a meeting, and it actually worked. He went a whole month before he used again, only this time he kept it to himself, and I knew we were headed for disaster. I begged him not to destroy the beautiful life we'd created, but I was wasting my time. Christian always did what he wanted, or whatever his demons told him to do.

Marianne was the only one who knew about the relapses. I felt she had a right to know as our roommate. Her friendship and support were the only things keeping me from falling into another immobilizing depression, which meant the world to me. It was hard pretending nothing was wrong around the others, but for the first time since Christian and I started dating, I had a friend, and that changed *everything*. She helped me stay positive and even helped me make an exit strategy for when it all turned to shit. She was my rock, and I was extremely grateful she was there.

It didn't take long for everything to come crashing down. Over the next month, Christian used more and more, until eventually he lost his job, and we were broke again. Our life was an emotional roller coaster, and although it was thrilling at times, I desperately wanted off. So I sat him down and told him it was time to leave. He bawled his eyes out when I told him it was over, and the pain I saw on his face reflected my own. "Sage, please don't do this. You're my soulmate, and I can't live without you. We belong together! You're the number one thing in my life. I *need* you."

"I am *not* the number one thing in your life. Don't kid yourself. At best, I'm third. *You* come first; coke comes second, and I fall somewhere in line after that."

"That's not true!" he shouted, stomping his foot.

"Yes it is, and you know it."

"It's not my fault I was born with this disease. Imagine how much I've suffered and how much I've lost because of it! When do I get *my* happy ending?"

"Believe me, Christian, I know that. But I can't keep watching my life fall apart because of your actions. I need to do this for me. I need to have control over my own life again."

"How will we even get home? We don't have any money. Maybe we could borrow some from one of your sisters or your parents . . ."

"Over my dead body will I ask my parents for money, and I'm not borrowing from my sisters, either. I'm not involving them in our drama. I'm not like you. I don't use people, and besides, you know that's not an option. Everyone in my family is broke."

"I don't use people!" he shouted, and then he spent the rest of the night trying to change my mind, but we both knew it was over. I honestly had no idea what we were going to do, but I needed to come up with something, and fast.

I needed time alone so I could clear my head and think. Marianne told me there was a full moon in a couple of days, so I made plans to go camping. I've always been drawn to the moon, and I figured it was the perfect time to do some deep soul searching. I headed to Playa Las Animas with a couple of friends, and we spent the day swimming, drinking, and eating the special cookies I'd baked, which were a big hit.

"These cookies are amazing. What a clever idea."

"Thanks. I made them with peanut butter to mask the taste."

"I would totally buy these if you ever decide to go into business."

"I would, too. It's dangerous smoking here. The police are so corrupt."

"Tell me about it. I got busted a few years ago with my friend, and the police harassed us for ages before I finally paid them off."

When the last water taxi departed, I waved my friends good-bye and pitched my tent on the beach. Now that the tourists were gone, the local residents wandered over to check me out. I was joined by a donkey, a couple of dogs, some chickens, and, of course . . . a rooster. My friends thought I was crazy to camp by myself, but I wasn't afraid. I desperately needed to connect with nature and the sounds of the ocean.

I talked to the moon for a long time that night. I turned over my options as I listened to the waves and the crickets. I asked the Universe for help. I knew that leaving Christian wouldn't be easy. I still loved him, but love wasn't enough anymore. I wanted to be happy. How the hell was I going to make enough money to get us out of here? Without a visa, I wasn't allowed to work unless I wanted to sell timeshare again, which I didn't.

I thought about the time Heather and I had gotten caught smoking, and I wondered how many tourists that had happened to over the years. Then I remembered what my friends said about my cookies and wanting to buy them. I thought about Wreck Beach, and an idea started forming.

It was risky and would land us in jail if we got caught, but I was desperate. I *had* to get us out of here. If Christian got caught with coke, we were headed to jail anyway, so I was fucked either way. When I got home, I shared my idea with Marianne. I needed allies to make this work.

"What if someone catches you? You could go to jail."

"I know. Believe me, I know. But here's the thing: no one will think twice about people eating cookies, and since edibles aren't known here—"

"—no one will be looking. Very clever. Where do you plan to sell them?"

"The blue chairs. Most of the tourists are Canadian, and I *know* they want it, but they're too scared to buy it. A fellow Canadian, however . . ."

"I see where you're going with this."

"Plus, we have a secret weapon—Christian. Gay men *love* him, and I'm going to use that."

"Very smart and very discreet. I'm impressed. Will Christian play ball, though?"

"That's the tricky part. I have to make sure he doesn't spend the money before I can save enough to get us home. He'll be working against me at all times. I'll have to outsmart him."

"Give the money to me. I'll hold on to it."

"That's a great idea, but you'll have to hide it. He's smart."

"Not a problem. Are you really going to leave him once this is over?"

"Yes, I am," I said sadly.

"But you two are so amazing together. You really are a wonderful couple."

"Marianne, I'm about to do something extremely illegal in a foreign country, something I would *never* do at home, all because Christian spent our money on drugs and left us stranded. So I don't care how perfect we are together. I've spent too many nights crying over this man, and I need it to stop."

"I admire you for making this decision when it's obvious how much you love him."

Tears came to my eyes. Marianne really was a good friend. "Don't sing my praises just yet. This will be really hard, and he's going to fight me every step of the way."

"I wish you didn't have to leave."

"Me neither. I love it here. But I need to go home, find a job, and get my finances in order. I owe a lot of money when I get home. Christian put me in debt and demolished my credit rating. I need to fix it and get my life back on track."

"Will you start singing again?"

"I have no idea. I'm not ready to think about that just yet, especially since it doesn't pay very well, and I'm tired of being broke."

"If you decide to come back, I'll be here for another six months."

I hugged her. "That means a lot. Thanks for listening to me, and I'm sorry you had to get involved in our drama. You're an amazing friend."

"It's OK. I've been there, and I totally understand."

There were about six of us who went to the beach every day over the next two months. As I suspected, Christian was amazing at networking, and we sold lots of cookies, but it was two steps forward and one step back. He was still using most nights, plus we still had to pay rent and buy groceries, all while trying to save enough money to get home. The nice thing was that the tourists talked to each other, and they usually came back for more, along with a couple of their friends, so business was good.

It may have looked like every day was a great big party on the beach (and it was), but make no mistake, my stress levels were through the roof. Everyone was having a great time except me. Every day that we were out there, we risked getting caught, and every night I had to fight with Christian not to spend the money. I begged him to stop putting us in danger, but in his mind, he was helping me earn it, so he got to spend it. Besides, he didn't want to leave, so he wasn't about to make it easy.

Every night we fought about money, but since I no longer held on to it, he couldn't find it. He was smart, though. He simply borrowed it from our unsuspecting friends, and I was forced to pay them back. Every day it was something new, but I finally managed to save enough money to buy two bus tickets to Los Angeles. My father would be providing us with free flights from there.

It would have been easier to leave Christian behind, but I couldn't do that. The guilt would have killed me, and the coke would have killed him, but none of that mattered anymore. After a year in Puerto Vallarta, we were heading home, and I was totally dreading it.

The bus ride took two days, and it was excruciating. We were lost in our own world of hurt and pain as we stopped over and over again, hitting every bus station from Puerto Vallarta to Los Angeles. It was incredibly hot in the middle of August, and I must have been dehydrated because for the second time in my life, I fainted. I woke up to a bunch of people shouting in Spanish, just as Christian came running over.

"Oh my God! Are you OK?" he asked, panic written all over his face.

"I think so. What happened?" I sat up, still feeling woozy.

"I was on the phone with my mother when I looked over and saw you faint. All of a sudden, you swayed in a circle and then boom! You fell straight backwards without even breaking your fall. Your head hit the cement really hard! Are you sure you're OK?"

Someone brought me a cold towel and a bottle of water, and then the driver opened the bus and let me sit inside. Usually he made everyone get off every time we stopped, but he was willing to make an exception. The locals were so kind that several of them returned with bottles of water and juice. I thanked them, but I was embarrassed to have caused such a scene.

Christian held my hand as we drove away. He was worried because he knew

I needed food and there was nothing he could do about it. He had spent all our money the night before we left, knowing it would be his last fix for a while.

"Oh, Sage. This is all my fault," he said as he held my hand.

"It's almost over Christian. Just two more days and we'll be home."

"But I won't have you in my life anymore, and I'm not sure I can stand it."

"You'll be fine. There was life before me, and there will be life after me."

"I just love you so much." His face crumpled and he started to cry.

"I know you do. I love you, too, but I can't keep doing this. I can't keep fighting. I can't keep crying. I can't keep living in fear. It's killing me, Christian. It's killing both of us."

"I know. You're right to do this, Sage. I don't blame you one bit, but I can't accept that this is the end. If I go home and get sober, would you take me back?"

"Christian—"

"Just hear me out. If I stay sober for six months, get a job, make money, will you take me back?" His eyes pleaded with me to say yes.

"I don't know . . ."

"But you're my soulmate! You have to know I'm not letting you go without a fight."

"I'll tell you what. You do what you need to do, and if you're still sober in six months, then we can talk about it, OK?"

"Really? That's all I need. Just a little hope and a goal to work towards."

When we got to the airport, we cried as we said good-bye. I felt like my heart was breaking in two, like half of me was being ripped away. It was hard to breathe, and for a brief moment I didn't want to let go. Leaving him was one of the hardest things I've ever done, but I knew it was the right thing to do.

"You get better, Christian, do you hear me? You're an amazing person with so many gifts. If you only knew how amazing you were, you'd be unstoppable."

"I *will* get better. I promise. I've learned a lot about myself this year, and I'm shocked at how low I've gone and heartbroken that I've hurt you in the process. I'm so proud of you for taking a stand and doing what's right for you. I know it's hard to walk away, but you're doing the right thing."

"How can you say that when this hurts so much?"

"Because I know this isn't good-bye. It's see you later."

He kissed me, and tears rolled down our cheeks as we walked away. As I sat on the plane, I thought about what he'd said and hoped like hell he was wrong. I knew he needed to believe we'd get back together, but I secretly hoped we wouldn't. I no longer believed in him or us. I had, however, learned a very valuable lesson from all this. I'd been in love twice in my life, and love did *not* equal happiness like the fairytales suggested. In fact, it did quite the opposite.

Twenty-Three

When I first got home, I stayed with Sienna, who was happy to hear that Christian and I were no longer dating. Then I reached out to an old friend, the kind you only see every couple of years but it's always like yesterday. I knew he was financially secure, so I asked if I could borrow some money until I found a job. I hated borrowing money from friends, but I didn't have much of a choice.

I found a catering job to get me through the winter, and then I found an apartment downtown. Luckily, Sidney was holding on to my old furniture, so at least I had the basics. She was going through her own struggles, and now that she and her husband were no longer together, she was figuring out just how much he'd manipulated her—something we had in common.

When I turned thirty, I went into early mid-life crisis mode, and it wasn't pretty. It's not that I necessarily felt old (although I did); it's that I'd had such grand ideas of who I wanted to be when I grew up and, well, to put it bluntly, my life was a steaming pile of crap and nowhere near the incredible life and career I'd once imagined for myself.

When I was twenty, I knew exactly who I wanted to be. I wanted to star in a Broadway show, do voiceovers for Disney, and sing jazz in some funky little nightclub. All things that were within my reach, yet here I was—thirty, and nowhere near that dream. In fact, I'd veered so far off my path I didn't even know where it was.

I was in the middle of this existential crisis when I decided to make some major changes. I mourned my breakup with Christian for months, but it was time to get my shit together, and first on the agenda was my finances. Starting from the bottom is one thing, but starting with someone else's debt hanging over your head is another. After some careful deliberation, I made the difficult decision to declare bankruptcy.

My debt wasn't that big, but I was only making minimum wage, so it felt like a mountain. The trustee was really nice and showed me a lot of sympathy, which made the whole process a lot easier. When someone lays their pride at your feet, a little understanding goes a long way.

In the spring, I found work as an extra on film sets. It didn't pay very well, but it was a start. It wasn't exactly what I'd hoped for when I put myself through acting school, but what can I say? I needed money, so it was time to buckle down and do what needed to be done. I was thirty now. I didn't have any more time to waste.

Christian still called every month, and hearing his voice made me sad. Despite everything we'd been through, I still loved him. The past six months had been lonely, but no matter how much I wanted to hate him, I couldn't, because I knew he had a disease and it wasn't his fault. He did a great job of programming me into believing that, just like my mother had when I was a child.

I remember how she used to cry in her bedroom, and how I could feel her pain as if it were my own. She used my empathy to manipulate me, and Christian did the same. I understand that now, but I didn't at the time. No one ever used words like *empath* or *narcissistic behavior* in those days. No one talked about boundaries or childhood trauma. We were just trying to survive.

It sounded like things were going well in Montreal until around April, when Christian had to go back to rehab. Since he wasn't able to call me anymore, he wrote letters instead. They were full of love and hope, apologies and amends, and although I loved hearing from him, I was glad he was there and not here. It had taken me eight months, but I was finally getting my life together, and the last thing I needed was Christian dragging me down.

I had just gotten home from work when someone knocked on the door. I wasn't expecting anyone, so imagine my surprise when I saw Christian standing there—with a suitcase. My first thought was fear. My eyes became saucers, and my mouth hit the floor as he stood there grinning, and although my body was frozen to the spot, my mind was racing in every direction. Seeing the look of shock on my face made him grin even wider, and he rushed forward to pick me up and twirl me in a circle. He was holding a bouquet of flowers, and he handed them to me.

"Surprise, baby!" he shouted joyfully. "I'm back!"

"What are you doing here?" I said, half laughing, half freaking out.

"You said you missed me, so I dropped everything to come and see you." His eyes sparkled as he looked me over appreciatively.

"You're here for a visit?" I asked hopefully. *Please only be here for a visit,* I prayed.

"Nope. I'm here to stay. I want to be with you, baby."

"But . . . you're supposed to be in rehab." Panic was spreading throughout my entire body as my heart started racing. I really hadn't been expecting this.

His face fell as he pretended to pout. "Aren't you happy to see me? I've come all this way to surprise you." When I didn't respond, he raised an eyebrow. "Can I at least come in?"

"Oh gosh, sorry, yes, come in. You just . . . surprised me."

"That was the whole point! After I read your letter, I couldn't stand to be away from you a second longer. And when you said you were lonely, I knew I had to rescue you. We belong together, Sage, and I'm never leaving you again."

Filter . . . filter . . . filter . . . so many things I wanted to say. "But what about rehab?"

"Oh, man. That got so weird." He put down his suitcase and looked around my studio apartment. "There were so many guys with mental issues, and after a while, the energy became so intense. I couldn't stand it anymore, but don't worry," he said when he saw the look on my face. "I did the work, and I feel *amazing!* Now get over here," he growled. "I haven't seen you in eight months, and I need to make love to you *right now.*"

He kissed me, and whatever protests were on my lips slipped away. I knew I shouldn't let him in, but what was I supposed to do? He had just flown across the country to be with me. It was kind of romantic, really. No one had ever made that kind of grand gesture for me before. Heck, no one had done *any* kind of gesture for me before.

I know this is hard to understand, but anyone who's ever been in a bad relationship where the sex is incredible will understand me when I say that great sex makes it difficult to leave. Sex is a powerful tool and a very intimate act. Christian knew exactly how to wield it. Ask any woman who's ever been in the same situation and she'll agree.

Sex is a very intimate act. You're literally allowing someone to plug into your energy. When that person is an energy vampire (like Christian), they know exactly how to steal your energy through your orgasms, leaving you satisfied yet energetically drained.

In my mind Christian was the only person who ever loved me. My parents didn't love me. My grandparents didn't love me. Luka definitely didn't love me. The world had proved to be a cruel and frightening place. Christian was all I had. No one had ever made me feel the way he did. When he wasn't using, he treated me like a queen, and those were the moments I held on to.

The reason I stayed was that I knew what our relationship *could* be, and I was constantly striving to return to that bliss. My brain told me to turn him away, but my resolve faded as soon as he kissed me. Even if this *was* a Romeo and Juliet romance that was doomed to kill us in the end, I figured it was better than dying alone.

By the time fall rolled around, Christian was so out of control that I knew I had to get rid of him, or have a nervous breakdown. I had no idea how to get through to him, but one thing was for sure: it was time for some tough love. When he'd first arrived, things had gone so well. He even had money this time around. The summer was full of adventure and laughter, and we were really happy for a while. Until we weren't.

Once again, our life was in the toilet, and I'd been asking him to leave for months, but he wouldn't listen. I was at my wits' end because I had no idea how to get through to him. How do you break up with someone who refuses to leave? He'd already stolen my electronics and jewelry (a new low, even for him), and now he wanted money. He always wanted money.

I felt trapped in an impossible situation, and the stress was taking its toll. My stomach was in knots, and I felt anxious all the time. I hadn't slept in months, and a fog was taking over my brain. The darkness was creeping in again, but I had to fight it. I didn't want to go back there.

The next time he showed up (stoned), I refused to open the door, but he was banging so loudly I was afraid he'd wake up the neighbors. The last thing I needed was a scene. He did the same thing when he showed up at my job. He knew I wouldn't draw attention to myself, so he used that against me. I was a nervous wreck because I never knew when he'd show up, and I was constantly looking over my shoulder.

I let him in to my apartment, but I told him this was the end. He wasn't allowed to stay this time. I told him to gather his things and get out. He immediately started crying and begged me to reconsider, but my mind was made up. No matter how much it broke my heart, I kept insisting he leave.

He got angry and asked for money, but I said no. We fought, and at one point, he grabbed me by the shoulders and started shaking me. That's when I lost it. There was a desperation in him I'd never seen before and I thought, *This is it. This is the breaking point.*

I started screaming, and he looked genuinely startled. I'd never made a scene before, and his fuzzy brain couldn't handle it. He covered my mouth with his hand (not to hurt me, but to make me stop), but it had the exact opposite effect, as you can imagine. I screamed even louder.

"Sage, please stop. You'll wake the neighbors," he whispered desperately.

I struggled to get away, but when he looked in my eyes and saw genuine terror, he immediately dropped his hands and started crying again.

"I'm so sorry. I would never hurt you. You *must* know that. I was only trying to get you to stop before someone calls the cops. Please, Sage, just let me sleep on the couch, and I won't touch you again I promise."

All of the fight seemed to have left him, but I was just getting started.

"Get. Out," I said evenly, as I pointed to the door.

"Sage, please," he begged, "I have nowhere to go, and it's cold outside."

I still wasn't getting through to him, so in my desperation, I started slinging insults, hoping that would work. Kindness never had. "You're nothing but a JUNKIE, and I want nothing more to do with you. Do you hear me, Christian? Now get out of my apartment!"

He gasped. I'd never called him that before, and I knew how much he hated that word. The look on his face and the way it hurt him broke my heart, but I was desperate to make him leave, so I said it again, all the while dying inside because cruelty isn't in my nature.

"I am NOT! How can you say that? I'm not some low life living on the streets. I'm a good man! It's not my fault I was born with this addiction!" He was sobbing as he said this, and I was, too, but I knew I couldn't back down. In the past few months, I'd tried being firm and I'd tried kindness. I begged, pleaded, and scorned, but nothing seemed to work.

"You're NOT a good man! You're nothing but a thief and a liar. I hate you!"

He gasped again. "How can you say that? I know it's not true. You love me. Do you think I like living like this? Do you think I like knowing how much this hurts you?"

"Get out of here!" I screamed, before I caved as usual. "GET OUT GET OUT GET OUT!" I was like a mad woman. I completely lost it. I started throwing his clothes out the window, just like those breakup scenes in the movies. I was screaming at the top of my lungs, and when he tried to embrace me, I lost it even more. The more he begged me to be quiet, the louder I got, until someone banged on the door, stopping both of us in our tracks.

"Police! Open up!"

The look on Christian's face was sheer *panic.* His worst nightmare was coming true. Someone had called the cops. He looked around for an escape, but there wasn't one.

"Don't open the door," he whispered. Paranoia is one of the worst side effects of shooting coke. Only this time it wasn't a hallucination.

Never in my life had I made a scene before. I'm an incredibly private person because that's how I was raised. You did *not* air your dirty laundry in public. If my father could've seen me now, he would've been so ashamed. Hell, I was ashamed of myself, but I'd have to deal with that later. For now, the police were my salvation, so I opened the door.

"Miss, we had a call about a domestic disturbance. Is everything OK in there?"

"No, it's not," I said, as tears ran down my face. "I need you to make him leave." I pointed at Christian who was cowering in the corner. The officer looked at him, then back at me.

"Has he hurt you, miss?"

I shook my head. "No. It's nothing like that. He's an addict, and he needs help. I'm trying to break up with him, but he won't leave."

One of the officers stayed with me while the other one walked into my apartment. "Sir, you heard the lady. You'll have to come with us," he said sternly.

"Sage, please don't do this. I love you, Sage. Please don't let them take me away."

The look of terror on his face was like a knife in my chest. I started sobbing uncontrollably. "I'm sorry, Christian. I can't do this anymore."

"Sage, please. I'm begging you!" he cried, and the knife twisted deeper. The officer pushed him out the door as he continued to plead. I could hear him all the way down the hall as he begged me to have mercy. I was shaking all over, and my breath was coming out in spasms as I watched the officer drag him away. I opened my mouth in a silent scream as my body filled with unbearable pain.

"Please don't hurt him," I said to the officer standing by the door.

"Would you like to press charges?" she asked, sympathetically.

"No. He just needs to detox, that's all. He's not a bad person, and he's not violent."

"Unfortunately, we can't force him into a program. He has to do that on his own." Then she put her hand on my shoulder. "You're doing the right thing, you know."

"It doesn't feel like the right thing." My face crumpled as fresh tears came to my eyes.

"If he comes back, call us, OK?"

I nodded as she turned to go. Then I closed the door and fell to my knees. All of my bravado was gone, and in its place was nothing but pain. Pain for me. Pain for him. Pain for that little boy who had been introduced to a needle so many years ago. As big wracking sobs took over my body, all I could see was the look on Christian's face as they'd dragged him away. His voice ringing in my ears . . . and that's when I broke.

I didn't hear from him for two weeks, and not one second went by that I didn't worry. It was October, and the weather was cold and wet. I wasn't even sure he had a coat. I lived in absolute fear waiting for that phone call, telling me he was dead, and I knew I'd never forgive myself if that happened. How on earth would I face his family knowing I was the one who sent him to live on the street? Had I sent him to die?

They call it tough love, but that's a serious understatement. It was hard enough watching him kill himself with drugs, but sending him to live on the street in the middle of winter? I wondered a million times if I'd done the right thing. I knew if something happened, it would be my fault. That night played over and over in my mind on an endless loop. The look of betrayal on

Christian's face as they they dragged him away was seared into my memory.

Eventually, he came back. He always did. Part of me was relieved, but the other part was gripped by fear. Fear that I'd never be free of him. When I opened the door, he practically collapsed in my arms, and I quickly pulled him inside so no one would see him. Not after that humiliating scene from a few weeks ago.

He was soaking wet and shivering uncontrollably. He'd lost so much weight his ribs were sticking out, and my guilt consumed me. He wept as he apologized for what he'd put me through, and I bawled as I begged him to forgive me. When he saw how broken I was, he grabbed my face and looked me in the eyes. "Don't be sad, my sweet *papillon*. You did the right thing. I'm proud of you. You didn't do anything wrong."

"How can you say that?" I wailed. "You live on the street, and I'm the one who put you there!" How could he be so kind after what I'd done? Why wasn't he blaming me?

"No, you didn't. Hey. Look at me. No. You. Didn't. I did that. Cocaine did that. But you—you are the most caring person I've ever known. You did the right thing, Sage. You did the right thing." He smiled gently, and there was genuine concern in his eyes.

"It doesn't feel like it," I whispered as tears streamed down my face. His forgiveness and understanding made it even more unbearable because I knew what I had to do next.

I fed him, gave him a hot bath, and let him sleep on the couch, but in the morning, I told him he had to leave. He was surprised, but I was adamant, and when I threatened to call the cops if he didn't leave, he knew I meant business. We'd crossed a line, and we both knew it. There was no turning back. I was broken.

Twenty-Four

I wish I could tell you that that was the end of it, but it wasn't. Even though he was gone, the darkness lingered for a long time. It had a hold on me, and it wasn't letting go. Over the past four years, Christian's demons and my own had made friends, and now they were ganging up on me. I was too tired to fight them, so I surrendered instead. After all, the darkness was all I'd ever known.

It's funny, because when I was a kid, I never cried. Even as a teen, I never cried, but then I went to theater school where they taught us how to tap into those emotions, and it was game over. Suddenly, everything was about how we were feeling. Suddenly, I was an emotional disaster.

I cried at movies, when I was angry, when I was sad, when other people were sad. Empaths don't have it easy. We feel everything, and we feel it very deeply. Half the time it's not even our own shit. Add my Virgo moon to the mix, and not only did I feel everything deeply, but then I spent weeks analyzing those feelings until I understood every nuance of why I (and others) felt that way. Sometimes it felt like all I ever did was self-reflect.

Christian and I played this game for several more years before I was finally free of him. Our journey took us back to Mexico, but this time we ended up in Cancun. I wasn't the same person when it was over, and I wondered if that carefree, life-of-the-party girl would ever come back. I doubted it. Nobody survives that kind of trauma unscathed. He'd taken something from me, and now I was even more jaded than when we met, seven years ago.

Seven years. That's how long it took me to break free. When it was over, I promised myself I'd never put myself in that situation again.

I had nightmares for a long time. Nightmares about Christian waking me up to steal my money or, even worse, dying and telling me it wasn't my fault. I went to some pretty dark places in those days, and then one day I decided enough was enough. It was time to snap out of it before I was completely lost. No one was coming to save me. This wasn't a fairytale. If I wanted to get out of this funk, I'd have to do it myself, so that's exactly what I did.

I was working at a hotel in Cancun when one of my guests called and asked if she could meet me. Her name was Angelou, and I liked her a lot. I think it was her calm demeanor that I found so inviting. She made me feel at peace, something I hadn't felt in a long time. She had an extra ticket for a tour to Chichen Itza, and she wanted to know if I'd like to accompany her. I love history, so I said yes.

When Christian and I first moved to Cancun in 2003, we were hired by a hotel. When he started using and got fired, I managed to not only keep my job, but to excel at it. I moved out, found my own beachfront apartment, and made a wonderful circle of friends. He continued coming in and out of my life for another two years before finally leaving Cancun. This time I stayed behind.

It's a two-hour drive to Chichen Itza, which gave Angelou and I plenty of time to get to know each other. I learned that she was a Christian, albeit a very open-minded one. I told her about my six-year brush with Christianity, and how the cult-like church had destroyed my family. She said she understood, and that many terrible things have been done in the name of God. It was an interesting conversation, and it was the first time I'd talked to a devout Christian since leaving the church.

When we got to Chichen Itza, we had a tour, and I learned a lot about the Mayan people. They were brilliant scholars, astrologers, and mathematicians.

The guide talked about the mysteries surrounding the pyramids, and the phenomena that happens on the equinox. I made a mental note to return and see it for myself one day.

Afterwards, Angelou and I climbed the pyramid. I was a little concerned because she was in her eighties, but she was a trooper. As we climbed, I was surprised by how tiny the steps were, which meant you had to do this sideways crawling thing. Then again, the Mayans were tiny people, so I guess it made sense.

When we got to the top, I peered over the edge while Angelou clung to the wall for dear life. As it turned out, she was deathly afraid of heights. I asked what she was doing up there, and she told me it was her dream to climb the pyramid, so that's what she did. As we sat there admiring the view, she turned to me and said, "Sage, I have something to tell you. A message meant just for you."

I was intrigued.

"Before I came to Cancun, I had a dream about you. I didn't know it was you specifically; just someone I'd meet on this trip. When I first saw you, I knew it was you in my dream, but I wasn't sure how to deliver the message. It's kismet that you're here today, and I can't think of a better place to deliver this message than on the top of this sacred pyramid."

I smiled, encouraging her to go on.

"You're trying to change your life, but you're stuck. You wonder why you can't get on with the next phase of your life, but it's simple. There's something that brings you great pain, and you must forgive this thing before you can move on."

I was momentarily stunned. I hadn't expected a message like that from a Christian.

"Forgive who?" I asked. I could think of dozens of people who'd done me wrong over the years.

"I'm not sure, but after our conversation, I think it's the church. Or maybe your mother."

When I got home, I walked along the beach, thinking about what she said. My relationship with my parents was still strained, but it was better than it used to be, especially now that they'd stopped going to church. I sat on the beach and wrote a letter to my mother, venting all of my anger and frustration, and then I did the same for the church. When I finished, I forgave them, burned the letters, and buried the ashes in the earth. I didn't want to hold on to my anger anymore. I didn't want to be bitter like Sidney, who still couldn't let it go.

October 1983

My parents were friends with a couple from the church who had two bratty kids. They were younger than us, stuck up, and super spoiled. Sidney and I couldn't stand them. Their family came over for Thanksgiving when I was twelve, and we had just finished eating when my mother started clearing the plates.

Until then, she always did the housework because she liked things done a certain way. She was a perfectionist, probably because she was trying to please my father, who expected nothing less than perfection.

"What are you doing?" asked Janice as my mother cleared the dishes. "Don't you have them to do that?" She nodded towards me and Sidney.

"What do you mean?" asked my mother.

Janice was a busybody who liked to stick her nose in other people's business, and she was about to stick her nose in ours. Church people were like that.

"Your kids are old enough to do that for you," she persisted. "You work hard enough already. You should relax. Take a load off and make *them* do it."

My mother's eyes lit up, and I'm pretty sure she was wondering why she'd never thought of that herself. She looked at me and Sidney and said, "I *do* work hard around here! And I'm the one who prepared this meal, so you girls should clean it up! Clear the table right now, and wash the dishes."

We had no idea how to wash the dishes, having never done them before. We looked to our father for help. "Don't look at me. Do what your mother tells you." That was pretty much his standard line when it came to us.

Here's the thing—this could have been a real teaching moment. My mother could have shown us how to wash the dishes, then let us do our thing, but that's not how it worked in our family. Instead, the two of them berated us from the kitchen table for over an hour, saying we were doing it all wrong, that we were stupid, and then they laughed at our frustration.

Even that stupid bitch Janice got in on it. Everyone was having a grand old time except for us. They made us do the dishes over and over again until we got it right, and there were *so many dishes* after Thanksgiving dinner. When it was over (several hours later), Sidney had the first in a long series of migraines. The worst part is that this was just the beginning.

Now that my mother knew we were her personal slaves, that's exactly how she treated us. Not only were the dishes our job, but so was the rest of the house. We did the vacuuming, the laundry, the dusting, the sweeping and mopping, and the bathroom. My mother still wanted it spotless, so she hovered over us, making sure we did it right and punishing us when we didn't.

If the house wasn't perfect, there was her never-ending criticism to contend with. If we complained, there was my father to contend with. For years, my mother looked for any spot we might have missed on a plate or cup, and if she found one, she put all the dishes back in the sink and made us start over.

Shortly after writing those letters, I met a shaman, and he was a fascinating man. He offered to do a re-birthing ceremony, so several friends and I took him up on the offer. That's one of the things I loved about Cancun. After seven years of darkness, I was ready to heal, and this was a good place to start, so I embraced the spirituality of the land and let it work its magic.

The shaman and his wife buried us in the sand, and then he placed a crystal on each of our heads. He said his prayers and left us there for about thirty minutes. The sand is Mother Earth, and being buried represented the womb. It was a very peaceful experience.

Afterwards, we bathed in the ocean, and the shaman told me that the salt water is a natural way to clean our energy. I guess that's why I've always loved the ocean. To me, the ocean is where I feel most at peace. I've always been drawn to it.

I spent five years in Cancun, and it really felt like home. I loved living on the beach, and I got to experience a lot of adventures while I was there—some good, some not so good. In 2005, Hurricane Wilma wiped out the entire Yucatan peninsula, and in 2006, we were hit with a swarm of locusts.

I'll never forget driving down the highway and seeing thousands of locusts flying towards us. They smashed into the windshield, and we screamed at the top of our lungs as one of the ten plagues of Egypt manifested before our very eyes. Afterward, we laughed so hard I nearly peed myself, and later that same day . . . I got Typhoid fever. I thought I would die I was in so much pain.

The good times far outweighed the bad, though. I loved swimming in the cenotes and watching the giant sea turtles lay eggs every summer. The pyramids, the people, the culture, the history . . . I loved it all, especially swimming with the whale sharks.

What's really crazy is that my father ended up moving to Cancun after losing his job with the airline. I got him a job at the hotel, and six months later, Sienna started working there, too. I really got to know my father during this time, and it was an interesting shift in our relationship. We'd never be close, but we managed to find a mutual respect, and that was enough. Eventually, he got his own apartment (in the same complex), and a year later, my mother arrived.

My parents were extremely popular, and every day they had cocktails in front of their unit with their new friends. It was weird seeing them drinking again, but I have to admit, they were a lot easier to handle when they were tipsy. Eventually, my parents returned to Vancouver, but they constantly talked about their exciting two-year adventure in Mexico.

I loved my time in Mexico, but six months after Sienna left, I got restless, so when the opportunity to work on a cruise ship came along, I accepted. I was hired for the front desk, which was odd since I had no experience, but I figured it was a great way to get my foot in the door. I had several singing gigs while I was in Cancun, and I was ready to get my career back on track.

I used my time in Cancun to heal, to connect with the ocean and the land. In the stillness, I found myself. I was thirty-seven years old, but it was never too late to embark on a new adventure.

TWENTY-FIVE

Working on a ship was a lot of fun, but as I suspected, I wasn't cut out for the front desk. Although my team was amazing and I loved my new family, the passengers were horrific, and I wanted to throw most of them overboard.

For ten hours a day, I had to listen to people complain. It was a wall of negativity coming at you all day, every day. You probably think I'm exaggerating, but I'm not. For example, one woman actually said to one of my colleagues, "Shut up, you stupid bitch, or I'll come across that desk and KILL you."

Most of my colleagues just stood there and took it. I don't know where they got their patience from, but I promise you, I'm not like them. I scolded people for being idiots, stepped in front of my colleagues when someone tried to bully them, and never hesitated to tell someone to walk away or I'd call security. My boss would say, "Don't take it so personally," or "Brush it off," but seriously, it's shit, and it's being thrown straight at you. You're going to wear it.

I lasted about three weeks before I handed in my resignation. My boss read it, crumpled it into a ball, and threw it in the garbage, which is shocking because she shouldn't have wanted someone like me at the front desk. I was far too mouthy.

"We love having you here, Sage. You're so funny, and you always speak your mind."

"Isn't that a bad thing? You're always telling me to rein it in."

"Yes, but you make us laugh. You can't quit. I deny your request."

"Um . . . OK, but don't say I didn't warn you."

My boss was an awesome lady, and when she found out I wanted to sing, she bent over backwards to help me. Eventually, I was introduced to a pianist, and when I told him I was hoping to make an audition video, he volunteered to help me rehearse the songs. Several times a week, I popped into the piano bar, and we always had a great time, laughing and joking as we rehearsed. One night, the cruise director came in, and the next day, I was told he wrote it into his nightly report, which was a great endorsement for me.

After a few months, I was ready. We arranged for a drummer and a bass player to complete our quartet, and the videographer agreed to film it. This might not sound like a big deal, but I promise, on a cruise ship, getting anyone to do anything when they're off work (which was after midnight) and then getting permission from their department heads (who rarely co-operated with each other) was a massive effort.

It was a packed house when I got there. The cruise director had invited his entire team, along with the captain and several guests. My own team was there, and I was happy to see their smiling faces. It was my first time singing with a trio, and I was super nervous. I'm always nervous when I sing.

Even if I didn't realize it, my mother's voice was always in my head, reminding me that I wasn't good enough and that I'd never amount to anything. It wasn't until my spiritual awakening (many years later) that I learned how to reprogram those thoughts. It took a while, but I finally learned how to be kind to myself and, more importantly, how to believe in myself.

The band was fantastic, and although I was seriously nervous, it went well. We even got a standing ovation. I was hyper aware of all the mistakes I'd made, but I'm my own worst critic when it comes to performing.

The next day, my name was brought up in the managers' meeting, and the cruise director requested I sing on every cruise. We had an overnight in Venice, and on the second night, we held a formal masquerade. It was awesome because everyone purchased a mask in Venice, and they looked so beautiful in their formal gowns and masks.

It was decided I'd sing a few songs with the nine-piece orchestra during their swing set, and I couldn't believe it when they told me. First a trio, and now an orchestra. This was incredible news, even if I found it a little intimidating.

Shortly after that, I was approached by the chief engineer, who asked me what on earth I was doing behind the desk. I laughed and told him that was the million-dollar question. It turned out he knew a lot of people, and he promised to forward my demo reel once it was ready.

All in all, it was a great contract, and six months went quickly. Even though I hated the front desk, I made a lot of new friends and loved the camaraderie that came with this crazy new life. I got to visit some unbelievable places and see things I'd only read about in school.

Standing at the ruins of Carthage was an incredible experience, and Cinque Terre was exactly how I'd imagined it. I almost wept when we saw an opera in Venice and when we went wine tasting in Tuscany . . . I thought I might never leave.

It's hard to explain what it's like working on a ship and visiting a different country every day. The pace is exceptionally fast, and it never stops. One day you're eating pizza in Naples, and the next day you're gambling in Monte Carlo. Work hard, play hard. That was our motto.

No wonder we all burnt out three quarters of the way through our contract. Working seven days a week for six months takes a toll, and I was burning the candle at both ends the entire time.

In November, about three weeks before my contract ended, I was at the desk catching up on emails when I saw one from Sienna. She'd come to cruise with me back in July, and it was fun showing her around the ports. She even got to see me sing with the orchestra. Since then, she'd been emailing me pretty regularly.

Hey Sage, I've been meaning to write for a few days, but things are a little crazy around here. Are you sitting down? Dad has a weird lump on his neck, and as it turns out, he has lymphatic cancer. He's currently at the hospital being poked and prodded like a guinea pig. They're doing a biopsy on his neck, and they extracted his bone marrow yesterday. Poor Dad.

They say he only needs a few rounds of chemo and then a maintenance program, and he can live up to another fifteen years, barring complications. They're optimistic, so don't panic, OK? Dad's in good spirits and ready to fight. I'm on my way to see him now.

I sat down with a thud. My relationship with my father was complicated, and I still resented him for the things he did when I was a child, but we'd come to a certain understanding as of late, and besides, he was still my father. Once I got over the initial shock, I called home. I told Sienna I was coming right away, but she told me to wait until my contract was over.

"But I feel so helpless all the way over here."

"Sage, I'm right here, and I still feel helpless. We all do. Finish your contract and come in three weeks. Trust me. You ARE coming here, right?"

"Yes. They're changing my flights right now."

Next, I called the hospital and talked to my father.

"Hey, kid. What a nice surprise. I'm so glad you called." The line was staticky, but I could still hear him. He sounded weak.

"How are you feeling?"

"I've been better, but we're working on it."

"Listen, I've already talked to my boss, and the company agreed to let me leave early."

"Don't be ridiculous! You're living the dream, and I want to hear all about it when you get here. Three weeks won't make a difference, believe me. I do have one request, though. I'd like you to be here for Christmas. Will you come here instead of going back to Cancun? This might be our last Christmas together, and I want all my girls in one place."

"You got it. Hang in there, OK?"

After I hung up, I went back to my cabin to start packing. Just when I thought things were turning around, life punched me in the gut once again.

Twenty-Six

I spent my thirty-eighth birthday on a plane worrying about my father's health, yet dreading moving in with my parents. I hadn't lived with them for over twenty years, and my inner child was screaming, while my adult self knew it was my father's dying wish and therefore the right thing to do. It wasn't lost on me that my parents had instilled in us the need to do the right thing, even though they never had.

It's a real mind fuck when the parent you've spent your life hating gets cancer. Your heart breaks because nobody deserves to suffer that way, yet it's impossible to express love for someone you don't love. In recent years, I'd learned to respect my father, and I even liked him, but I couldn't say I loved him. So on top of everything else I was feeling, I had to deal with the guilt of not being able to truly comfort him. Like I said—mind fuck.

As far as the living situation went, it wasn't my father I was worried about. We learned long ago not to talk about anything personal. Small talk was safe ground in our family, and since Dad loved history, and I'd just come from Europe, that's what we talked about.

My mother was a different story. She still had the tongue of a snake, and boy, did she love causing drama. It was hard enough handling her at family dinners, but now I was living under her roof. Spreading discord and lies was still one of her favorite games, so having all of us (except Sidney) in one apartment was a lot to handle. At least we weren't helpless children any more.

Burnaby 1981

"Girls, go outside and play. Don't come back until six o'clock," said my mother one sunny afternoon when I was ten.

"OK!" we said. We liked it outside. Outside was good. Outside was freedom. When we were children, we *always* played outside. All the kids did. At six o'clock, we returned to find my mother standing in the doorway, a furious expression on her face.

"Where the hell have you been? Dinner was an hour ago!"

"What do you mean?" we said, totally confused. "You told us not to come back until six o'clock. It's six o'clock!"

"How *dare* you talk back to me!" Bam. Back hand across the face. Man, we hated that back hand. My mother's wedding ring was pointy and sharp, and it always left a mark. "I told you to be back at five o'clock!" she yelled.

"But Mom, we all heard you, and we swear you said six!" Bam across the face.

"Are you calling me a *liar?*" she challenged, with a gleam in her eye. Sidney and I made eye contact while Sienna hid behind us. This was a trap, and we knew it. No matter what we said, we were in trouble. My mother smirked. "That's what I thought. You're both grounded for a week." She turned to walk away.

"But Mom!" we said in unison, and she whipped around.

"Would you like me to make it two weeks? Or perhaps you'd like me to tell your father when he gets home?"

We shook our heads. It was never good when she told our father.

"I hate that fucking woman," said Sidney, once she was out of earshot.

"She just lied," I said, shocked. "Why would she do that?"

"She's been doing that for years," said my older, wiser sister. "She's batshit crazy."

"What are we going to do?"

"Nothing. We can't win against someone who keeps changing the rules. I think that's the point. Besides, Dad always takes her side, so we're screwed no matter what we do."

"She sets us up to fail, and then she punishes us," I said, amazed that she would do that. She was our *mother*. Her job was to protect us.

"*Now* you're catching on," said Sidney.

When I first got to Vancouver, Dad had a huge lump on his neck, and it was quite a shock. I felt like I needed to comfort him in some way, yet I didn't know how, and I don't think he wanted me to. It's funny, because even though I was an adult and extremely good at expressing myself to everyone else, I was somehow reduced to a child just by being under their roof.

Or maybe being in their presence always did that to me. As children, we were told to be seen and not heard, so the words didn't come because we never expressed any kind of emotion in our family. Even hugging was an incredibly awkward experience and never initiated by us.

Christmas ended up being a lot of fun that year because everyone was on their best behavior for once. Sidney's and Bailey's boyfriends were there, so between them and Sidney's kids, there were a lot of people to act as buffers between the rest of us. It was also our first family Christmas involving booze, which helped a lot. We laughed all day (for the first time ever), and everyone had a great time.

Usually, we didn't bother with presents (except the children), but this year we decided to go all out. I brought everyone gifts from Europe, and my dad was ecstatic when he opened the box of treats I brought especially for him. I figured edible gifts were the way to go since anything else seemed pointless.

My father loved food and had a serious sweet tooth (like me), so I brought two kinds of olives from Greece, a box of Turkish Delight from Turkey, a jar of pesto sauce from Tuscany, and two boxes of cookies (along with some honey lager) from Dubrovnik.

My father almost cried when he saw the box of cookies in his own language, and I could see it stirred up memories from his childhood, which is exactly what I was aiming for. He slapped my mother's hand when she tried to steal the Turkish Delight (a first), then he hid everything in his bedroom and said he wasn't sharing (also a first), so I knew I'd hit the mark.

We took a lot of funny photos that year, and everyone got tipsy, then my sisters and I went outside to play in the snow. We don't usually get snow in Vancouver, but we were having one of the worst snowstorms in twenty years, and it dumped two feet on Christmas Eve alone.

Although it was pretty, I have to say I was freezing my ass off. I didn't own any winter clothing (let alone a coat or boots), and after living in Cancun for five years, I was struggling with the below-zero weather.

In January, I went back to Cancun and stayed with a friend for a month just to thaw out. I also needed a break from my parents. It was nice swimming in the ocean again, and we even went camping in Tulum under the full moon. It was a much-needed vacation.

When I got back, I started taking my father to chemotherapy since my mother didn't want to go. He never wanted me to stay, but I made sure to drop him off and pick him up. He was still in good spirits and *never* complained, even when he started throwing up and we knew he was in pain. That was typical of my father. He was trying not to inconvenience any of us, although sometimes we wished he would. He's the only reason I was even there.

The longer I stayed in Vancouver, the more boredom set in—and eventually the winter blues. To go from working on a ship where it never stops to doing absolutely nothing was hard. With no job and no friends, I was stuck at home, and the more time I spent with my mother, the more she got on my nerves. Biting my tongue to keep the peace was something I'd been doing my entire life, but I was starting to lose patience with her constant nagging and petty games.

She said whatever she wanted, while the rest of us had to hold back, because we knew talking to her was futile and would only end in an argument. You can't have a real conversation with someone who acts like a six-year-old and refuses to see reality. Thankfully, the only person she really cared about was Bailey, so she spent most of her time in Bailey's room, gossiping and complaining about the rest of us.

When I look back on it now, I see just how wrong we were about Bailey. I think deep down, we resented her for being the favorite, but the truth is that Bailey was the biggest victim of us all. My mother said she loved her, but it was really about control. By filling her head with lies and turning her against her sisters, she kept her in complete isolation—siphoning her energy until there was nothing left—yet we were so wrapped up in our own pain, we never saw how broken she was.

When the three of us left home, we never looked back, so we never realized that in Bailey's eyes, we'd abandoned her, leaving her to fend for herself. We had always assumed that because my parents never hit her, that she had it easy, but abuse comes in many forms.

I had a lot of time to think about my past in those days. It was hard not to. I thought about my childhood and all the people who came and went over the years. I thought about Luka, Jamie, and Vivian, and I wondered where they had ended up. We were so close once, and I still missed them.

I had plenty of friends overseas, but an email isn't the same as human contact. It was weird being back in Vancouver and realizing I didn't know anyone anymore. There were a few girls from college who I saw every couple of years, and maybe one or two from my restaurant days, but that was it. Everyone else had either fallen away or moved away.

After thinking about Jamie for several weeks, I decided to reach out because strangely enough, he's the one I missed the most. We had been such good friends once, and I missed those days. So much had happened since that fateful day when he'd walked into my apartment with a bottle of Baileys. I wondered if he still hated me. Weirdly enough, I had nothing but love for him.

I searched online, but I couldn't find anything. He didn't have Facebook, and I couldn't believe that in this day and age, I couldn't find any information on him. I wondered if he'd moved away or changed his name just to spite me, like he'd threatened to do all those years ago. It would have been exactly like Jamie to do such a thing. Even now, I rolled my eyes at how silly he could be. *Jamie, Jamie, Jamie. Where are you?* I wondered.

I tried very hard to keep myself busy that winter, and Dad was doing the same. He wasn't allowed to go outside, and like me, he wasn't used to having so much time on his hands. The winter was long and dark, and I struggled to stay positive when all I really wanted to do was bolt. I put on thirty pounds from the lack of activity, which only made it worse.

In May, my mother and I had a blow out, and I knew it was time to leave. There were far too many people under one roof, and sleeping on the couch was getting old. I needed my own space. My father asked me not to leave, but we both knew I couldn't stay. It wasn't lost on either of us that this was exactly what happened the last time I left home.

"I'm sorry, Dad, but I can't be in the same house as her anymore, and you don't need that kind of energy while you're trying to get better. This is your house, so I'll go. It's time, anyway. I've been here for months."

My dad shook his head. "I'm sorry you have to leave. There's just no reasoning with your mother when it comes to Bailey. I gave up years ago."

I had never heard my father say a bad thing about my mother EVER, so I was surprised by this rare moment of honesty. Apparently, he wasn't as blind as he pretended to be.

"I'm worried about her, you know," he said, interrupting my thoughts. "I'm worried about who will take care of her when I'm gone."

I took a moment to answer because I knew what my father wanted to hear, but I had no intention of making that kind of promise, even if he was dying. After leaving home as a teen, I only saw my parents a couple times a year, and they knew nothing about my personal life until they moved to Cancun. Then I saw them every day, but we still weren't close. My father and I had bridged the gap a little, but my mother . . . not so much.

"You know that's not going to be *me,* right?" I said slowly. I was expecting a lecture, but instead he only said, "Yes, I do."

"Good." It may not seem like much, but in our world, this was the equivalent of a long conversation and probably the most honest one we ever had.

Once I moved out, I continued to struggle. In fact, things got a lot worse. I couldn't rent an apartment because I didn't have any furniture, and I didn't want to be locked into a lease since I intended to return to ships once this was over. On top of that, I was running out of money, so the only thing I could do was answer ads for roommates.

First, I moved in with a girl who turned out to be a psychopath. I thought for sure she'd murder me in my sleep, but the crazy part is that she lived in the exact same townhouses we lived in when we joined the church. What a trip that was. Next, I moved in with an old man who was nice enough, but after a few months, I had to leave because he didn't like the way I fried chicken.

I hated being stuck in limbo. I applied for jobs for months, but the economy was in shambles, and no one was hiring. "You're overqualified" seemed to be the general consensus. Mentally, I was in a bad place, and I felt completely alone. I wanted to run away, but I couldn't leave my father when he was sick.

I finally got a part-time job that fall, and once I had money coming in, I was able to move in with a Korean girl who had a one-bedroom apartment in the west end. She was cold and had no interest in me, but it was a good location, and it was affordable, which is all I really needed. She had converted the living room into a second bedroom, and since I didn't own any furniture, I ended up with a mattress on the floor and nothing else.

After six months, Dad wasn't any better, so they ordered another two rounds of a super chemo that made him violently ill. When that didn't work, they sent him back to the hospital for a stem cell replacement, and while he was there, Bailey came down with the H1N1 virus. Sienna told her to stay with her boyfriend, but my mother refused to let her out of her sight.

The stem cell replacement went so well that the doctor sent my father home early, or at least that's what they told us. We suspected it was budget cuts, and we were frustrated that we couldn't afford to send my father to a private hospital. He was supposed to be in the hospital for weeks, but the doctor released him after eight days, even though several nurses voiced their concerns over his lack of an immune system.

Four days later, Dad was back in the hospital with a forty-degree temperature and the H1N1 virus. I was livid when I found out. Sienna told me I was the only one allowed to visit him, since everyone else had been exposed to the virus. I cannot express how hard it was to watch my fifty-seven year old father suffer in those days, as the fever wracked his already fragile body with violent chills.

Day after day, I sat there watching him suffer. I wasn't even allowed to give him a blanket because they needed to bring down his fever. I watched as my father cried out in pain, going in and out of consciousness, begging for someone, anyone, to give him a blanket because he was so cold. I rubbed his feet and gave him a head massage, but I felt helpless as I sat there, watching him waste away.

For an entire week, he threw up everything they gave him, but finally his temperature came down, and once again, they sent him home. My father joked that they kept sending him home because they needed the bed for the next guy, but I feared that was true.

Canada has a free medical system, and I always thought that was a good thing, but the system is overtaxed, and it was failing us. All we kept hearing about were "budget cuts," and it was heartbreaking knowing that if we weren't so poor, we probably could have given my father better care.

There was so much left unsaid during those visits. I wanted to talk about things that were important, like our childhood. I wanted my father to acknowledge that they hadn't been good parents. I needed him to apologize for beating us so I could forgive him and finally get closure before he died. He owed me that. But he was a proud man, and even now he couldn't say the words I so desperately needed to hear.

I was angry at his stubbornness and sad that he was dying. I raged against his selfishness and cried because he suffered. The turmoil in my head ripped at my heart and soul. There he was asking about my mother again, even though she didn't love him, yet it never occurred to him to mend what was broken between him and his daughters, the ones who visited him every day. After all these years, he was still choosing her over us.

After my father died, I mourned him for a long time. They say there's five stages of grief, but for several months I was trapped somewhere between anguish and rage. I kept seeing my sisters' faces as we stayed night after night in that hospital, watching the life leave my father, until the doctor pulled the plug on my thirty-ninth birthday—exactly one year after I'd arrived.

I watched as the pain from the present mixed with the pain from the past, so we could re-live it over and over again. I knew there were things that had never been said, and once he was gone, they never would be. I felt sorry for my mother who lived with this man for forty years, and I hated her for the same reason.

When my anger subsided, it was replaced with unbearable pain, and then I started having nightmares as memories from my childhood tried to surface. My demons haunted me day and night, and I almost broke under the weight of them. The fact that I had no one to turn to in my darkest hours made the loneliness even worse. I understood that I was truly alone in this world, and once again, no one was coming to save me. My loneliness left a giant hole in my soul, and it was several months before I could breathe again.

TWENTY-SEVEN

In the spring, I returned to ships, but this time I was working for the entertainment department as cruise staff. I had a bit of a rocky start in the form of two crazy roommates (the first one was a hoarder, and the second one liked to wake up in the middle of the night to feed her potato chip addiction), but other than that, I had a great contract. Being cruise staff was very different from being a purser, and I loved the new job.

Our entire department was close, so I never lacked company, either on the ship or in the ports. I was grateful to be surrounded by amazing people again, especially after the extreme loneliness I'd felt in Vancouver. Now that I was back on ships, not only was I in a much better state of mind, but the job was extremely physical, so I was losing a lot of the weight I'd gained while I was home, and it was doing wonders for my self-esteem.

Things were going really well until about four months into my contract, when I volunteered to be a model for the acupuncturist. He put needles in my neck, but he must have done something wrong because a few hours later I was in severe pain and couldn't turn my head. My boss sent me to the doctor's office, where I was given painkillers. I told the doctor it felt like a pinched nerve, but he said the pills would take care of it.

Two weeks later, I was back in his office with seriously lopsided shoulders.

Once again, he issued pain killers, but this time, I didn't take them. I didn't want to mask the pain, and I certainly didn't want to become addicted. What I wanted was for someone to listen to me.

Fast forward two weeks, and I started having pins and needles in my hands, and then they went numb. Once again, I found myself in the doctor's office, only this time my boss got involved. It quickly became an HR issue, and then I had everyone's attention, but not in a good way. One of my friends warned me about signing anything, or saying anything that could be used against me. She told me the company had a reputation for getting rid of people with medical issues, and I needed to be careful.

I experienced this firsthand when the HR manager sat me down and suddenly became all business, when just the night before he was hitting on me. This sudden change of attitude proved my friend right, and I made sure to cover my ass. I was immediately taken off duty, which sucked because Sienna and her boyfriend were coming to cruise, and I was gutted when I was put on medical leave for their entire visit. Overnight, I went from being the golden child to being a social pariah, as my team was ordered not to talk to me.

I'd been looking forward to showing Sienna and her boyfriend around the ports, but instead I had to go to several doctor's appointments. After an MRI, they found a pinch in my spine, so I was sent home to undergo six weeks of physiotherapy. I ended up back on my mother's couch because I had nowhere else to go, and besides, she needed help with the rent now that Sienna and Bailey were gone. I couldn't believe I was back there already. Sometimes it felt like all life ever did was kick me in the ass.

Things moved slowly over the next couple of months, but eventually I got better and was instructed to see a specialist. Although medical care is free in Canada, the company ordered me to go to a private doctor of their choosing. In the end, my friend was right: the company fired me, but only after they manipulated my test results. I know this because after my visit, the doctor said everything was fine and I was able to return to work, then two days later he suddenly changed his story and said I *couldn't* work, while refusing to take my calls.

Once again, I felt utterly defeated, and the depression moved in, except this time I didn't let it last very long, and to give credit where credit is due, my mother was pretty supportive throughout this ordeal. She felt bad when I got fired, and when I came down with the flu, she brought me an extra pillow and made chicken noodle soup. It was always unnerving when my mother was nice because there was usually an angle, but on this occasion, I think it was real.

One afternoon, my mother pulled out a photo album and said she wanted to show it to me. I didn't even know it existed, so I was quite surprised. When she opened it, I saw pictures from my childhood. She found one of her and my father when they were teenagers and pointed to it.

"This was taken shortly after we met. Look how young we were!"

"How did you two meet anyway?" My mother never talked about her past, but she was clearly feeling nostalgic, so I figured it was a good time to ask.

"I used to live with a girlfriend when I first left home, then one day I came home and he was there, in the living room. They were having a party. Look how handsome he was."

"He looks like a hippie."

"It was 1969. We all looked like hippies." She turned the page and pointed to another picture. "Oh, look! This is our wedding day. We got married in Victoria."

I leaned in and took a closer look. "I thought you got married in Ontario and then moved to Victoria," I said, confused.

"No, no, no. We got married in Victoria. We dated for a couple of months when I found out I was pregnant with Sidney. As you can imagine, I panicked, so I called your father, but he never answered. I left several messages with his mother, but he never called back."

"What happened?"

"Well, his parents found out we were dating, and they were livid when they realized I was Catholic, so they shipped him off to Victoria without telling anyone."

"Really?"

"Oh, yes. He went to live with some of their friends. When weeks went by and I still hadn't heard from him, I went to his house, but his mother turned me away. I went back a few days later, and she turned me away again, only this time I told her why I was there."

"What did she say?"

"She told me I was nothing but a Catholic whore and offered to pay for an abortion, except as a Catholic that wasn't an option."

I was stunned, and my face said it all. I'd always known my grandparents were assholes, but this was shocking. I could only imagine how scared my mother must have been. Your boyfriend suddenly disappears, and then you find out you're pregnant. What a nightmare. Especially in 1969.

"So what did you do? How did you find him?"

"One of the ladies in the house overheard our conversation and took pity on me. I think she was an aunt or something. After your Baba slammed the door, this woman came out and handed me a phone number. She told me where he was."

"And then what happened?"

"I called him, and he immediately said we should get married. He flew me out to Victoria, but I wasn't sure. I never wanted marriage or children, and I really struggled with the fact that he wasn't Catholic."

"I didn't think you cared about that."

"At the time, it was a huge issue. Your dad was raised Orthodox by birth, but he never actually went to church. I, on the other hand, was raised in a very strict Catholic home, and I even went to a Catholic school. I figured I was already in trouble with God for getting pregnant, so I worried what would happen if I married a non-Catholic."

"What changed your mind?" I asked, fascinated by this story.

"I went to a Catholic church and talked it over with a priest. He told me it didn't matter what religion your father was, as long as he believed in God."

"A *priest* said that?"

"I know, right? It was quite a progressive thing to say in the seventies."

"That's for sure. And wasn't it *your* mother who offered to pay you to divorce Dad?"

She stiffened at the mention of her mother. "Yes. She held that money over my head for years. She always referred to your father as *that foreigner*, and in the end she never gave me a cent." She turned the page and came to another photo. It was one of me as a baby. It was summer, and we were at the beach.

"Who's that holding me?" I asked, as I studied the grainy photo.

"That's Baba," she said coldly.

"But I thought we never met her."

"Oh, she came all right. Shortly after you were born. She wanted your dad to leave me and demanded that he bring you and Sidney back to Ontario so she could raise you as Orthodox."

My mouth dropped open. "She came to visit just so she could convince Dad to leave you? What a bitch. No wonder you hated her so much."

My mother had a faraway look in her eyes. These must have been painful memories for her. "Yes, I always feared that one day she'd get through to him and win. That he'd take you girls and leave me," she said, almost to herself.

I wondered briefly if that's why she always made him choose between us and her. Yes, we were broken children, but my parents were broken, too. We were a family of broken people.

I had a much better understanding of my parents after that. I always thought they were awful because that's just how they were, but after hearing this story, I began to see the bigger picture. Their lives weren't easy, either, and I felt sorry for them. I wondered how many other secrets my mother was keeping, but she'd already closed the book, both literally and figuratively.

Twenty-Eight

It didn't take long to get hired by another cruise line, and my next contract was very exciting. I was sent to Australia, where I got to see over forty countries in nine months, and then I did back-to-back contracts in Europe, Scandinavia, and Russia. I was currently staying in Cancun, sorting through the boxes I'd left behind when I joined ships over four years ago.

While I was there, I heard about a shaman who did readings, so I set up an appointment and brought my friend along. When we got there, the shaman instructed me to write my name on a piece of paper, which he placed under a glass bowl filled with water. He explained that he'd go into a trance-like state, so we should write down everything he said. Then he began to speak Spanish in a soft, clear voice.

"When your mother was four months pregnant, she had some kind of fear about your father. She never gave you any love while you were in the womb. You weren't wanted by her."

My friend and I looked at each other in surprise. I hadn't realized we were going back to the beginning.

"This continued throughout your childhood, leaving you to feel very alone. This loneliness is a major theme in your life. You're surrounded by people, yet you feel it deep in your heart. It consumes you."

Woah. He'd just hit on something I'd been feeling my entire life. This profound feeling of loneliness that I couldn't escape. I was awed by his insight into my childhood, something I still couldn't remember.

"When you were seventeen, you made a big change and took control of your life."

My friend looked at me questioningly. "I left home," I whispered.

"You are a warrior, a traveler. You seek to know the world." He paused, as if listening to someone. "There's an aunt on your father's side. She practices dark magic. She put a curse on your father's bloodline. Her energy surrounds you and affects you."

What? I didn't even know Dad *had* an aunt, but as I thought about it, it made sense. My ancestors came from the old country. Putting curses on people went back generations, and it wouldn't have surprised me if Baba had asked this aunt to put a curse on us after her visit when I was a baby.

"Ten years ago, you met a man. He had a strong hold on you. The relationship was very bad. Darkness controls him, and you were greatly affected by this darkness." He suddenly looked sad, like he couldn't believe what he was seeing. It reminded me of Lilith when she'd tried to read my palm all those years ago.

"You lost something important in that relationship. You took the wrong path. You've been on the wrong path ever since."

My friend gave me another questioning look. "Christian," I whispered, but I was almost in tears, thinking of all those wasted years and the career I'd given up because of him. It was like losing ballet when I was ten.

The shaman reached up and touched his throat. "You have a gift, but you don't use it. This is where you lost your way. You're meant to use this gift. It will bring you great success."

I looked at my friend. What the heck was he talking about?

"You're a singer, dummy! He's talking about your voice."

Oh right. How did I not think of that?

"Mother Mary is here, and she has a message for you. She says the angels weep every time you sing, and so does she. She is always with you, walking beside you."

My music career was going absolutely nowhere these days. I taught choir and all the dance classes on the ship, but I didn't get to sing very often. Cruise lines no longer hired jazz bands, and although I had a few supportive cruise directors over the years who allowed me to sing every once in a while, most of them were assholes who were afraid to share the spotlight. Dealing with their enormous egos was the toughest part of my job.

"There have been many men in the past, and there will be more in the future. Most have bad intentions. So far you have natural walls that have protected you, but you must be careful. Your path is brightly lit but blocked at the moment. Beware of jealousy in the people around you, especially women."

I felt this a lot while working on cruise ships. Sometimes I worked with the most amazing people, and other times I was surrounded by petty, jealous people who made my life a living hell. It tended to be one extreme or the other in my experience.

"These people are jealous of your gifts and wish to harm you. You must learn to protect yourself from them. Strengthen your aura. Don't absorb their energy. Your aura is pure white and very bright. People are attracted to your light, but they either want to steal it or control it. Don't let them."

"Ain't that the truth," I muttered under my breath.

"You work on the water. This is a good job because it suits your gifts. It's also bad because you're surrounded by people who steal your energy. It will consume you if you don't learn to protect yourself. Stop absorbing the energy. Push it away."

When the session was over, we dove a little deeper, and then I set up a second appointment to remove the curse from my family's bloodline. We had enough problems without a curse hanging over our heads. They might not believe in this kind of thing, but I did, and I wanted to be free of it.

For the past year, I'd been thinking about leaving ships, but I had no idea what I was supposed to do next. After six years, I was tired of working on ships, and for the first time in a long time, I missed being at home with my sisters and their kids, especially since Sienna had a new baby.

I knew if I stayed in Vancouver, I'd have to face my demons, but I kind of felt like *Forrest Gump* after he ran across the country several times. I was tired of running, and not only that, I was tired of being lonely. I'd never find a partner if I stayed on ships.

Yes, there was more of the world I wanted to see, but what I really needed was to find balance, and I desperately wanted my own place. Every time I came off a ship, I had to scramble to find somewhere to stay, which made me feel like a burden. I wanted a home, a place to call my own, and I wanted my art on my walls instead of in boxes. I was restless again, but this time to settle down.

When a colleague suggested I try tour guiding, I was intrigued. When I found out how much it paid, she had my full attention. The money was decent, I'd still get to travel, and my skills would be put to good use. She was definitely onto something.

I made up my mind to quit when I suddenly got an email asking me to come back early. My initial thought was to say no, but then I saw it was a world cruise, something I'd been asking for for years. I figured it was the perfect way to end my career, knowing I'd have no regrets when it was over, so I said yes.

Sidney had recently moved into Sienna's basement suite, and after all these years, we were getting to know each other again. I told her she should take advantage of my privileges while she still had the chance, and she actually listened for once. She ended up booking off five weeks in the fall to come cruise with me. It's amazing that we're only a year apart, yet we lead such different lives. I'd traveled all over the world, while she'd never even left North America.

I worked with the most phenomenal women that contract. The three of us were inseparable, which everyone found hilarious because Kendra was in her twenties, Lily was in her thirties, and I was in my forties. We were an odd pairing for sure, yet somehow it worked.

About three months into my contract, I was eating lunch in the officer's mess when an extremely attractive man walked in. I gauged him to be in his mid-thirties, so he was a little young for me, but damn was he hot. He had thick black hair, smoldering eyes, and a wicked smile. He was exactly my type, which meant he was trouble.

"Who's *that?*" I asked the stage manager. She turned to see who I was talking about. "Oh, that's Matheus. Would you like to meet him?"

"Noooooo," I said, shaking my head for emphasis.

"Why not? He's super hot and really nice."

"That's exactly why I don't want to meet him. He's too hot. He's got trouble written all over him. Besides, he's a little young for me."

"So what? You're leaving in three months. What does it matter?"

A few nights later, I was on duty when I ran into Matheus near the shops. It was formal night, and I was wearing a red satin dress. It's my favorite because it's a Marylin Monroe replica, which suits my hourglass figure. Since we hadn't been introduced yet, I stuck out my hand. "Hi. I'm Sage, by the way."

"I know," he said smiling, "I'm Matheus. It's nice to officially meet you. You look gorgeous, by the way."

The next time we met was in the crew bar. The girls were a permanent fixture, but I only went there once a week. We were at a table laughing our asses off when Matheus suddenly joined us. We ended up having such a good time, and not wanting the night to end, we headed to my cabin for one more drink.

As soon as we got there, Matheus received a page, so he stepped out to answer it. Twenty minutes later, he still wasn't back, so the girls left, and I went to bed. I was almost asleep when I heard a knock on the door.

"Where is everybody?" he asked when I opened the door in my pajamas.

"They went to bed."

"But I thought we were having drinks."

"We were, and then you ditched us for a booty call, so the girls left."

"But I was only gone a few minutes!"

"Actually, you were gone *thirty* minutes. Rude, by the way."

"It wasn't a booty call," he said as I gave him my best *oh please,* look. "It wasn't. I mean, she tried, but I'm not interested in her. It's *you* I'm interested in. You're . . . *gorgeous.* Oh, wow. I can't believe I just said that out loud. I must be drunk."

A little thrill went through me, but I decided to play it cool. "Let me get this straight. You left my cabin to see a girl. You were gone half an hour but insist nothing happened, and now you're hoping to get some from *me?* Wow. You're barking up the wrong tree mister. I don't do one-night stands anymore. They're messy, especially with someone who ditched us."

He was sitting in an armchair in the corner while I sat on my bed. This playful banter went on for quite some time. The booze had loosened his tongue, so he was talking more than he usually did. In fact, we ended up talking for almost an hour, and the more I got to know him, the more I liked him. He was nice, and he seemed kind, which is not what I was expecting.

"Sage, I really like you," he said seriously.

"I like you, too, but don't you think I'm a little old for you? I mean let's be honest here. You're seriously hot, player. Shouldn't you be hitting on one of the dancers or something?"

He looked offended by that. "Pffft! No thanks. I'm not looking for someone who's empty headed and shallow. I've always preferred older women. They're mature, and they actually have something to say. Besides, I kind of have a thing for pin-up girls."

"Really? Me, too! I have tons of vintage dresses."

"Believe me, I've noticed. Every man on this ship has noticed." He stared at me with a longing I hadn't seen in a while. I think I blushed. Damn, he was cute, and if he stayed much longer I'd definitely cave. I was trying to put up boundaries now that I was in my forties, but that doesn't mean I didn't feel things in my girly parts.

"I want you, but I can't give you what you ask," he said sadly.

"Why not? I'm not asking for much. I just don't want to be a one-night stand. I'm not a child anymore. And in this environment, where I have to see you every day, no thanks. I'm not looking to marry you, either, just something in between. Will we last a couple of weeks or a couple of months? I don't know. It lasts until it stops being fun. So if you're up for that great, but I'm not a one-night stand. I'm worth more than that." Boundaries, damn it.

"I'm not a player. I've had three relationships in the last ten years, all with lovely women who I hurt very badly when I told them I couldn't marry them. None of them deserved that, and I don't want to do that with you."

"Why couldn't you marry them? You obviously loved them. I can see it on your face."

He told me how his first girlfriend had betrayed his trust when she tried to trap him into marriage. It clearly had a profound effect on him because fourteen years later, he still carried the scars. The only good thing to come of it was a daughter, whom he loved dearly, but it was also a constant reminder that women couldn't be trusted. My heart broke for him as he told me the story. I could feel his pain, and I understood it completely. I had trust issues myself.

The more I got to know him, the more I liked him. He was a nice guy who was fucked over by an evil woman and not at all the player I expected him to be. Damn, why was I always attracted to broken men? Maybe because deep down inside . . . I was broken, too.

He stood up. "It's late. I think I should go."

When he got to the door, he suddenly stopped. I thought he was coming in for a hug, but instead he pinned me against the wall. Time stopped as he kissed me with so much passion my heart skipped a beat. Holy shit, he was a great kisser, and had he thrown me on the bed right then and there, I probably wouldn't have resisted. It had been a long time since anyone had kissed me like that, and from the look on his face, he felt it, too.

Without hesitation, he leaned in a second time, pulling me into his arms for an embrace that made my toes curl. The kiss was so passionate we were both out of breath by the time it was over. He pulled away and studied my face. He seemed torn between his desire to rip my clothes off and his desire to respect my wishes.

"I think I better leave now," he said as he opened the door.

The next morning, I told the girls what had happened, and they squealed with delight. The two of them always fawned over boys, but this was a first for me. I hadn't fawned over anyone in years. A few days later, when Matheus hand-delivered a fan he'd repaired for me, we kissed once more . . . and then I didn't see him for a week. When we arrived in Singapore and the ship went into dry dock, I didn't see him at all. Not because he was avoiding me, but because dry dock throws everything into chaos.

Since we were docked in Singapore for two weeks, I arranged for Sidney to meet us there. That way she could hang out with us for a couple of days before boarding the ship. By the time she arrived, we knew the city pretty well, and we had an absolute riot showing her our favorite spots. She and the girls totally hit it off, which was a good thing because whenever I had to work, they took care of her.

One evening, I came home to a message on my answering machine. It was Matheus wanting to know if I'd like to have dinner. The poor guy was working so hard he hadn't left the ship since we'd arrived, and I felt bad because he sounded exhausted, while I'd been having a great time. I went to Little India and bought us a feast, then I went to a Portuguese bakery and bought a few of their famous tarts.

We had a delicious dinner in his cabin, and he was really touched by the tarts. He was Portuguese, so they reminded him of home. We got comfy on his bed and put on a movie, but he was already falling asleep twenty minutes in. When I tried to sit up, he pulled me back down, and we had a lovely make-out session, but he was so exhausted that the next time he dozed off, I decided to let him sleep and quietly slipped out of his cabin.

It was Sidney's birthday the day she boarded the ship, so we decorated my cabin with balloons and a big welcome sign. The F&B manager arranged a chocolate cake and champagne when he heard it was her birthday. Then I found her a cabin in the crew area, which was awesome because it meant she didn't have to stay with me.

Sidney got along with everyone onboard and even managed to find a lover to keep her occupied while the rest of us worked. I told everyone it was her first vacation (a mind-blowing concept for the rest of us), so everywhere she went, the crew spoiled her, and for the first time in her life . . . she felt like a princess. It was fun seeing the look on her face every time she discovered a new port, and I was happy I could give that to her. After years of terrible hardship with her ex, she deserved a little fun.

Every night, the four of us had dinner together. Sometimes we couldn't line up our schedules, but with a little finesse, we made it work. "Family dinner" was super fun and soon, we attracted quite the entourage. When the F&B manager saw us having these great big dinner parties, he started dropping off bottles of wine, and it quickly became a ritual. Everyone who sat at our table was boisterous, and we were so loud I thought for sure the other officers would complain, but they were charmed by the laughter and camaraderie coming from our drunken table.

One night, Matheus joined in, and he and Sidney really hit it off. I was bummed when I had to leave because I hadn't seen him since we had dinner in his cabin, and I wanted to spend more time with him. When I saw Sidney a few hours later, she was grinning from ear to ear.

"I have something to tell you that will make you smile," she teased.

"Listening . . ."

"When you left the table earlier, I saw Matheus watch you leave. He didn't take his eyes off you until you were out of sight, and when he turned back to face me, I was like, *OMG. You like my sister!*"

"Really?"

"Oh yah. The look on his face was unmistakable. He's got it *bad*. We ended up talking about you for quite some time. He really likes you, but he's wrestling with his demons."

"I know. His first girlfriend really messed him up."

"I told him to go for it because you're the most amazing woman he'll ever meet, and you always speak the truth, so he can trust you when you say you don't want marriage from him."

"That was nice of you to say."

"I mean it. You're amazing, Sage. You've traveled all over the world by yourself, and you're so positive all the time. I'm glad we get to spend this time together. Thank you for arranging this trip for me. I love you, sis."

"You're welcome. You deserve it. And when did you become so sappy?"

"I know, right? It happened when my kids were born. I wanted to say all the things I never heard growing up, like I love you."

"I'm sorry. I don't know what that words means," I said, and we both laughed.

It was nice having Sidney onboard. After she'd left home, I'd seen her only a few times a year, and when I lived abroad, years would go by without any communication. I understood why she kept us at arm's length. Part of it was our childhood, and the rest had to do with her ex. It took a long time to recover from that relationship, and it was nice to see her smiling again. In fact, I'd never seen her so happy. Sidney had a tendency to be grumpy and negative, but she was the life of the party while she was on that cruise.

As for Matheus, I won't bore you with our on again/off again flirtation. All that matters is that he talked to Sidney more than he talked to me, and it really pissed me off. I knew he liked me, and Sidney fed that narrative the entire month she was onboard, but it was starting to sound familiar.

Three weeks later, we were at it again. "He's in love with you, Sage. That's why he's avoiding you. He's scared you'll hurt him."

"Oh, that's just perfect."

"What's wrong? I thought you'd be happy. The man's crazy about you."

"That may be, but I've already played this game. Twenty years ago with *Luka*. He wanted me too, but he put me so high on a pedestal he couldn't reach me. Why do men keep doing that? Why do they keep putting me in a glass box? I'm not doing this again. If he wants me, he'll have to man up."

After she left the ship, I got my wish. He came over one night after work. One thing led to another, and we finally went to bed together. We listened to Bon Jovi as we made love, but then something very strange and familiar happened. Right in the middle of sex, he suddenly caught my eye, so I smiled, but he didn't smile back. In fact, I saw a moment of panic, then it was like he flipped a switch, completely shutting off his emotions. We were still in the throes of passion, but the energy totally changed, and I didn't know why. What was happening in his head?

When we finished, I wanted to ask him about it, but he booked it out of there so fast I was left feeling hurt and confused. It was Luka all over again. Why did the Universe keep doing this to me? Didn't I deserve to find love? What was wrong with me that I kept repeating this pattern, yet I didn't recognize it until it was too late? I'd asked myself these questions before, but this time it was different. I was worried.

Here I was again, alone and crying over a boy. Why did I keep doing this to myself?

Twenty-Nine

Even though I didn't realize it at the time, I was finally asking the right questions. Not *why does the Universe keep doing this to me,* but rather *what am I doing that keeps attracting the same kind of painful relationships?*

When we ask these questions, the Universe moves heaven and earth to show us the answers, and if we don't listen, it shows us even louder. Sometimes it smashes us right in the face, and we wonder *what the hell?* Then we realize we completely missed the ten previous messages. We've been living in darkness for so long we've forgotten how to listen to the Universe, but that doesn't mean it stopped talking.

Once I left ships, I had no choice but to rent a room from my mother, something I dreaded with every fiber of my being. For the past few years, I'd been staying with Sienna and her family in between contracts, but with a second baby on the way, she told me there simply wasn't room.

My mother couldn't afford her apartment now that she was living alone, and for years we told her to move to a smaller place, but she had a million excuses for procrastinating. I suspected it had a lot to do with my father. Either way, it was mutually beneficial for us to live together until I could find a job. Her entire apartment was covered in half-empty boxes as my mother *pretended* to pack, but after five years, the only person she was fooling was herself.

The clutter made me insane, but I think for my mother, it was a security blanket. The boxes filled three bedrooms, lined the hallways, and spilled into the bathrooms. The kitchen counters were so cluttered you couldn't even see them. My mother refused to throw anything away, even spices that expired in 1983. The clutter made me claustrophobic, but I was starting to understand that for *her*, it was a wall of protection from the outside world.

For the most part, we didn't argue, but that's because I was a pro at biting my tongue. My mother was hoping I'd stay indefinitely (so she wouldn't have to move), which put her on her best behavior. As for me, I realized I was no longer angry with my mother. Actually, I felt sorry for her. It's not like she chose to be bipolar, although it *was* her choice to ignore it.

She rarely left the apartment these days, choosing to live in a fantasy world she'd created in her mind. She constantly talked about the exotic places she'd visit one day, and how she was moving back to Mexico, but it was just that— talk. We'd never be friends because our history was too painful, but I'd learned the value of tolerance and forgiveness over the years, and seeing her now helped me understand both her and her disease.

When I learned that forgiving her didn't mean I had to <u>like</u> her, I was able to let go of my anger. So whenever she got on my nerves, I reminded myself that this was *her* apartment, (even though I paid rent), and I did my best to keep my thoughts to myself in order to keep the peace. In the meantime, I sent my resume to all the local tour companies. The tour season started in May, and if I didn't get a job by then, I didn't know what I'd do.

In February, I went to Egypt and Jordan and had an incredible time. On our last night, I saw a full moon, so I sat outside and talked to her. I asked her to help me find a job and bring me true love. After all, one of the driving factors for leaving ships was the loneliness that constantly haunted me. Coming home was about facing my demons, finding balance, and laying down roots. I'd traveled all over the world and I certainly wasn't finished, but what I needed now was a place to call home and someone to share it with.

Things moved quickly once I got back from Egypt. I was hired by a tour company and began training in the spring. I also found a great little apartment, close to Stanley Park, which made me very happy. It was like Christmas when I opened the boxes that had been in storage for almost seven years.

I'd bought a lot of great art while working on ships, and it was exciting to see the pieces displayed in all their glory. It might have been the world's tiniest apartment, but it was a work of art by the time I was finished with it. Plus, it was all mine. No more clutter. No more dust. No more tiptoeing around someone else.

I loved my new job and the freedom it provided me. The scenery was so beautiful, and showing it off was incredibly rewarding. Being an explorer made me an excellent tour director, and I bent over backwards making sure my guests had the best experience possible.

In September, Bailey came to visit with her new baby. She asked me to come over so we could go for a walk, but when I got to my mother's, she changed her mind and decided we should stay in. I was only there a few minutes when Mom started playing her usual games, and I don't know what came over me, but something snapped. For the first time in my life, I spoke back without filtering my thoughts.

"*You're* changing his diaper?" said my mother, smirking. "As if you know how to change a diaper. You've never even had kids."

"You honestly think because I don't have kids that I don't know how to change a diaper? I was changing Bailey's diapers when I was thirteen in case you've forgotten."

"You did no such thing!" my mother said hotly.

"I most certainly did."

"That's not true!"

My eyes nearly bugged out of my head. "You're kidding, right? And the worst part is you had those cloth diapers, and we always had to scrape the poop off them. It was revolting."

"What are you talking about? We never had cloth diapers. You're being ridiculous."

I don't know if it was her bitchy tone or just the way she was showing off in front of Bailey, but she triggered something and I dug in. Realizing she was losing the argument, she did what she does best—switched tactics and went into self-pity mode. She locked herself in her room and didn't come out until I was gone.

The next day, I got a scathing message from Bailey about how cruel I was, and how my mother had cried all day because of me. I was floored when I read the message and decided enough was enough. It was time to put up boundaries between me and my mother. I was tired of fighting, and I was tired of holding back. I didn't make the decision to be cruel or to punish her. I figured it was simply time, because making her cry wasn't the answer, either.

In October, an old friend came to visit, so several of us got together. I hadn't seen him in fifteen years, and I hadn't seen the girls since I'd quit the restaurant back in 1998. It was fun catching up with them. It reminded me of the good old days, and I found myself reminiscing.

When I got home, I pulled out an old photo album, which made me even more nostalgic. The girls posted photos of our reunion, and the next thing I knew, there were several messages from people I hadn't talked to in years. As I looked through my photos, I was overwhelmed by both happy and sad memories.

I'd lost so many friends over the years, and now that I was home, I felt those losses very deeply. Not only because I didn't have any friends in Vancouver, but because those were some of the best years of my life. As I flipped through the pages, I came across photos of Vivian, Heather, Luka, and Jamie. Photos I hadn't seen in years. Camping, singing, dinner parties—I hadn't given them much thought in the past seventeen years, but now that I was home, it was impossible not to. Once again, I wondered what had happened to them. Were they married? Divorced? Did they have kids? Were they happy? Did they ever think about me?

All day, I exchanged messages with the old gang, and then I had a sudden impulse to look Jamie up. I hadn't found anything the last time I'd tried, so I wasn't expecting anything to turn up, but I figured it couldn't hurt. I typed his name into the search bar, and there he was. Just like that. I was so shocked to see his picture, I actually gasped. I clicked on his profile and saw an older version of Jamie, with his arm around a teenage girl I assumed was his daughter. She was beautiful.

I thought about how close we had been in our twenties, and it made me wonder: did he still hate me? We were such good friends once upon a time. Was there any chance we could be friends again? There was only one way to find out, so I sent him a message.

> *Sweet, sweet Jamie . . . my old friend. It's been a long time. I'm back in Vancouver, and I was looking through some old photos that made me think of you. I hope you're doing well.*

My finger hovered over the send button because I had no idea how he'd react to my message. After a moment, I hit send. Then all I could do was wait.

THIRTY

October 2016

A wave of happiness washed over me when I received a message several hours later. Just seeing Jamie's name made me smile. Had it really been seventeen years since we'd last spoken? Was I really old enough to say *seventeen years ago?* I thought about him many times over the years, but only now did I fully realize how much I'd missed him.

> *Hello, old friend. Is that really you? I can't tell you how surprised I was to get your message. When did you get back, and where have you been all these years? As for me, I'm a firefighter, and I have a daughter, but last year my world was turned upside down when my wife ripped the rug from under me. She had an affair with my best friend, filed for divorce, and took me for everything I'm worth. It broke me in ways I never could have imagined."*

I shook my head. Some things never changed. Jamie was feeling sorry for himself, which is exactly how I remembered him. It made me smile. It's funny because this was a quality that had irritated me when we were younger, yet now I somehow found it endearing. It made me feel safe, like there was at least one thing in my life that was consistent.

I wrote back, and we ended up texting for hours. He told me all about his ex-wife and how controlling and manipulative she was. How he felt like a shell of the person he used to be. How slowly, over time, she destroyed him—something I could relate to. Eventually, we made plans to get together, and I could hardly contain my excitement. Several weeks later, when I saw him standing in my doorway with a bottle of wine and a box of strawberries, I couldn't help but grin. When he smiled and his dimples appeared, I grinned even more.

He was older and had a few extra pounds on him, but other than that, he hadn't changed a bit. When we hugged, my entire being filled with joy. I don't know how to explain it, except to say that after years of running away, I finally felt like I was home. Jamie felt like *home.*

"I can't believe you're actually here. Where have you been all these years? Tell me everything. The last time I saw you, you were dating that French guy."

"Christian? My God, that seems like a lifetime ago." I told him about Christian's drug problem and how hard it was to break free. How it changed me. The lessons I'd learned and the scars that were left behind.

"Oh, Sage. I'm sorry you had to go through that alone. I should have been there!"

"Don't be silly. How could you have known?"

"You must really hate him for what he put you through."

"No. I don't, actually. He has a terrible disease, and although he caused me a lot of pain, I have to take responsibility for my part in it. I'm the one who stayed, so that's on me."

"Wow, you're a much bigger person than I am. I'm definitely not that forgiving. Speaking of which . . . I owe you an apology," he said sheepishly. "That night . . . when I came to your place . . . I said some *terrible* things, and you didn't deserve that. Can you ever forgive me?"

"Oh, Jamie. That was such a long time ago. You don't have to apologize."

"Yes, I do. I was an asshole."

"OK. You're right. You *were* an asshole. But I forgive you."

"Really? Just like that?"

"Just like that. Speaking of the old days, are you still in touch with Luka at all?"

His face suddenly hardened. "Don't say his name! Never say his name!"

I was momentarily stunned by the vehemence in his voice. "Jamie, you can't be serious. Are you still mad at him? It was seventeen years ago."

"He stole you away from me, so he wasn't really a friend, was he?"

That's not exactly how it happened, but he was getting worked up, so I thought it best to change the subject. "Tell me about your daughter."

"Oh, Sage, she's brilliant. She's the light of my life, but ever since the divorce, it's been difficult. She-who-shall-not-be-named has poisoned her against me."

I laughed. "She-who-shall-not-be-named?"

"I met her a couple of weeks after you and I parted ways. We dated for a year before we got married. I should have known it was doomed to fail. When Maya was born, she was so tiny and perfect, but we argued about how to raise her. Then she refused to go back to work, which put a lot of pressure on me. We ended up moving to Langley to be closer to her parents, but she hated my family, so I stopped talking to them."

"What's wrong with your family?"

"She thinks they're racist. Actually, they *are* a little racist. Not my immediate family but the extended one. They don't mean it. They're from a small town, and they're a little backwards, but they're good people."

"If you were so unhappy, why did you stay so long?"

"We made a commitment, and besides, it's not like it happened all at once. Things changed over time, and I didn't notice. She didn't like me drinking or smoking, so soon that became the new normal. Then it was something else. On and on it went, until one day I woke up and realized she was controlling me."

I knew this story well. The same thing had happened to me with Christian. "Oh, Jamie, I'm so sorry. Believe it or not, I know exactly how you feel."

"I feel so deceived. She manipulated me for years. I even changed my name because she refused to take mine! I can't even tell you what that did to my father."

Wait a minute. What? "You changed your name?" I asked.

"I thought I was being progressive by taking her last name. Changing it back was the first thing I did after the divorce."

I knew it! I knew he changed his name. I knew him so well.

"After she kicked me out, I was such a mess. I didn't even know who I was anymore. She tore me down for so long there was nothing left."

Tears slid down his cheeks, and my heart broke when I saw how much pain he was in. My poor, sweet, sensitive Jamie. He looked so fragile. All I wanted to do was protect him. The boy I remembered was arrogant and proud, but I didn't see any of that now. Life had humbled him, and I knew the feeling. I was humbled, too.

We talked for several hours and drank three bottles of wine before I noticed how late it was. Although I only drank a few glasses, I was already feeling it, and I was surprised that Jamie wasn't. Then again, he was twice my size.

"We should get going if we want to eat. It's almost eight o'clock."

"Good idea. I'm up for anything but Greek."

"I thought you loved Greek food. Oh . . . is your ex Greek?"

"Yes."

"What's her name, if you don't mind me asking?"

"Paige."

That stopped me in my tracks. Did he say *Paige?* Clearly, he didn't see the irony, but it wasn't lost on me. She practically had my name. As we stepped outside, he grabbed my hand like it was the most natural thing in the world. I wasn't sure if it was intentional or habitual, but I liked it. His hand was warm and strong. During dinner, we talked and laughed for hours, and it felt like no time had passed at all.

I was glad to see that he still had a wicked sense of humor. It was one of my favorite things about him. We laughed and laughed, and when we got back to my apartment, I suggested he spend the night. We'd already consumed four bottles of wine, and I didn't want him driving. He agreed but said he'd sleep on the couch. Boy, did that sound familiar.

"Oh, Sage. I'm so glad you're here. I haven't felt this good in a long time."

We were sitting on opposite ends of my love seat, facing each other with our legs intertwined. He looked at me for a long time, then he grabbed the back of my neck and pulled me towards him, except once he was a millimeter away, he stopped. He held me like that for a full minute as he wrestled with his demons.

I wondered if he was waiting for me to bridge the gap, but I had no intention of doing that. Not because I didn't want to, but because I wanted him to make the first move. Eventually, having made the decision not to kiss me, he sighed and leaned his forehead against mine, not wanting to lose the connection just yet. We must have stayed like that for fifteen minutes, neither of us saying a word before he finally pulled away.

"I'm sorry. I don't know what's happening right now, but I'm not ready," he whispered, his eyes pleading with me to understand.

"It's OK, Jamie. This is . . . unexpected, and a bit strange." Understatement of the year.

"How is it that you always show up when I need you the most?" he asked in awe.

"I'm not sure, but this kind of feels like kismet. A year ago, I was standing on a ship when I suddenly had this incredible longing for home. At the same time, you were divorcing someone who made you miserable, and now here we are, both of us getting a second chance."

"I *really* missed you Sage. I can't believe you're here. Sometimes, I'd hear a song on the radio that reminded me of you, and I'd wonder where you were. I never allowed myself to dwell on it because I was married, but you were always there in the back of my mind. It was always you, wasn't it? You were the one that got away."

"You know, Jamie, I think it was you I was searching for all along, and I never even realized it. I've always had this list of qualities my 'perfect guy' would have, and I didn't realize until right now, it was you I was describing all along."

"I loved you so much, Sage. It made me crazy seeing you with *him.*"

"I'm sorry, Jamie. I never meant to hurt you. I didn't know you had feelings for me. You were so angry all the time, and I couldn't understand why."

"I was jealous and stupid."

Although he didn't end up sleeping on the couch, nothing happened that night. We weren't ready, and I was glad we weren't rushing into anything. A week later, he came over again, and we ended up in a similar embrace. I wondered if he'd ever find the nerve to kiss me. Luka, Matheus, Jamie—there was a theme here, but this time I recognized it, and I refused to do the chasing. If he wanted me, he'd have to make the first move.

"I'm broken, Sage. I have intimacy issues, and I'm not sure I know how to love. I don't think I'm ready for this—yet here you are."

"Maybe we needed to be broken so we could learn how precious our friendship is. The way I see it, this is a gift. When I worked on ships, I observed a lot of couples. The ones that impressed me were married for fifty years, yet they still held hands. I asked them what their secret was, and they said it was marrying their best friend. They said when all the passion simmers down, what you're left with is conversation, and if you don't have that, you have nothing."

"I like that," he said. "But what if I'm not ready?"

"I'll tell you what. Let's work on our friendship, and we'll take it from there. I'm not in a hurry. I mean, jeez . . . we waited this long." I laughed.

"That's what women always say, but they don't mean it," he said, bitterly. "I've dated two women in the past year, and they both tried to push me into a commitment."

"Hey," I said, turning his face towards me. "I'm not like other women, and you should know that by now. I will say this, though. I'm done trying to convince men to want me. So please hear me when I say I'm not going to make the first move. I will never kiss you first, so the ball's in your court. You have all the power here."

"But I'm so broken," he repeated.

"And you think I'm not? Jamie, I need you to listen to me. I tried to fix Christian, and it ended very badly, but I learned a valuable lesson. I understand you're broken, but only you can fix that. I will always listen, I will always be a shoulder to cry on, but I won't fix you. I've learned my lesson. I need to be really clear about that. Whatever happens next, I won't fix you."

THIRTY-ONE

By the third visit, I noticed a big change in Jamie. He was smiling like he didn't have a care in the world, and there was a hop in his step. It reminded me of the old Jamie. The boy I met back in college.

"Guess what happened today? I was walking past a mirror when I saw my reflection, and you know what I saw? *Me.* I haven't seen me in a long time. Even the guys at work noticed it," he said proudly as he hugged me.

"Oh Jamie, that's wonderful!"

"I'm so glad you're here, Sage. You've changed my whole world just by being you. No one has ever seen me the way you do."

"I see you Jamie Montgomery. I've always seen you."

A few days later, he went to Panama to visit his best friends, a couple he knew from work who moved there several years ago. Although we texted every day, I still missed him. When he got back, he told me he still had a week off and asked if I'd like to go on a road trip to meet his family. I thought it was a wonderful idea, even though I figured it was a test. They didn't like Paige, and he wanted their approval before making up his mind about me. I wasn't offended, though. Actually, I looked forward to meeting his family.

After his mother died, his father had sent him up north every summer. She had seven siblings, so there were plenty of aunts and uncles to take care of him.

Since they lived in a remote town in northern B.C., they taught Jamie how to hunt, fish, build things from scratch, and a bunch of other manly things. He spoke very highly of them.

On the way up, we stopped at his father's house and spent the night. Jamie was nervous because they didn't have a good relationship, but nothing happened while I was there. Actually, I liked his dad a lot. I found him to be quite charming. We had dinner and looked at old photo albums, laughing as he regaled us with stories. It was a short visit, but we promised to stop in again on the way back.

The drive was absolutely beautiful. The snow turned the landscape into a winter wonderland, and we stopped several times to admire the view. The mountains and valleys went on for miles, and the snow shimmered in the sunlight.

When I met his aunt and uncle, I complimented them on their wall of canning, so his aunt filled a box with jars and insisted I take them home. Jamie shook his head in amazement. "She only ever sends me home with a few jars. How did you do that?"

The next day, we went to his grandfather's house, and he told me stories about the time he was bitten by a cougar. Then he brought out some old newspaper articles and gave them to me. Jamie couldn't believe it. He'd been asking for those articles for years. The following night, when we had a family dinner at the second uncle's house, the first thing Grandpa said when he walked in the door was, "Where's Sage? I want to see Sage."

"Grandpa, what about me? I thought I was your favorite," Jamie said, and everyone laughed.

Later that night, I was in the kitchen with his grandpa while everyone else was in the living room. "Sage," he said very seriously, "I have to tell you something." He was ninety, so he talked quite loudly, and I watched as every head in the house turned to hear what Grandpa had to say, while pretending not to listen.

"What's that, Grandpa?" I asked.

"I love you," he stated matter-of-factly, and my heart melted.

Jamie was in the other room, and I saw his jaw drop open. When we'd first arrived, he told everyone we were just friends, but I don't think they bought it. That night I was sent home with more canning and an offer to come back and build a house on their massive property.

I was touched by everyone's generosity. Having never received love from my own family, I was overwhelmed by their affection. Jamie was lucky to have them, and it was clear how much they loved him. Those were such fun days, getting to know Jamie again.

Although we slept in the same bed for a week, nothing happened. I didn't mind because just being in his arms made the nights less lonely. We were up before dawn, and we used that time to get to know each other as we lingered over our coffee and tea. One morning, I came out of the bathroom in nothing but a towel, and Jamie let out a low growl. His eyes betrayed his desire.

"Sorry," I said as I ran past him. "I left my tea on the counter."

"You're making me crazy," he said in a low voice.

"Who, me?" I said innocently, batting my eyelashes.

By the time we went to a party at his third aunt's house, Jamie had stopped pretending we were "just friends" and openly flirted with me. It was a wild party, and everybody got drunk and a little crazy. I had a few drinks, but I've always been more of a toker, so I was OK.

Afterwards, as we sat on the couch in the privacy of our loft, he rubbed my shoulders and traced his finger along my arm. It was slow and sensual, and I thought for sure we were going to make out . . . and then he stopped. I waited a few minutes until I realized he was sound asleep. Now it was my turn to growl.

The last aunt we visited wasn't as warm as the others. She sat in her chair, rocking back and forth in a manic fashion while talking a mile a minute. I knew there was mental illness on his mother's side, and now I was seeing it firsthand. Actually, I had my suspicions about several of them. When we talked about it later, we joked that it was amazing we were even sane, given our gene pools.

On our way back to Vancouver, we stopped at his dad's house. He cooked a lovely meal and even chilled the wine glasses, which made Jamie's eyes bug out of his head. His father was obviously trying to impress me, and I thought it was cute, especially since every one of them hated his ex-wife.

"How do you *do* that?" he asked after his dad went to bed.

"What do you mean?"

"My entire family's in love with you! My dad chilled wine glasses! I think they like you better than they like me. They *never* send me home with gifts, yet I have a box of stuff all for you!"

I laughed. "Don't worry. I'll share."

A myriad of emotions crossed his face as he continued staring at me. "What is it about you that makes me so crazy and always has? No matter how hard I try, I can't get you out of my head. Even when we were kids, you were like that. Luka and I talked about it all the time. How there was something about you that we couldn't quite describe. You were so talented and full of life. It was overwhelming when we were younger. And now, here you are again, and I still can't get you out of my mind."

"So why are you trying so hard?"

"I don't know."

He leaned in for a kiss, and then he stopped when he was almost there, just like he always did. His eyebrows knit together as he turned away. "For some reason, the timing is always off with us. Maybe we're not meant to be together. Maybe we're just meant to be friends."

That was it. This time I lost my temper. I could understand that he was conflicted, but this was ridiculous. "Is that what you really think, Jamie? That we should only be friends?" I was pretty sure we were way past that.

"I don't know. Maybe," he said as he pulled away.

"Really? So what happens down the road when I start dating someone else?"

Anger flashed across his face, and his voice went up a notch. "Then that would be the end of us! I'm not watching you with another man ever again."

"Really? So what's your plan, exactly? You and I are friends, but I'm not allowed to date anyone else? I'm not allowed to get laid? And let me guess . . . you are. Is that how this works? Because I'm fairly sure we already tried that, and I *definitely* lived that bullshit with Luka."

"I don't know," he said, frustrated.

"Let me explain something to you, and I want to be very clear. I came home because I'm lonely, and I want a partner to share my life with. If you want to be friends, that's great. I can do that. Just know that I'll be dating while we're friends because that's what I want for myself. Do you think you can handle that?"

"No," he said miserably.

"Then what the fuck are you waiting for? You missed your chance seventeen years ago because you said nothing. Now I'm sitting right here—right in front of you—and you're about to let me go again, all because you don't have the balls to take what you want."

He gasped. "How *dare* you!"

We glared at each other for several minutes, but eventually he realized I wasn't backing down or apologizing. His shoulders sagged, and he blew out a breath because he knew I was right.

"Damn you," he whispered, right before he kissed me.

THIRTY-TWO

Jamie and I were a great love story. Everybody thought so. It had started twenty-two years ago, twisting and turning in different directions until finally bringing us here. I was thrilled that after all my shitty relationships, the Universe was finally rewarding me with true love, and with Jamie of all people. When I originally called him, I hadn't expected our reunion to be romantic. It was hard wrapping my head around it to be honest.

Not in a million years had I seen this coming, but now that it was here, I was determined to make it work. I was finally getting my happily ever after. Sure, Jamie could be irrational sometimes, but he was worth it because he was also funny, kind, thoughtful, and caring.

Besides, if there's one thing I've learned in my forty-five years on the planet, it's that no one's perfect. No relationship is, either. The important thing was that his good traits outweighed the bad, and I knew with time, the trauma from his marriage would fade, and so would his rage.

Jamie told me that I was saving him, but in truth he was the one saving me. My entire life, I'd felt invisible, like I didn't fit in, but he saw me for who I *really* was, and that meant the world to me. I didn't have to put on a brave face when I was with Jamie. I could be myself. It's funny because it was always like that, even when we were younger. We knew each other so well that we didn't even need words to communicate. It's like we were connected, and we could always sense what the other person was feeling.

He complained that he'd put on weight and wasn't a young man anymore, but that only meant I didn't have to stress about my own weight, something that had plagued me my entire life. He worried he was broken and had nothing to offer me, but somehow that made me feel less threatened, like I didn't have to work so hard to hide my *own* broken. Besides, at our age, it's hard to find someone without baggage. Believe me, I tried.

In some ways, Jamie was a lot like Christian. They were both tall, strong, handsome men with an extremely sensitive side, and I loved that contradiction. Strong on the outside, soft on the inside. I was the opposite, but I figured it brought balance to our relationship.

Now, don't assume that just because we kissed it was smooth sailing from here. This is Jamie we're talking about, and he never made anything easy. At least he wasn't boring, I'll give him that. On my birthday, he invited me over after his daughter left. Langley is on the border of suburbia and farmland, and in my opinion it's very . . . meh. I knew asking me to take the bus for two hours in the middle of winter was another test, but I didn't mind. Besides, I wanted to see where he lived.

When I walked in, I could tell a bachelor decorated. All the furniture was black, and the only things on the wall were an old shotgun and an enormous print from IKEA. It lacked personality (and color), which is such a dude thing to do; build a cave and decorate it in black. This was a house, not a home, and it desperately needed a feminine touch.

"I bought you something," he said when we got upstairs. "It's not much, but I thought you might need them."

"You bought me a present? I love presents." I opened the bag to find a pair of slippers, something I mentioned needing a week ago, and I loved that he remembered. "Thanks! I actually need these." I immediately put them on.

"I thought so," he said, smiling to himself. I got the idea that his ex never gave him any praise, and I knew what that felt like. He seemed so beaten, so down, and I knew that all he needed was a kind word to lift his spirits. Both of us had been through so much in the past twenty years, and we were trying to feel our way through this new version of ourselves. It was familiar, yet it was still a mystery.

"I hope you like pasta," he said as he put a pot on the stove.

I watched as he poured two glasses of wine from a box and handed me one. Next, he pulled out a jar of store-bought spaghetti sauce and poured it into the pot. As I watched him cook, I'm not gonna lie, the food snob in me was mortified, but I didn't let it show. I made a mental note to teach him how to cook. Now that he was a single dad, he needed to know these things.

As if reading my mind he said, "Sorry, I'm not much of a cook."

"Are you kidding? A man's making me dinner. I can't think of anything better than that." And I meant it. I love it when a man cooks for me, and the fact that it was my birthday made it even more special. My birthdays had a way of going sideways.

He shook his head in wonderment. "My ex always criticized me, but you constantly find ways to build me up. How do you do that?"

I shrugged. It was pretty simple, really. "I think you're amazing," I said sincerely.

He left the stove and came over to where I was standing. He kissed me passionately. Suddenly, a new song came over the radio. It was a merengue, and Jamie put out his hand. I took it, and he twirled me into his chest and then expertly dipped me. I giggled like a school girl, and he grinned. We danced, and it was exhilarating. I'd forgotten that Jamie knew how to dance.

When I was on ships, I was the dance instructor, and I always envied those couples. A lot of single women came to my classes, and there were never enough men to go around. Whenever a man showed up with his girlfriend or wife, we *all* envied them. It was romantic watching them dance, and I'd always hoped that one day, it would be me. Now here I was, dancing with my own sweet, handsome prince.

We ate dinner, and then we watched a movie while cuddling on the couch.

Just me and Jamie and his two enormous cats. How we loved cuddling, Jamie and I. Whether on the couch or in bed, we were a perfect fit, and we couldn't get enough of that simple pleasure. I think we realized how precious time was and didn't want to waste another second.

When it started to snow, he asked if I'd like to go for a walk, and I immediately said yes.

"Really? Just like that?"

It was after midnight, and I guess he wasn't expecting me to say yes.

"Heck yah. The first snowfall is always the prettiest. Let's get out there before anyone else does."

He studied me for a minute, and then he smiled. He jumped up and pulled me up with him. "I love my new life," he shouted joyfully, and I laughed at his silliness.

We held hands as we walked around the block and caught snowflakes on our tongues. We were the only people outside, and we laughed as we played like children. We felt young and free, which was a nice change for both of us. When we got back, we made hot chocolate, and then we went to the basement to find his old journal.

"I found it recently while I was going through some of this stuff, and I couldn't believe it. I read a few pages, and there you were, all over the place. I was dating so many girls at the time, but you were the one constant." He stopped and looked up at me. "You were always the one, Sage. I was so in love with you it hurt, but all you wanted was him."

I remembered those days well. What a stupid love triangle we were in. If only I hadn't been so caught up in my feelings for Luka, maybe I would have seen what was right in front of me.

"I'm sorry," I said quietly. "I was young and stupid and blinded by my love for Luka."

"Thankfully we're a lot older now, right?" He smiled, lightening the mood.

While he was digging around, I noticed a bunch of paintings leaning against the wall.

"What are these?" I asked as I sifted through them.

"They were my grandmother's. She was an artist."

They were a bit flowery for my taste, but some of them were good. "Jamie, you should hang these up. Your walls could use a little art."

"Really? My ex hated those paintings."

"They're a bit dated, but it's better than nothing, and if they belonged to your grandmother, I'm guessing they're special, right?"

His eyes lit up, and a smile spread across his face. "You're right. Pick the ones you like, and I'll take them upstairs." He was excited now. "You know what else I have? An old cabinet of hers. Let me show you."

When Jamie said *old cabinet,* what he really meant was a beautiful, vintage cabinet from the fifties. "Jamie, this is gorgeous! Why on earth is it hiding down here?"

"My ex never let me put this stuff in the house. She said it was old junk, stuff I inherited from dead people."

"Your ex sounds like a bitch, so it's a good thing you're not married to her anymore."

He grabbed me and kissed me. "You get me, don't you?" he said as he searched my eyes. I smiled and nodded. "But . . . you *really* get me, don't you?" he repeated.

I smiled softly. "I really do."

The next day, we decorated his townhouse with our new treasures. By the time we were finished, his place looked completely different, and he was gobsmacked by the transformation.

"You're a miracle worker! This place looks amazing. Seriously, you should be an interior decorator. You have a gift." He hugged me tightly. "Thank you, Sage. This place finally feels like home. My daughter's going to love it."

It was a long dark winter that year, but I didn't mind because I had Jamie to keep me warm. We split our time between my place and his, as we slowly fell into a rhythm. As a firefighter, he worked shift work, so he had Maya on his four days off, and I had him the four days he worked, which gave me plenty of time to myself.

Christmas Eve turned out to be a rough one for both of us. Sienna threw a dinner party and invited my mother, whom I hadn't seen since the incident with Bailey. I was dreading it and almost didn't go, but once I got there, I went out of my way to be civil because I'm an adult. I can't say the same for my mother, who was definitely NOT civil. She has a way of sucking the air out of a room, and although I tried to avoid her, she still got under my skin.

When it was over, I hopped on the bus and headed to Jamie's. All I could think of was how badly I needed a hug. I knew a hug from Jamie would make everything better, and I couldn't wait to be in his arms. As my childhood haunted me on that long bus ride, I sank deeper into despair, but by the time I arrived, I'd made a decision. I was done letting my mother do this to me. It was time to put up stronger boundaries. It was time to walk away for good.

When Jamie pulled up, he took one look at my face and said, "Good. Because I'm in a bad mood, too." His comment shattered me as I realized there'd be no comfort from him tonight. He didn't even hug me when I got into his truck, which was a first.

After months of listening to his sob stories, he couldn't even be bothered to listen to mine. As we drove to his place, he vented about not having his daughter on Christmas, how awful his ex was, and how unfair life was, but instead of making him feel better, I kept silent. Dealing with my mother was exhausting, and I didn't have the energy to make him feel better.

We spent the evening in complete silence. He was lost in his rage, and I was lost in my pain. We sat a foot apart while watching a movie and kept our hands to ourselves. Only the cats were in the mood to cuddle. We went to bed, and by the time I woke up, he was already at work. I hadn't given him his present yet, and as I'd find out later, it hadn't even occurred to him to buy me one.

I spent Christmas Day by myself, crying over his selfishness, but by the time he came home, I'd managed to plaster a smile on my face. We had to go to his brother's house for dinner, where I was supposed to meet his immediate family, so I couldn't afford to be upset or to make a bad impression.

As soon as he got home, he apologized for his behavior, and I immediately forgave him, but secretly, I was sad it had even happened in the first place. You only get one "first Christmas," and this would always be ours. Sitting on the couch, a foot apart, watching a movie in silence.

We had a similar experience when Valentine's Day rolled around. We were driving in his truck when I asked if he wanted to make plans. He ranted about how Valentine's Day was just a ploy to spend money, how love is an illusion that ends with women screwing you over, and how it was all a bunch of bullshit.

At first, I was offended, but then I remembered how Christmas played out and decided it was time for some tough love. I had no intention of letting him destroy another holiday just because he was bitter about his ex. I'd waited a long time to have someone to celebrate the holidays with, and this was not how I'd envisioned it.

"Is that really how you feel, Jamie?" I asked in my serious voice.

"What?" he said, distracted by his own bitter thoughts.

"Do you really think love is just a bunch of bullshit?"

"Yes . . . no . . . maybe. I'm just in a bad mood." When I didn't respond, he looked over at me and grabbed my hand. "Sorry."

"Jamie—my *friend*. I realize Paige hurt you, and you're bitter, and for that I'm sorry. Jamie—my *boyfriend* . . . fuck you."

He gasped and opened his mouth to respond, but I cut him off. "Valentine's Day is about spending time with the ones we *love*. It's not about gifts. I don't give a shit about the gifts. I get that you were pissy about Christmas because you didn't get to spend it with your daughter, and I get that you've had many holidays with your wife, so this might not seem like a big deal to you. But I've spent the last forty-five Valentine's Days alone, and this is the first time in my life I actually have someone to spend it with, so for once can you please take *my* feelings into account?"

He went to speak again, but I wasn't finished. "I was actually looking forward to our first Valentine's Day, so I really need you to get your head out of your ass and start treating me like I matter, or we're going to have a problem. "

"I thought you dated Christian for seven years. Didn't you spend the holidays together?"

"Oh, please. Christian was never around for special occasions. The 'pressure' always sent him on a bender, so I generally spent them alone and crying."

His face instantly softened. "I'm really sorry that happened to you, Sage."

"Thanks," I mumbled.

"Really. I'm sorry. And I promise I'll do better." He squeezed my hand and smiled at me. "Let's be better than them, OK?"

Thirty-Three

Jamie had a lot of anxiety, and after a tough day at work, or spending time with his daughter, it always got worse. I usually noticed it when we were watching movies. His knee bounced up and down like a jackhammer, and sometimes he'd pace for a full ten minutes before sitting down, like he wasn't quite sure what to do with himself.

I was able to calm him down by simply placing my hand on his knee or patiently waiting for him to stop pacing, but when he told me he made an appointment to see a doctor, I was relieved. He had a tough job, and I knew it affected him. The doctor told him he probably had PTSD and gave him two types of medication: a daily pill to help with his anxiety and pills for the days when it got really bad.

"Is this because of your job?" I asked.

"Yes. She thinks I should be talking to someone on a regular basis."

"I agree. Bottling it up only makes it worse."

"People always think it's what I *see* that gives me nightmares, but it's the things I *hear*. When you arrive on a scene and a woman is screaming because her child was killed in a car accident . . . when you hear pain and suffering in her voice, that's what really haunts me."

"I imagine it does," I said, but Jamie was lost in his own thoughts. I reached out and grabbed his hand. "You know, if you ever want to talk about it, I'm right here, right? I think a professional can help, but I'm here, too, and I'm a great listener. I hope you know that."

His smile was sad. "Thank you, Sage. My ex always told me to check that stuff at the door, so I was never allowed to talk about it."

"I'm really starting to hate that woman."

"That makes two of us."

After he left, I did some research, because the doctor was right—this was more than anxiety. I couldn't put my finger on it, but it was setting off warning bells in my head. I thought it was because Jamie reminded me so much of Christian, the same way I reminded him of Paige. We were quite the pair. Our theme song was *Issues* by Julia Michaels. The lyrics described us perfectly.

I didn't know anything about PTSD, so I decided to look it up. I read an article, and it talked about panic, stress, anxiety, excessive sweating, depression, insomnia, and aggressive or self-destructive behavior. It went on to say that the person might be easily irritated, they may lash out in anger, and they may be prone to abusing drugs and alcohol. I sat back in my chair. Damn. That sounded exactly like Jamie. His terrible sleeping patterns, his unpredictable mood swings, and the contradicting stories he told me about his marriage.

He always blamed Paige for everything that happened, but as more of the story unfolded, it was obvious that Jamie had checked out of his marriage long before Paige filed for divorce. One night while he was drunk, he told me he'd spent the last two years of his marriage hiding in his man cave, not talking to his wife or daughter because he was "tired of their bullshit."

For two years, he slept downstairs, yet he blamed the divorce entirely on Paige. He was so blinded by his resentment that he couldn't see the truth, because in his mind nothing was ever his fault—a quality I did not enjoy.

Thank God I was there to pull him back from the abyss whenever he started spiralling. His thoughts were so dark sometimes that I had to remind him *never* to say them to anyone else. His hatred for his ex was eating him alive, so when he finally went to see a counselor, I was relieved. In my world, it takes a real man to admit he needs help.

In the spring, Jamie decided it was time for his daughter and I to meet. He and I had been dating for five months. He let her invite a friend so she'd have someone to talk to while the four of us went out. She was shy and didn't say much, but later she told him she wanted to work on a cruise ship when she grew up, so we counted that as a win.

After several successful outings, the next step was to have me sleep over. We bent over backwards trying to make it easy on her, but she was a typical teenager, and in her eyes, I was the enemy, so she gave us a fair amount of attitude. Having a miserable teenager sending me daggers wasn't exactly my idea of a good time, but she was Jamie's daughter, so I sucked it up. Besides, I understood teenage girls and their mood swings. It was Jamie who was having a hard time with her "spoiled, ungrateful attitude."

When I took Jamie to Piers Island to meet my friends, he fell so in love with it, he asked if we could return with his daughter and her cousin. The trip was a huge success. We ate really good food, played cards, and did an Easter egg hunt in the forest. Then Jamie and I looked at properties. I'd always dreamed about retiring on the island, so I was thrilled that he loved it as much as I did. I also found it entertaining that we were looking at property before we'd even said "I love you." Then again, Jamie never did anything normal, and the property was for the future, not now.

I'm not sure what happened, but the next time I came over, Maya announced that she hated my guts and never wanted to see me again. She didn't say it directly to my face, but to Jamie while she was hiding in her bedroom.

It was her fifteenth birthday, and we'd planned a really fun day, except she refused to leave her bedroom while I was still in her house. I told Jamie I should leave, but he was furious and wanted to teach his daughter a lesson. We left and took a drive for about an hour before he dropped me off at the bus station. When he got home, they had a massive argument.

"I was so mad I was shaking," he told me later. "We were screaming at each other, and just like her mother, she was pushing all my buttons. I was freaking out, but I think I took it too far, because at one point, she said I was scaring her. Damn it, she needs to grow up. When I was her age, I took the bus to school and had a job. She can't even get off her ass to get a glass of water. The other day, I asked her to grab something from the basement, but she refused to go down there because *it's too scary*. What a crock of shit! She's just lazy because her mother spoils her."

I let Jamie rant about his daughter, and I was careful how I responded. Being the girlfriend is tricky when someone has kids, so I listened while keeping most of my opinions to myself. I knew that anything I said might come back to haunt me if it all went sideways.

"I know you're mad, and I don't mean to contradict you, but just so you know . . . I'm an *adult*, and I'm scared of your basement. It's kind of a girl thing."

"What? What's wrong with my basement?"

"Do you know what men fear most about a woman?" He shook his head, not sure where I was going with this. "That she'll laugh at him."

"OK . . ."

"Now guess what a woman fears most about a man?"

He shook his head again. "I have no idea."

"That he'll kill her. Let that sink in for a moment. Men only have to worry about their egos, but as women, we worry about our lives. Every single day. As females, we're pre-programmed to fear men and serial killers. We're born with a sixth sense when it comes to danger because it's always there, no matter how old we get."

I watched as he pondered that, and then I continued. "If someone wants to break into this house, they'll enter from the basement, so it's quite natural for girls to fear the basement, especially at night. It's a dark, scary place where monsters hide. When you work nights, I hate going down to the basement by myself. It scares me."

"Huh. I never thought of it like that."

"Of course not. Look at you. You can defend yourself against an attacker, whereas I'd be dead in five minutes. Men have a natural advantage that we don't, so you should cut Maya a little slack. She's just a child."

"She's a teenager," he said stubbornly.

"She's still a child."

He stared at me for a minute and then he shook his head in wonderment. "How do you do that?"

"Do what?"

"You have this unique perspective on life and such a patient way of explaining it. I swear, talking to you is like holding up a mirror. I don't always like what you have to say, but you're usually right." He sighed and shook his head again. "Maya was a total bitch to you, yet here you are defending her. You're an amazing human being, Sage." He wrapped his arms around me. "Have I told you lately how much I like you?"

I smiled. "I like you, too."

Thirty-Four

In May, I went back to work, which was both a blessing and a curse. My tours were really long (sometimes four weeks), and we missed each other like crazy, so we had to come up with ideas on how to make it work. We promised to talk every night, even if it was only for a few minutes, and whenever I was close to home, Jamie moved heaven and earth to come see me. We actually found it exciting, meeting up in fancy hotels, and we made the most of these stolen moments by taking long walks, eating delicious meals, and drinking gorgeous wines like *we* were on vacation.

He offered to water my plants while I was away, and once a week he spent the night so my neighbors would see activity in my apartment.

I'd just come home from my second trip when I walked into my kitchen and found a pile of moldy dishes on the counter. Now if there's one thing everybody knows about me, it's that I'm an impeccable neat freak, so you can imagine how mortified I was when I saw those dishes sitting in the exact same place I'd left them in a month ago.

What really pissed me off is there were only a few of them, and I would have washed them on my last night in town, except Jamie had begged me to leave them, *swearing* he'd do them in the morning. I told him he'd better not forget because if I came home to dirty dishes, I'd be pissed. So imagine my surprise when a month later the exact same dishes were still sitting there, covered in mold.

What really sent me over the edge is when I brought it up, he brushed it off and said I was overreacting. Instead of apologizing, he pointed out how he was doing me a favor by coming over in the first place. I found this attempt to manipulate me unacceptable, and although I tried to be the bigger person and let it go, I couldn't. After Christian, I promised myself I'd never be manipulated again.

Jamie had disrespected me (and my home) and that was not OK. I had to follow so many rules when I was at his place, but he seemed to think he could do whatever he wanted when he was at mine. The patriarchy loves its double standards.

When I discovered several empty bottles of booze in my recycling bin, I got even more upset. I had just purchased those bottles, and he drank them without asking me or saving me a drop. Not only that, he'd added a sports package to my TV, without even asking. I barely had any channels because I couldn't afford them, and now I had to pay for a package I'd never watch.

I knew if I mentioned these things, I'd sound cheap, but he'd overstepped, and the more I thought about it, the more upset I got. I sat down to write him a text so I could get it off my chest before he came over. I took my time, making sure I worded it ever so carefully. I wanted to tell him how I felt, not start a fight. A few minutes later, he sent a reply. "Oh, you just *had* to go there, didn't you? You just *couldn't* leave it alone. They're just dishes, Sage. For fuck's sake, get over it already."

I was stunned when I read his reply. He'd never spoken to me like that before. I'd been so careful to construct my text in a non-threatening manner, while he just lashed out as if I'd been nagging him for weeks. We exchanged a few more texts, but it only got worse, so eventually, I stopped and tried to make sense of what was happening. It didn't take long to figure out that he was confusing me with Paige. Whereas I saw this as our first fight, he treated it like a continuation of the fights they'd been having for seventeen years.

This wasn't good, and it wasn't the first time either. I wondered how long I'd have to pay for Paige's sins, and I felt sick that we were fighting when I hadn't seen him in weeks. Now that I understood what was going on, we needed to talk about the things that triggered him so we could avoid these arguments in the future. I knew his PTSD made him overreact sometimes, but I needed to lay down some boundaries.

As I sat there, I realized something else was bothering me. This was the second time I'd come home to empty liquor bottles, and I was starting to worry that Jamie had a drinking problem. His ability to throw them back and stay sober was quite impressive, but after nine months, his drinking hadn't slowed down, and that made me nervous.

It didn't matter how much I loved him; this was one nightmare I wasn't willing to repeat. He reminded me so much of Christian sometimes it was frightening, and I wondered if that made me better able to handle the situation or stupid. The question is, how do you ask someone if they're an alcoholic without it sounding like an accusation, especially someone with a short fuse?

For the rest of the afternoon, I was on edge, wondering if he'd still come over. Would he act like a child and go home, or would he come and talk about it like an adult? I honestly wasn't sure. I saw how he treated his ex-wife, and it wasn't good, so when I heard a key in the door a few hours later, I was relieved.

"Hi," I said when the door opened. "I wasn't sure you'd come."

"To be honest, I almost didn't, but I respect you too much to leave it like this."

We talked for hours, and I even found the courage to bring up his drinking. At first, he got angry and said he didn't like ultimatums, but I explained this wasn't an ultimatum; it was about me and my boundaries. He had an entire list of things I wasn't allowed to do or say because they reminded him of Paige, and I bent over backwards to avoid anything that triggered him, but this was a two-way street.

I told him what it had been like living with Christian, and eventually he admitted he'd been a little careless lately. He said his daughter had voiced the same concern and promised to do better for both our sakes. When he actually refrained from alcohol for two weeks, I thought, *an alcoholic couldn't do that. Maybe I was wrong about him.*

After that argument, things got better, and eventually he found the courage to tell me he loved me—another thing I let him do first, no matter how many times I'd wanted to say it.

We had only a couple of days each month to see each other that summer, but we certainly made them count. We went to concerts, took his canoe out on the lake, went to the movies, went camping, and threw lots of dinner parties for his friends and family. Jamie had a very active social life, and I loved being part of it, especially since I'd been so lonely every time I came home in the past.

In the middle of summer, when I had two weeks off, we went camping, and then we took a road trip to Kelowna to visit his sister. Kelowna is in the middle of wine country, so we wine-tasted our way there and did the same thing on the way back. We loved it so much we even joined a wine club. It felt like such a grown-up thing to do. I was pleased when Jamie told me he'd never be able to drink wine from a box again. "Yes!" I joked. "My work here is done!"

While our relationship was growing stronger, things with his daughter continued to deteriorate. They fought constantly, and for months he'd threatened to kick her out if she didn't change. Neither of them was willing to apologize for the blow-out on her birthday, and the rift between them grew. Although I tried to stay out of it, I warned him to be careful because if he *did* kick her out, she'd never come back.

One night in August, they had a fight, and Jamie did what he did best—he went down to his man cave to brood and drink. When he went upstairs the next morning, she was gone. She'd called her mother in the middle of the night and had snuck out while Jamie was passed out in the basement. He was livid when he found a note with the number to a suicide hotline and nothing else. He screamed at Paige for taking her without waking him up, and she yelled at him for being so drunk he hadn't even noticed she was gone.

It got really ugly, and I was glad I was on the road and didn't have to deal with the fallout because secretly, I thought Jamie had fucked up. For months after that, he cried about how he was desperate to repair his relationship with his daughter, yet he refused to do the one thing she wanted—apologize for ruining her birthday.

On my last trip of the season, he came to see me in Whistler, and we had a wonderful time. I knew he was still upset, so I made sure to pump him full of positive energy like I always did. After dinner, he sat me down for a talk.

"I was thinking. It seems silly to spend so much money on an apartment when you basically live with me. You're not even home half the year, and it's such a waste of money. What do you think about moving in with me?"

I deadpanned, "Wow. That was such a romantic proposal. How could I possibly refuse?"

He laughed. "You know what I mean."

"I'd love to move in with you Jamie, but are you sure you're ready? I don't want to give up my apartment to find out you've changed your mind in a year. You're pretty protective of your space, and if I move in, you realize my stuff comes with me, right?"

"I thought about that, but I'm sure you'll do an amazing job of decorating."

"Well, that goes without saying, but there's more. By moving me to Langley, you'll be stripping me of my independence. As you know, I don't drive. Have you considered what that means? You'll have to drive me everywhere. I'll be totally dependent on you."

"I know. I thought about that, too, and I don't mind, but what about you? You hate Langley."

"I do, but I love *you*, and that's all that matters."

"Is that a yes, then?" he said hopefully.

"I have one last concern. I cannot live in a dirty space, as you well know, so how are we going to handle that? I've got the winter off, so I'm happy to do the cooking and daily chores, but your place is huge, and I have no desire to clean it by myself."

He smiled. "I've actually come to appreciate how OCD you are. My ex wasn't a good housekeeper, but you're amazing. I always know exactly where everything is, and I love that."

"Look at how grown up we are. If we were still in our twenties, we'd just move in and deal with the fallout later. I love how we're able to talk about these things before they become a problem. Now, how are we going to split the bills? Can I even afford to move in with you? I don't make nearly as much money as you do."

He suddenly looked nervous. "Listen, I'd love to support you—"

I put up my hand. "Stop. I'm not looking for a free ride. I just need to know how much it's going to cost."

"Oh, Sage. You never cease to amaze me. Thank you for understanding. Paige took everything from me, and I'm not ready to support someone else just yet."

After we sorted out the bills, I got up to limp my way to the bathroom. I'd taken a nasty fall back in April, injuring my hip, and despite the fact that I'd been to three different doctors in five months, it wasn't improving. Mainly because they kept telling me nothing was wrong with me.

As someone who's always been active, I was extremely distressed by my inability to walk more than a few blocks before the limping kicked in. Not only was I putting on weight, but by favoring my right hip, I was developing severe pain in my left foot.

"Babe, I can't believe you're still limping after all this time. Now that you're finished working, we're going to make your hip our top priority. I'm taking you to my chiropractor when we get home. We'll do whatever it takes to make you better, OK?"

"I'm so frustrated I could scream. I'm tired of living on painkillers, but the doctors won't listen to me. I feel like I'm going crazy. If one more person tells me nothing's wrong with me, I'll lose it." A tear slid down my cheek, and he brushed it away with his thumb.

"Hey. *I'm* listening, and I promise we're going to fix this. Let me take care of you, OK?"

"OK." I whined pitifully, as he wrapped his arms around me. Someone was finally taking care of me for once.

Even though I hated Jamie's townhouse (it was cold, dark, and lacked privacy), living with him was amazing. Waking up every morning with him besides me, hearing him yell "Luuuucy. I'm hooooome!" when he walked in the door, or simply cuddling in front of the TV. It didn't matter. Sure, I still spent most of my time making him feel less sad, or less angry, or less unhappy—but I'd gotten good at it, so by this point, it was second nature.

He showed his appreciation by driving me to endless appointments as we tried to figure out what was wrong with my hip. His townhouse had a lot of stairs, and my hip was so bad I struggled to climb them sometimes, yet I never complained. I was too happy and too in love for complaints. Besides, Jamie did enough of that for the both of us.

Like most new relationships, we had a lot of fun in those days. Since I wasn't working, I threw myself into the role of Domestic Goddess. I'd cook elaborate meals and bake sumptuous desserts, having it all on the table by the time he got home. He'd rave about how beautiful his place looked and how delicious everything tasted. Both of us were happy.

He told me the guys at work were impressed with how happy he looked, and a little jealous of how exciting our lives were. On his days off, we'd cook together while drinking wine, and I really cherished those moments because I've always felt that the kitchen is the center of any home. Our lives were full of activity and family gatherings, and every morning I woke up thanking the Universe for blessing me with such a beautiful life.

I decorated his place with great care, making sure to put his things in prominent positions and always asked his opinion so he wouldn't feel left out. I knew Jamie, and I bent over backwards making things easy for him. He did the same for me.

In November, we flew to Panama to stay with his friends, the same ones he'd visited last year. I was nervous about meeting them because I knew how much he loved them, and if I didn't get their stamp of approval, I knew we'd have a problem. Panama wasn't a vacation; it was another test.

Everyone in Jamie's life hated Paige and they warned him not to marry her, but he ignored them, and it was a disaster. He didn't want to make that mistake again so this time, he was getting everyone's approval. I didn't mind. Most people love me.

Jamie met Paul and Jackie when he first started working at the fire department. They were practically family. He talked about them all the time, and I knew he looked up to Paul as both a mentor and a friend. They were his favorite people in the whole world.

They picked us up from the airport, and I found them to be nice people, but it was clear I was the outsider. We spent our days talking and cooking while the three of them got drunk. I enjoy drinking and had a few cocktails myself, but drinking to get drunk has never been my thing. I don't like the way it makes me feel, and I especially don't like the hangover.

After a few days, I asked if they wouldn't mind showing us around, since this was my first time in the area. I was shocked to learn that Jamie had never ventured off their property before.

"These trips aren't about sightseeing; they're about getting drunk and catching up with old friends," he told me.

We ended up going to some ancient ruins, and then I convinced everyone to go zip lining. When the instructor asked if this was our first time, they all said "yes," and then he looked at me. "Oh no, I've done this tons of times," I answered, but later Jamie scolded me. He said I was showing off and had ruined it for his friends by one-upping them. I was horrified by his comment, and made sure not to do that again.

As the days passed, I found it more and more difficult to listen to the three of them repeat the same conversation over and over. They were so drunk they didn't even realize they were doing it, and I never said a word because they were nice people and because Jamie was having a good time. I made sure never to talk about my travel experiences (even though they talked about theirs) because I didn't want to outdo them again.

When we left, we promised to return the following year. We made plans to rent a yacht and sail around the islands. I knew I'd always be an outsider with this group, but Jamie loved them, so that was all that mattered.

"So . . . did I pass the test?" I asked once we were on the plane.

He laughed. "With flying colors. They absolutely loved you. They said you were smart, funny, and a fabulous cook. They're really happy for me." He kissed me softly. "Everyone loves you, Sage. It's hard not to. How did I get so lucky?"

Thirty-Five

When I lived in Cancun, I worked with a lady who told wonderful stories about Uganda. She'd been there a dozen times and went gorilla trekking with every visit. I remember thinking how incredibly brave that sounded. Kama was so in love with Uganda that it was her dream to open an orphanage, and for that I truly admired her. Due to the red tape, it took longer than expected, but eventually she opened a school in Kisoro.

It thrilled me that my dream of seeing Uganda was finally coming true and that Jamie and my two Aussie friends were joining me. I booked the trip through a local tour company and made arrangements to visit the school while we were there. That plus gorilla trekking, chimp trekking, and a dozen game drives were the highlight of our vacation.

Our first stop was the Ziwa Rhino Sanctuary, where we got an up-close-and-personal view of the rhinos as we walked beside them. Then we continued north to Murchison Falls. Jamie and I chose the glamping option while my friends chose to upgrade, so we usually ended up on opposite ends of the property. Jamie and I loved camping, and Africa was the ultimate dream, so that's why we chose it. That night, we slept with the sound of crickets in our ears, and in the morning, we got up before dawn for our first game drive.

I quickly realized there'd be no grooming on this trip, since it was difficult to see anything in the dark. Unlike our friends who were staying in a hotel room, we had little to no electricity. We'd brought headlamps, but the amount of bugs (not to mention bats) stalking us as we tried to brush our teeth encouraged us to get ready quickly. Luckily, I'd brought a hat and wasn't fussed about make-up. Of course, every morning our friends arrived looking perfectly refreshed while we looked like a couple of hobos.

On our way to the first game park, we saw an elephant, and since this was everyone else's first time to Africa, the excitement was through the roof. When the sun came up, it turned the entire savannah a burnt orange, and just as I was taking a photo, a giraffe walked by. It was pure magic. Africa is always magic. I got to see South Africa when I worked on ships, and in 2011, I spent three glorious months there.

Jamie was so overwhelmed he almost cried. He was hyper and speechless, and it brought me such joy to see him react that way, because it's exactly how I feel every time I travel, and I wanted him to love it as much as I did. He'd shown me his world over the past fifteen months, and now I was showing him mine.

"Is this what you've been doing for the past twenty years?" he asked me in awe.

"Ummm . . . yes. Basically."

"Wow. This is exceptional. It's the most beautiful thing I've ever seen, and it's all because of you. *You* did this. Thank you for opening my eyes to a whole new world." He bent down and kissed me. "I love you, Sage."

For the next few hours, we saw all kinds of wildlife. Our guide had the personality of a noodle, but he was a great spotter, and he never rushed us. He even let us get out of the vehicle to pose for photos (when it was safe to do so) and stopped to show us tracks left by a python. It was fascinating, but I'm not gonna lie, I hadn't considered pythons when we decided to go camping.

After a delicious lunch, we took a lazy cruise down the Nile where we saw hippos playing alongside crocodiles. The cruise was four hours long, and we had *such* a wonderful time, but as we disembarked the vessel, Jamie was so drunk he almost fell over. When I got back from the bathroom, I saw him pouring our bag of emergency trail mix down his throat.

After a trip to Morocco during Ramadan (where I starved), I had learned to bring my own snacks on vacation to help with my hypoglycemia (low blood sugar). So you can imagine my panic when I saw him with the trail mix, especially since he devoured everything in sight when he drank, not to mention that *he's* the one who lectured me whenever I let my sugars drop.

"Babe! Don't eat all the trail mix!" I said when I saw him. It's not like I could run out and buy more.

"Don't tell me what to do," he snapped angrily.

"I'm not. I just know how you get when you're drunk." I said playfully, "and those are for *emergencies.*"

"Oh, so they're only for *you?* Everything's always about *you*, isn't it?"

"What? Of course not. I just meant . . ."

"You know what? Fuck you," he said, and threw the bag at me. "They're all yours. I won't touch them for the rest of the trip."

I was stunned by this abrupt mood swing and desperately tried to calm the situation down before it got out of control, but it was too late. The switch had already been flipped. He moved to his own seat, turned his back to me, and passed out. I couldn't believe it. For the next several hours, he slept. We were on the vacation of a lifetime—on a damn *safari*—and he slept.

When we came across a lioness, I tried to wake him, but the only thing he said was, "If I wanted to watch a cat lick its own ass, I can do that at home." That was, in fact, what the lion was doing at that moment, but it's hardly the point. After that, I left him alone because I was so embarrassed. How could he act that way in front of my friends? Can you imagine if I'd acted that way in Panama? I told myself to be patient because he had PTSD and this was one of the side effects, but it still burned.

When we got back to the campsite, he said he was going to bed. I didn't stop him, nor did I follow him. In the morning, neither of us said a word. I was waiting for him to apologize, but he clearly had no intention of doing that.

We boarded another cruise, and as the sun rose over the mountains, it cast pink and red hues across the sky. It was exceptionally romantic, and our friends were cuddling, yet we were sitting on opposite sides of the boat. Missing out on this romantic moment made me incredibly sad. His insane mood swings were one thing at home, but now he was ruining our vacation, and that pissed me off.

We were about three hours into the cruise before he finally sat down beside me. "Sage, we can't keep ignoring each other like this," he said softly.

"I'm mad at you," I said as tears slid down my cheeks.

"I know you are. I was drunk, and when you told me what to do, it got under my skin. I don't like being bossed around."

"You're mean, and you say hurtful things when you're drunk. No matter how mad I get, I never say anything I'll regret later because I love you even when I'm mad. But you—you *aim* to hurt me. You call me names and lash out like I'm the enemy."

"I'm so sorry. I don't know why I do that. You don't deserve it."

"No, I don't."

"It won't happen again. I promise."

"Good. Because I really hate it when we fight."

"Me, too. Come here." He kissed the top of my head. "I'm sorry I made you cry."

After that, we were back to being the lovey-dovey couple we usually were, although he refused to touch that trail mix for the rest of the trip, not even when he was hungry. I thought I could be stubborn, but Jamie took that word to a whole other level. As for how childish he was acting, that reminded me of my mother.

In Kibale, we went on our first chimp walk, and then we visited the local village. We gave the children a soccer ball and played a game with them (and the cows), then slept to a symphony of frogs. The next day, we traveled north, and when we got to the hotel, the manager upgraded our friends to the Royal Suite while completely ignoring us, even though we were sitting at the same table and the property was deserted.

By now, we were used to our friends getting special treatment, so it didn't really bother us . . . until we saw the suite. At every property, they'd shown us their room, but we weren't living in luxury (or even comfort), and although it wasn't intentional, it felt like a slap in the face.

Jamie really resented it and constantly complained, which put me in an awkward position because I knew my friends were just excited. I reminded him that camping was our choice, but I admit, it was hard not to feel like second-class citizens as we walked to the very back of the property to some sad-looking tents reeking of mold. It was by far the worst campsite we stayed at on that trip.

Determined not to let this get us down, we carried on (showering beside the hornets' nest), but things got much worse when it started to rain in the middle of the night, and the tent started leaking. It quickly became a torrential downpour, and within minutes, the bed was completely soaked. We ended up huddling in the corner as we tried to stay dry.

When the thunder started, it was so loud we jumped, and Jamie screamed, which made me laugh. My big, strong fireman was scared. The storm lasted forever and got closer by the minute, until eventually it was on top of us. We peeked outside and saw several bolts of lightning strike the campground, causing the bed and tent to shake. It felt like we were literally inside the storm.

"What happens if lightning strikes our tent?" I asked Jamie.

"I'm not sure, but I'm not gonna lie, this is kind of freaking me out."

"Oh God, we're going to die!" We both laughed as we held onto each other for dear life.

The next morning, it felt like we'd been hit by a truck, and listening to our friends go on and on about how awesome the storm was, how comfortable their beds were, and how lovely their room was didn't help. Jamie's resentment grew, and so did his complaining.

Luckily, we had the most incredible stay on the Kazinga Channel, which put us both in a better mood. We saw every animal imaginable, and that night, we slept to the sound of elephants calling across the channel and a hippo eating grass outside our tent. Every night was a different sound that only added to the magic.

We had an incredible time in Uganda, but nothing compared to seeing the gorillas. I was a little nervous about the trek. Between the hard beds and strenuous hikes, my busted hip was taking a beating, but I was determined not to let it get in the way. Besides, I had plenty of painkillers on hand, a lesson I'd learned after my last trip to Africa, when I fractured my ribs and sprained my ankle.

The hike through the rainforest was difficult, but it was worth it. We got to sit with a family of gorillas (including a baby and a silverback), which was humbling and precious, to say the least. We were overwhelmed after the exceptional experience, and as we drank Baileys while looking at the mountains, a mist moved in, and that's when I finally understood . . . *Gorillas in the Mist.*

When we got to the hotel in Kisoro, Mukisa (my friends' liaison) was waiting for us, and what a lovely young man he turned out to be. We went on a long walk to the top of the mountain, and then we wound our way through the market. In the morning, he took us to a local village. Mukisa explained that this was a new tour he'd put together in an effort to help support local families. We were more than happy to try it out.

When we came down the hill, we saw a crowd gathered outside, ready to welcome us. They were singing, dancing, and drumming, and after a few minutes, they led us to a small area at the back of the house. The two male dancers were incredible, and I couldn't take my eyes off them. They twisted their bodies at odd angles, jumping sky high while the drum beat its rhythm. They played off each other's energy and it was primal, spiritual, mesmerizing. I could have watched them all day.

We sat on a wooden bench, and the children gathered behind us as the adults led a demonstration and Mukisa interpreted it for us. At first, they were shy as they showed us how to grind corn, weave a mat, and balance baskets on our heads. How strange we must have seemed to them, coming to their home to learn how to do daily chores.

Since we failed at most of them, we made fun of ourselves, which helped lighten the mood. When a fiery old lady slapped my hand for messing up the weaving, everyone gasped and froze, waiting for my reaction. I burst out laughing, and the entire village, who until that moment had looked so stern, laughed with me. After that, the energy changed as everyone relaxed and joined in on the fun.

The ladies dressed my friend and I "for a trip to the market," then strapped their babies on our backs. I was laughing at how huge her baby was, while mine was a tiny newborn. Of course, neither of us were laughing when the babies peed down our backs.

After more dancing and drumming, it was time for lunch. We washed our hands and were ushered into the house to sit at the table as guests of honor. Jamie (who's a bit of a germaphobe) and Letty (who's a bit of a princess) were worried about eating with their hands, but I told them they were not allowed to insult these people, who'd given us a much larger portion of food than what they took for themselves.

Once we'd finished eating (it was delicious), Mukisa sang the first line of "Oh Happy Day," and he almost fell over when I sang the next line.

"You know this song?" he asked me.

"Of course I do! I directed a choir for five years. *Sister Act* was my inspiration."

We sang the song together, and not only were the adults completely surprised, but the children (who were sent outside while we ate) came rushing over to see what was going on. They may not have understood the words, but they certainly understood the music.

There must have been a dozen faces in the window as they clamored over each other to get a better view. Everyone listened with rapt attention, then I asked if they could sing one for us. Not only did they sing a beautiful song, they sang it in four-part harmony! I almost cried.

Next, it was my turn, and when I finished, one of the ladies came over, knelt in front of me, and put her hands on my knees. She had the most genuine smile, and when she gestured for me to sing again, I did. She listened carefully, and then she sang it back to me. I can't even tell you how happy that made me. My heart was overwhelmed with joy, and I knew she felt it, too.

She was a kindred spirit, and I can't explain it, but at that moment, we bonded. Pleased with herself, she sang a song in her language and gestured for me to repeat it, which I did. Everyone cheered when I got it right. She clapped her hands, and the next thing I knew, chaos broke out. The boys grabbed the drum and started dancing and singing again while the rest of us stomped our feet to the frenzied rhythm.

"Mukisa, this is amazing! Is it always like this?" I asked as I filmed the song.

"Never! Usually, they're pretty shy. I didn't even know they could sing!"

When it was time to leave, one of the male dancers stood up to make a speech and Mukisa interpreted it for us.

"Thank you for coming to our village and our home. You're family now, and you'll always have a place here. Today, we bonded in a way we didn't even know was possible. We hope one day you'll return and stay with us as our honored guests."

He turned to look at me and Jamie. "Today I learned what true love looks like. Never in my life have I seen two people who love each other the way you do. I can only hope to be as happy as you are one day."

I was so moved I almost cried. We all did. We thanked them for their wonderful hospitality and promised to visit if we ever made it back. This was one of the most precious experiences of my life, and I knew it would live in my heart forever.

When we got back to the hotel, we went our separate ways and agreed to meet in an hour. Everyone needed a shower, especially Letty and me, as we were still covered in baby pee. As I got ready, I thought about the speech the male dancer had made, and once again I thanked the Universe for blessing me with such a beautiful partner and an amazing life. There are so many things we take for granted in the western world, and these vacations were a constant reminder of just how lucky we are.

Once everyone was ready, it was time to leave again. I was finally going to my friend's school! It had been ten years since we'd first talked about it. We were greeted by the director when we arrived. He was a tall, quiet man who told us the children were excited to meet Mama Kama's special friends. In fact, they'd been preparing all week.

First, we took a walk to each of the three classrooms. There were three cement buildings and two wooden shacks. The smallest classroom had huge gaps between the slats of wood that made up the walls, so they hung UN bags to keep out the cold. Seeing that tugged at my heart.

The children smiled shyly as the teachers introduced us, then asked questions so they could show us how smart they were. I was having a wonderful time, but Jamie was growing more irritable by the minute. He kept complaining about Letty's "constant need for attention." I told him he was being silly and everyone was having a great time, but he wouldn't let it go.

"This is *your* dream and *your* moment, Sage. She should take a back seat for once."

"Don't do that, babe. This isn't about me. It's about the children, and she's just excited. We all are." I could tell he didn't agree, but he let it go.

After the tour, we were led to the soccer field so we could watch the show the children had prepared. They sang, danced, read poetry, and even dedicated a rap song to Mama Kama. I was so proud I was bawling the entire time. When the show was over, we presented them with a soccer ball, and once again, the boys played a game while I took photos.

After the game, we gave the director a suitcase full of school supplies, with a few toys thrown in for the younger children. They were excited as the teachers handed out the gifts, then one of the teenage boys came over, holding a plastic ruler.

"What is this?" he asked me in awe.

"It's a ruler."

"Oh . . . it's beautiful," he said, as he turned it over. "And what does it do?"

I explained it to him, and his eyes grew as a smile spread across his face. He was holding it like it was the most amazing thing in the world, and my heart broke a little. We take so much for granted, and this child was fascinated by a cheap plastic ruler. It made me wish I'd brought so much more.

After leaving Uganda, we flew down to Cape Town to visit one of my friends, and both of us were looking forward to a hot shower and clean clothes. Camping was an exceptional experience, but our tired old bodies were in pain. We were in for a big surprise when we got there, though, because Cape Town was having a severe drought.

We were only allowed to have sixty-second showers, and toilets were only to be flushed when absolutely necessary. Since we come from a country with millions of lakes and rivers, this was a shock. The locals had been living under these conditions for almost a year, and if they didn't get rain soon, they'd be out of water in three months. I couldn't even imagine how they'd survive without water. This trip was a constant reminder of how blessed we were.

It was fun seeing Cape Town again, and seeing it with Jamie was even better. After all these years traveling by myself, it was nice having my lover and friend by my side. We walked the beaches hand in hand, listened to the street musicians down at the V&A Waterfront, drank copious amounts of wine, and had a picnic on Table Mountain. All in all, it was an exceptional vacation.

Believe it or not, after being home for only a week, it was time to leave again. We flew to Australia to board a ship to Papua New Guinea, but first, we spent a week with my friends from Uganda, who lived on the Gold Coast.

I was worried that Jamie wouldn't be civil (since he clearly didn't like them), but he promised to be nice for my sake, especially since we were their guests. So far, they had no idea how Jamie really felt about them, and I wanted to keep it that way because they're nice people, and more importantly, they're my friends.

They went out of their way to show us a wonderful time and when they found out Jamie had spent a year in Byron Bay back in the nineties, they took us there so he could see it again. He was ecstatic as we explored his old hangout, and we even went to the youth hostel where he worked back in his Hare Krishna days.

"Oh, Sage, I've walked this beach so many times thinking about you and wishing I had the courage to tell you how I felt. You were always in my thoughts, and now here we are, twenty years later, walking this same beach, and you're finally mine." He leaned down to kiss me. "It was always you, even then, and now that I have you, I'm never letting go."

"I wish I could have been here, back in those days, with you."

"You *were* here. You were with me every second of every day."

Thirty-Six

By the time we got home, we were pretty jet-lagged. In the past two months, we'd been to Uganda, South Africa, Australia, and Papua New Guinea. It was a hell of a start to the new year, and I was on such a high, even though my entire body ached. Whatever was happening with my hip, being cramped in a tiny seat on several long flights hadn't helped. I could barely walk, yet I was so happy I thought I'd burst.

Not only had we just returned from an epic adventure, but our home life was pretty amazing as well. Even Jamie was happy . . . for a minute. Within a week, he was back to complaining about work and all the injustices life had thrown at him. I'm not gonna lie, his constant whining was pissing me off. I mean, seriously. We'd just returned from Africa, where people have real problems.

What's truly amazing is that with nothing new to complain about, Jamie simply recycled old complaints. He actively looked for things to complain about, and although I reminded him how incredibly lucky we were, I soon realized he *wanted* to be miserable, because that's how he garnered attention. It was exhausting having to constantly build him up and send him on his way, only to have him return sulking and angry again.

"Babe, every day we were in Uganda, you wished your daughter could've seen how hard it was for those kids, walking ten miles in their bare feet to get water. You get pissed off when she complains, yet listen to yourself. How is this any different? We just had an epic vacation. We go camping all the time; we do road trips and wine tours; you have a woman who loves you, a beautiful home, a great job, friends. I really don't understand why you're unhappy. Can't you just choose to be happy, instead of focusing on what you don't have?"

"I can't help it. It's just how I'm wired. I think I'll go downstairs and sort my head out for a while. Do you mind?"

"No, of course not. Do what you have to do."

An hour later, I went downstairs to check on him, but he was on the phone. I smiled and asked who he was talking to.

"Can I have a little privacy?" he snapped.

"Of course. Sorry," I said, taken aback. What the heck was that all about? By the time he came upstairs, he looked really upset. "Is everything OK?" I asked, cautiously.

"Not really. That was Paul and Jackie calling from Panama. We had a huge argument."

"Really? Why?"

"They said I don't talk to them anymore now that I'm dating you."

"What? That's crazy. Did you tell them we were away?"

"Yes, but they were drunk. Anyways, I don't want to talk about it. Can we drop it?"

"Of course," I said, but that wasn't the end of it. Whatever had happened on that call, he had a hard time shaking it off, and it was odd that he didn't want to talk about it. We talked about everything. Luckily, the weather was improving now that it was spring, and we started camping on his days off. This always had a calming effect on Jamie. In fact, it was the only time he was completely relaxed. His knee stopped bouncing; his pacing subsided, and his anxiety vanished.

Our love of nature was something we had in common, and we always had a great time, but as soon as we got home, he was right back to feeling sorry for himself. It occurred to me that I always wanted the world to be a better place, while Jamie needed it to be worse so he'd have something to complain about. That's where he got his power—from the pity he received.

I no longer wanted to feed this "poor me" drama, so when he wanted to hide in his man cave instead of watching TV with me, I didn't argue. I didn't like it, but I didn't argue. Many years ago, *The Celestine Prophecy* taught me a valuable lesson about how couples (and people in general) try to steal each other's energy. Jamie definitely fell into the category of "poor me."

I was familiar with this part of him, and I accepted it, but it didn't mean I had to feed it. If he chose to act that way, it was his choice. So when he came home in a bad mood and wanted to watch the game, I figured it was best to let him self-soothe because I'd meant it when I said I wouldn't fix him. Besides, he'd come upstairs eventually, and by then he was usually in a better mood.

Only it never lasted. Over the next few weeks, his mood continued to darken, and as it did, he started looking for a fight. I didn't even realize it at first, because it was so subtle. He started moving things around, things most people would never notice, but he knew I would. I was so used to cleaning up I'd put them back without giving it a second thought, so it certainly never occurred to me that he was doing it on purpose, trying to get a rise out of me.

When that didn't work, he started moving bigger things and made sure to put them where they were totally in the way. Except this time when I put them back, he yelled at me and accused me of being a control freak like his ex. I found myself constantly on edge, not knowing what mood he'd be in when he got home, yet I still refused to engage in an argument because fighting isn't in my nature.

Eventually, he stopped helping me clean the house, and then he asked me to stop washing the dishes after dinner so I could sit with him instead. He wanted me to leave them until morning, even though he knew I hated waking up to dirty dishes, yet I did it to keep the peace. Women do that, don't we? We've been trained from a young age to make excuses for other people's bad behavior, especially men.

When none of these tactics worked, Jamie started criticizing me, and his favorite topic was my hip. I was already horrified by the amount of weight I'd gained, the constant pain I was in, and the mobility I'd lost, but now on top of everything else, I felt guilty for how it was affecting Jamie. He made a point of reminding me that after Paige's back surgery, she'd stopped hiking, camping, and road tripping, and how much he resented her for that.

"I didn't sign up for this, Sage," he reminded me with every appointment. It felt like no matter what I did, I'd always be compared to Paige.

More and more, Jamie spent time downstairs getting drunk, and the darker his mood got, the more I shrank. I was so afraid of doing something to set him off or making him mad that I walked on eggshells for weeks. Everything infuriated him, and I constantly found myself apologizing.

"I can make my own lunch, Sage! Stop fussing all the time," he'd say, even though I'd been making him lunches for a year and a half and he used to love it.

"Sorry."

"Can't you walk any faster? It's ridiculous that your hip isn't better yet. All I do is drive you to appointments."

"Sorry."

"We need to buy groceries *again?* When are you going to learn how to drive?"

"Sorry."

I don't know how many weeks this went on, but at some point, I was tired of hearing myself apologize, and apparently so was Jamie, because the next time I apologized, he flipped out. "Oh, for Christ's sake! Stop apologizing already! I'm sick of hearing it!"

And *that* snapped me out of it. "Jamie, what the fuck is going on with you? I've been walking on eggshells for weeks, and I can't stand it anymore. You're tired of hearing me apologize? How do you think I feel? I realize you're having an existential crisis, but it's not my fault, and I'm tired of you taking it out on me!"

"Oh my God. You're right. You haven't done anything wrong. I'm just on edge lately."

"Babe, I'm really starting to worry about you. You're drinking all the time—"

"Yeah, well you smoke pot, so how is that any different?"

"Yes, I smoke pot, but I don't smoke it before I go to work. I do it after, in order to relax. You're putting away a six pack before your afternoon shift, and I'm worried you're going to get fired or, worse, hurt. I know you've been doing it for years, but that's the problem. You're getting careless because you've gotten away with it for so long. Lately, you've been falling asleep on your day shifts. You even slept through an alarm!"

"Yeah, that was bad. The guys weren't impressed. I'm lucky they covered for me."

"I'm only saying this because I love you. You need to take better care of yourself."

"You're right. I will. I promise."

But things didn't get better. They got worse, so by the time I started my first tour, I was happy with the distraction, and figured a little time apart might be good for us. Even so, I missed him like crazy while I was gone, especially when he told me he wouldn't be joining me at any of my hotels that summer, something we'd really enjoyed the previous year.

We promised to talk every night, but two days into my first tour, a tragedy happened. The fire chief's daughter was killed by a drunk driver, and the entire department was shaken. Jamie took it especially hard because he imagined how he'd feel if it had been *his* daughter, and once that thought got a hold of him, he couldn't let it go. Without me there to stop it, he spiraled into a deep dark hole.

I called every night, but he never answered. He'd text me during the day, but he never wanted to talk on the phone. His texts were alarming, and at one point, I worried he was suicidal, but there was nothing I could do from so far away. He spent all his time in his man cave, drinking, smoking, obsessing over his ex, and creating homemade weapons.

He was so drunk that he became careless with his tools and hurt himself more than once. He sent me a photo of a massive cut on his leg and a huge gouge in his hand. Both of them needed stitches, and I begged him to see a doctor, but he only laughed and said he was fine. I was wracked with guilt for not being there when he needed me, and worried sick that he'd do something even more reckless, even though I knew it wasn't my job to fix him.

Thirty-Seven

I felt it as soon as I walked in the door. A strange darkness penetrated the air, immediately putting me on edge. Jamie clearly hadn't cleaned the house while I was gone, and although I was horrified by what I saw, I didn't let it show. I didn't want to set him off. Evidence of what had transpired over the past month was all over the place. It was even worse than I'd anticipated.

The basement was utter chaos. The ashtray was overflowing, empty beer bottles littered the floor, and an assortment of homemade weapons stood in the corner. Alarm bells rang in my head, yet I remained calm because I sensed he was waiting for me to say something.

I wasn't the only one on edge. I could feel his anxiety from across the room. In fact, he hadn't stopped sweating since picking me up from the airport, a clear sign he was in distress. Upstairs was littered with fast food containers, but what really grossed me out was the fridge. It was so dirty I wasn't even sure it was sanitary, and the only things in the crisper were rotting vegetables.

My heart sank as I realized how serious this was. I'd known it would be bad when I got home, but this was shocking. Jamie was in crisis, and it was up to me to pull him out before he self-destructed. I loved him so much, and it tore at my heart to see him this way. His PTSD was in overdrive and had been for a month.

I waited until he was at work before I started cleaning, although I never touched the basement because that was his space, and I respected his privacy. None of that mattered though, because the second he walked in the door, he was angry. He said that by cleaning up, I was insinuating that he *wasn't* clean. I tried reasoning with him, but it's hard to have a logical conversation with someone who isn't rational. The loving and caring man I'd fallen in love with had somehow disappeared and in his place was a stranger.

I was extremely concerned, but instead of letting me in, he pushed me away. When I asked if he'd remembered to take his pills, he lashed out, saying he hadn't taken them in a month and never planned to take them again, and that was the end of that. The alarm bells got louder.

He immediately started criticizing me, but I wasn't about to be bullied again, so instead of apologizing, I pushed back. We had a fight, and then we didn't speak to each other for four days. I was waiting for him to apologize for the awful things he'd said, but he didn't. Instead, he acted like a petulant child.

After work, he'd immediately go downstairs, refusing to eat dinner until I went to bed. Then, in a drunken stupor, he'd come upstairs, eat the leftovers, and sift through the cupboards before passing out on the couch. I was seriously distraught over the situation, especially since we were headed to Alaska in a few days.

I'd taken time off work and had planned the trip entirely for him, because he'd never been to Alaska and was dying to see it. My friends were putting us up, and I'd arranged a week of exceptional activities all for him. After all, I'd been to Alaska a million times back when I worked on ships.

We still weren't talking even as we boarded the plane. We didn't talk the entire flight, but thirty minutes before landing, I decided enough was enough.

"Jamie, we have to sort this out before we land. We can't do this in front of my friends."

"I know. You're right."

"I don't understand what's going on. You don't talk to me; you're always angry, always on edge. I was gone for a month and missed you like crazy, but I get the distinct feeling you didn't miss me at all."

"I know. I've done a lot of thinking lately, and I've decided that the only thing that matters is getting my daughter back."

"OK . . ." *Where was this going?* I wondered.

"After you told me to kick her out . . ."

"Hold on. I did NOT tell you to kick her out. In fact, I'm the only person who stayed out of it. If anything, I'm the one who thought it was a bad idea."

"Really? I thought it was you who suggested it. Anyways, it doesn't matter. I need her in my life, Sage, and there's no way she'll come back as long as you're living with me." Boom.

"What are you saying? Are you . . . breaking up with me?" I whispered in horror.

"Well . . . I . . . yes," he said nervously.

"Oh my God. You're breaking up with me, and you're doing it on a plane? How could you? We're about to land, and you thought *now* was the time to do this?"

"I tried telling you yesterday, but you were angry and didn't want to talk."

"You should have tried harder," I hissed, "knowing you had a bomb to drop."

He reached for my hand, but I pulled away. I was in shock. I knew we were having problems, but I hadn't seen this coming. "I can't do this right now. Not here . . ."

I ran to the bathroom and shut the door. I cried for thirty seconds, and then the captain announced that we were landing, so I had no choice but to return to my seat. I couldn't even look at Jamie because I knew I'd lose it, and the last thing I wanted was a public meltdown.

When we finally landed, I bolted. I raced through the terminal like a madwoman, and when I saw my friend, I threw my arms around her, whispering urgently in her ear. I knew Jamie was behind me and that I only had a few seconds to convey what was happening.

"Jamie broke up with me ten minutes ago, and I'm about to lose it. Please help."

I pulled away just as he came up behind me. My friend looked at me long enough to convey that she understood, and then she turned to Jamie without skipping a beat.

"Hi! You must be Jamie. It's nice to finally meet you."

For the next few hours, I tried to keep it together as we ate dinner, but I was a lot quieter than usual and it didn't go unnoticed by Scott, who had no idea what was going on. He kept asking if I was all right and wanted to know all about our trips, but I didn't feel like talking about the good times.

Jamie kept trying to catch my eye, but I still couldn't look at him, or I'd start crying again. The stress of holding my feelings at bay and pretending to smile was so overwhelming that by the time we were finally alone, all I could do was collapse on the bed and cry.

Not sure what to do, Jamie sat in a chair on the opposite end of the room. For the next ten hours, I sobbed my heart out while he sat in the chair and watched. I could feel his anxiety from across the room, but I didn't have the energy to worry about him when my heart was literally breaking in two.

Not in a million years had I seen this coming, despite the fact that we'd been so disconnected lately. I'd figured it was just a phase and he'd get over it. In the morning, we sat down and decided it was best we went home. We couldn't stay with my friends under the circumstances, so I moved our flights to the following day, and then we walked up to the house to let them know, except they weren't home.

They left us a note saying we probably needed our privacy and to help ourselves to whatever we wanted. They also left car keys in case we wanted to go out. Both of them had been through nasty divorces, so they understood the situation. I was grateful for that, even though having my private life play out in front of them was humiliating.

After lunch, we took a drive to clear our heads and that's when I learned what was really going on. Jamie confessed that it had all started when Paul and Jackie called from Panama a few months ago. What they'd really said was that they hated me and thought he should break up with me at once. I was floored by this revelation, not to mention pissed off.

"I don't understand. I thought they gave me their stamp of approval. Why did they change their minds four months later?"

"I don't know. I thought it was weird, too. They said that, upon reflection you were exactly like Paige, so I told them to fuck off."

Now that I had this new piece of information, everything made perfect sense. The way he'd snapped at me when I'd asked who he was talking to, the way his mood had suddenly changed, the constant criticism that had followed. It didn't matter that he'd defended me on the phone—the seed had been planted and took root, growing stronger every day until he actually believed it.

Moving things around, trying to get a rise out of me—Jamie's fractured mind played tricks on him, and I knew there were times when he couldn't tell the difference between me and Paige. Then the chief lost his daughter, he stopped taking his medication, stopped eating healthy foods, and started drinking even more heavily. Needing someone to blame, he convinced himself that I was responsible for his daughter moving out. Jamie had always had a hard time owning his own shit.

"Oh, God. What have I done?" he suddenly said, obviously connecting the dots as well. "I don't want to break up with you, Sage. I panicked on the plane when you asked if that's what I wanted, but I don't. Oh, Sage . . . my sweet Sage . . . please forgive me. I can't even imagine my life without you. You're the only thing that makes sense to me."

I'm not a fan of games, and I certainly wasn't enjoying the roller coaster of emotions he was putting me through, but I loved Jamie, and it made me sick to see how much he was hurting. I knew his mind played tricks on him, so I decided to give him another chance.

"Of course I forgive you, but let me be very clear about something. Don't mistake my kindness for weakness. You get to break up with me exactly one time. The next time, it's for real because my heart can't take any more of this."

"Oh God, Sage. Thank you. Sometimes, I feel like I don't deserve you."

"While we're on the subject, we need to lay down some ground rules for when I'm away, or we won't survive. You can't keep ignoring my calls, and you can't shut me out! Talking about what's going on inside your head is the only way to fight the darkness. You know that. It's impossible for me to do my job if I have to worry about you all the time, and it's not fair. We're supposed to be a team."

"You're right. I was just in a bad place. To be honest, I scared myself with the places my mind went. It was really dark, Sage," he said quietly, and I could see the fear in his eyes.

"I know it was. I could feel it. Maybe if you went back on the pills . . ."

"No! I already told you. I don't need those anymore."

Thirty-Eight

Now that we weren't breaking up, it sucked that we'd already changed our flights, but what was done was done. That afternoon, we flew home, and since we still had a week off, we went camping in our favorite spot, except it wasn't exactly the zen experience it usually was. Jamie drank so much he almost fell into the fire (twice), and he was so restless he chopped wood all day while shouting "I love my life" at the top of his lungs.

He loved chopping wood, so this was nothing new, but there was something manic about his "good mood" that made me nervous, because I knew it wasn't real. Something was *very* wrong, and now that he was off his meds, he couldn't hide it.

Over the next few weeks we got along quite well, although he still spent a lot of time in the basement and he never wanted to cuddle anymore. He claimed he was too hot and he *was* sweating a lot, but I knew that wasn't the real reason. The more he pulled away, the more I tried to hold on, while still giving him space. The juggling act was doing my head in, but I stayed calm, cool, and collected the entire time in order to keep the peace.

When I left for my second tour, we texted each other every day, but he was always busy when I wanted to talk on the phone. Then at the last moment he decided to come see me at the Hotel Vancouver, and I was super excited, except he was so wasted I had to rush him upstairs before any of my guests could see him. I wasn't sure what pissed me off more: the fact that he was driving drunk (something he was doing more and more often) or that he dared to show up that hammered. Imagine if I'd done that to him at his job.

Not wanting to ruin the mood, I swallowed my anger until he was sober, then I gently explained how foolish he was for risking his life and my job. His selfishness was off the charts, and I was losing my patience. After that visit, he stopped texting me altogether, but this time I didn't fight it. I needed to think.

Thankfully, work gave me something to focus on during the day, but in the evenings, my mind wandered. Something was nagging me, but I couldn't put my finger on it. The past few months played over in my mind as I struggled to make sense of what my subconscious was trying to tell me.

Jamie's erratic behavior reminded me so much of Christian that one night I sat down to make a list of all the things that were bothering me. I felt guilty for making such a list, but I figured if I wrote it down I'd be able to get a clearer picture of the situation, because one thing was for sure: we couldn't carry on this way. I closed my eyes, took a deep breath, and started writing.

Childish, petty, petulant, moody, hot-headed, stubborn, immature. He was even like that back in college. I thought about the terrible things he'd said to me. Things that no one should ever say to someone they love, even when they're mad. Especially when they're mad.

Aims to hurt when he's angry, no forgiveness, it's never his fault, quick to blame. That made me think of all the terrible things he'd said about his ex-wife and child. Things that were very inconsistent, and stories that changed depending on his angle. *Rewrites the past to suit him, and then believes it.*

I thought about our camping trip and all the weapons in the garage. *Manic, hyper, starts a thousand projects but never finishes them.* I sat back and looked at my list. It didn't paint a pretty picture. *Alcoholic, selfish, poor me, suicidal, mood swings.* I remembered him when he was at his worst (which was lately), and if I'm being honest, twenty years ago. *Constant criticism, often cruel, mean, bouts of rage.* Never-ending rage about the ex, the boss, the kid, Asian drivers, women drivers, women in the fire department, the #Metoo movement, traffic—you get the picture. *A little bit racist at times, misogynistic.*

I sat back, and it felt like someone had punched me in the gut. Life gets real when you make a list. It's why I didn't want to do it in the first place. All this time, I'd thought it was Christian Jamie reminded of, but in reality, it was my mother.

It was so blatantly obvious I couldn't believe I hadn't seen it before. No wonder he'd changed so much when he stopped taking his pills. Jamie was bipolar. Suddenly it all made sense, and just like that, my entire world came crashing down. I knew I couldn't stay with him now that I knew the truth, because this was one problem that wouldn't go away.

My mind reeled from the deception. Not Jamie's, because I was pretty sure he had no idea, but the Universe. What kind of cruel joke was the Universe playing on me? After all those years of loneliness, it had finally brought me the greatest love of my life, and just when I let down my walls and believed I was getting my stupid, fucking, happily ever after . . . *this* happened.

I felt my pain so deeply, it reached right into my soul and kicked my inner child in the face. The familiarity. The deception. The knowledge that I'd have to walk away. And then, I broke under the weight of it and cried all night. My chest filled with unbearable pain as I was wracked with sobs. At first, I yelled at the Universe for deceiving me yet again, and then I turned inward, and asked myself why I kept repeating this pattern.

I was nervous as hell heading home because I had no idea what I was going to do. I knew this was a deal breaker, but I also knew how much I loved Jamie. Part of me hoped he'd go back on his medication, but if there's one thing I've learned, it's that people always stop taking their medication when they "feel better."

I wasn't even home for twelve hours when he started in on me. He attacked me for doing the dishes while his uncle was over, because once again I'd come home to a dirty house. We were drinking coffee in the kitchen while I washed the dishes, but he demanded I stop, and when his uncle joked that all women clean while they chat, he told me I was selfish for not honoring his wishes.

After his uncle left, we had a huge fight. "How come you never do what *I* want? What about *me*? Why isn't it ever about *me*?" he yelled, as he slammed his fist on the counter, then he went to his man cave and ignored me for the rest of the day. By the time I went to bed, we still hadn't made up, and I tossed and turned all night. In the morning, he came into the room to get his clothes and saw that I was awake.

"Good morning," he said sheepishly.

"Good morning."

"Listen, about yesterday. I'm sorry. I shouldn't have lost my temper like that. You're only here for two weeks, and I don't want to fight."

"I don't want to fight, either."

He smiled, but it was sad, and he could barely look at me. He turned to leave, but I stopped him. We needed to talk about what was going on.

"Jamie?"

"Yes?"

I hesitated because once the words were out of my mouth I knew I couldn't take them back. "You don't want me to live here anymore, do you?"

His face crumpled, but this time he looked me in the eye. "No. I really don't."

I nodded as tears filled my eyes. This was really happening, and I could hardly contain my grief. "Ok. I'll um . . . try to find an apartment, but I don't know how I'm supposed to do that while I'm still on the road."

"Don't worry about that right now. We've been friends for twenty-five years, and I don't want to lose that, so let's keep this civil, OK? Take all the time you need. There's no rush. I realize I just completely blew up your life." *Understatement.*

"My last trip ends in October, so I won't be able to look for an apartment until then, if that's OK?" It was only August, and I still had several more tours to lead.

"Of course it is. I'm sorry, Sage. None of this is your fault, and you don't deserve this. You're such a good person, and it's not that I don't love you. I just need to be alone right now. I'm really fucked up, and I don't know what's happening to me."

"Jamie, I'm worried about you."

"I know you are, and quite frankly, I'm worried about myself. Sometimes I feel so angry I can't control it, and other times I'm so depressed I just want to end it. I think there's something wrong with me, but I don't know what." Once again, he turned to leave.

"Jamie?" I said cautiously.

"Yeah?"

"I . . . ummm . . . I think I might know what's wrong with you, but I don't want you to get mad. Please know I say this as your friend. I've been doing a lot of thinking lately, and I think you might be bipolar." I held my breath as I waited for him to explode, but he didn't. In fact, he did the opposite.

"I think you might be right," he said, sadly. "I've often wondered that myself."

"You have? Oh, Jamie, it explains so much. The depression, the mood swings, the criticizing . . ."

"Yeah. She used to say the same thing. She put up with it as long as she could."

What??? "Wait. This isn't the first time you're hearing this?" I asked, dumbfounded. He shook his head, and then I understood. "Paige thought you were bipolar, too."

He nodded, and suddenly more puzzle pieces fell into place. No wonder he was always adamant that I never meet her. All those terrible things he'd said about her—they really applied to him. He'd twisted the story to suit his own narrative, just like my mother did. I kicked myself again, wondering how I could be so blind. If I was being totally honest, the signs were there right from the beginning, but I was too busy making excuses for him to see it for what it really was. Bad behavior.

"Oh, Jamie. I'm so sorry. The good news is they have medications that can help you. You don't have to do this alone."

"You're right. I think I'll call my doctor and make an appointment."

"That's a good idea. I'm really proud of you."

"Thanks. I'm heading downstairs now. I think I need to be by myself for a while."

And that was it. That's how we broke up. A five-minute conversation between friends. I stayed upstairs most of the day, trying to sort through my emotions, but I was pretty numb. In the late afternoon, I went downstairs to make sure he was all right, but by then he was well into a case of beer and apocalyptic zombies.

"I'm making dinner. Would you like some?" I asked over the noise of the television.

"I don't want dinner. In fact, I don't want *anything* from you. After you said that terrible thing about me, you can go fuck yourself for all I care!"

"Seriously? You just broke up with me, but I'm the bad guy?"

"You know what? I think *you're* the one who's bipolar. Yeah, that was going on. You're the one who's bipolar. This is all your fault!"

"Jamie," I said, but he wasn't listening. His eyes were wild, and I could tell he'd been concocting this story for a while.

"Your mother's bipolar. Clearly, it runs in your family. How do you know you don't have it?" He jammed his finger into my chest.

I sighed. It ran in his family, too, and we'd always talked about it, but I kept that to myself. "Because I'm fairly certain that if I did, my sisters would have mentioned it by now. If it makes you feel better, we can go to the doctor together, and I'll get tested, too. If I'm bipolar, I'd like to know."

Oh man, he didn't like that at all. His face turned scarlet, and before I knew it, he was standing right in front of me, all six foot two of him. He towered over me in a threatening manner as he continued to glare at me, and then he stuck his finger in my face. I let out a gasp, but he was in such a rage he didn't even notice.

"Fuck you!" he shouted. "You want to know what Paul and Jackie *really* said about you when they called? They said you were bipolar. Exactly like Paige. I was so mad I actually defended you, but now I see they're right. YOU'RE the problem here! Not me."

I didn't flinch, nor did I break eye contact, but on the inside, I was filled with fear. Staring back at me were the exact same demons I'd seen in my mother's eyes all those years ago. The day she'd watched my father beat me. It was the face of pure evil.

I was so shocked by the familiarity of it that I froze for a second, and then I got angry. I narrowed my eyes and lowered my voice to a deadly calm, just like I had all those years ago when I told my father he'd never break me.

"First of all, thank you for proving my point. Second, you need to back the fuck off. *Right. This. Second.*"

He didn't move. He continued glaring at me instead.

"Jamie, you're scaring me." It was the exact same thing his daughter had said last year, when he'd lost his temper on her birthday.

The corner of his mouth flickered into a triumphant smile, and then he let out a snort of disgust as he turned away. "My wife, my kid, *you* . . . fucking women are all the same." But I was already heading for the door. I needed to get out of there before he hurt me. Whatever was standing there in the basement, it wasn't Jamie.

THIRTY-NINE

I'd always wondered if blocking out my childhood would bite me in the ass one day, and now I had my answer. Over the next four months, I was forced to re-live my childhood trauma as Jamie continued to find new and creative ways of punishing me for my "sins." Now that I was the enemy, he no longer felt guilty for his actions because in his mind, I deserved it. So he dropped all pretense of civility until he became the ugly monster from my nightmares.

Most of the time, he completely ignored me, which was its own kind of torture, but every once in a while, he'd come upstairs long enough to grab a six pack and fire off a couple of insults. His rejection, paired with his look of disdain, were so familiar that sometimes it felt like I was putting on an old coat. After all, we'd played this game before, him and I, twenty years ago when he came back from Australia and treated me like shit for two years before telling me to fuck off.

What a sanctimonious ass he'd been in those days. I'd always chalked it up to jealousy, but now I knew the truth. His bipolar was showing even back then. How could I have been so stupid? How could I have been so blind? I was angry at him for so expertly luring me into his game and angry at myself for letting him do it. Fool me once, shame on you. Fool me twice . . .

The similarities between him and my mother became so obvious I was haunted day and night by memories I'd forgotten, yet now I couldn't escape. I'd never liked Jamie's house because it was cold and dark, and I hated it even more now that it was my prison. The energy inside those walls was so toxic I could barely breathe. Perhaps it was my broken heart or the enormous weight of my grief, but I swear it felt like something was sitting on my chest, weighing me down even further, and sometimes, it even felt like it was choking me.

I still had to lead two tours before the season ended, so luckily I was away for weeks at a time those first two months, but every time I came back, he got worse. He made it clear I wasn't welcome and constantly nagged at me to move out, but I didn't have time to look for an apartment when I wasn't even in town. When I *was* home, I wanted nothing more than to run away, but I had nowhere to go.

For miles and miles, there was nothing but busy roads and construction sites. There weren't any parks or green spaces of any kind, so I couldn't even take a walk. By moving me to Langley, Jamie had successfully cut me off from the rest of the world, just like Christian had done all those years before. Isolation and separation—the first rule in every narcissist's handbook. How I longed for my freedom, and how my soul ached to connect with nature.

It took every ounce of my strength to protect myself from Jamie's hatred, so I shut down my emotions, not allowing myself to cry because I was afraid that once I started, I wouldn't stop. I didn't have any friends to talk to, so my only comfort came from his two gorgeous cats, who never left my side. Cats are clever that way. They always know when we're hurting.

After months of dealing with the Rage Monster, Jamie came to pick me up after my last tour, and he was in a great mood. He hugged me for the first time in ages and even asked how my trip went, but this only made me nervous because I knew it wasn't real. My mother used to play these "I'm going to be nice to you for a minute" games, too, right before she attacked.

I couldn't understand what had brought on this sudden change in mood, but I found out later, it was because he'd met someone new. In fact, he'd met her long before we'd even broken up, and there there were probably others before her. I knew his ex-wife had accused him of cheating, and he always denied it, but he used to do the same thing back when we were in college. Once a cheater, always a cheater. I had said it back then, and I should have followed my own advice.

After my last tour, he started going out all the time and told me he was no longer available to drive me anywhere. I walked for miles to get to my appointments, limping the entire way. He barely looked at me for months, but now every once in a while, just before leaving the house, he'd come upstairs and get this sad look on his face. Out of nowhere, he'd grab me, pull me into his arms and say, "Oh, Sage. I'm so sorry."

I was so surprised by these sudden "acts of kindness" that I didn't know what to do. I'd freeze in terror, my body stiff and my arms hanging limply by my side as he locked me in a bear hug. Was this a joke? Was he toying with me in his sick, sadistic way, or was this genuine regret? Was my old friend making an appearance for a minute, or was this another ploy meant to knock me off balance? I didn't want to hug him, and I didn't want him "comforting" me either, but he wouldn't let go.

He'd stand there waiting until my rigid body finally relaxed and slowly my arms would come up to hug him. As soon as I did that, he'd kiss the top of my head, mutter some regret, and the moment was over. If I dared to say anything he'd snap, and the Rage Monster would be back in a flash. After all, the hugs had nothing to do with me, they were just his guilt and self-pity coming to the surface for a minute.

I couldn't let my guard down for even a second, even though it was exhausting holding it up all the time. Those hugs shattered my spirit because I was so desperate for human contact, yet the only person I was getting it from was my tormentor. It was Christian all over again.

As Jamie continued to play this new game, I wasn't sure what was worse: his pity or his rage. His torture was slow and drawn out, but it was also familiar, like that old coat. My mother loved her mind games, too. My past and my present—I couldn't separate them.

Once I moved out, things got better, but it took a minute. My heartache lasted a long time because I loved Jamie, and even though I didn't want him back, it didn't make it any less painful. Besides, he wasn't done hurting me just yet. He still had a few tricks up his sleeve, and it seemed like the Universe wasn't finished with me, either.

An old friend invited me to the Bahamas over Christmas so I could heal, but the trip was an absolute nightmare once I realized that she, too, had issues. She and her friend ganged up on me like cruel teenagers, treating me like shit the entire time, and all I could think was, "*OK, Universe, I get it already. I attract people with mental illness. But why?*

I was so emotionally and mentally exhausted, it felt like the life had been sucked out of me. Honestly, if the Universe wasn't trying to tell me something, I didn't know what was going on. I was like a magnet for energy-sucking vampires lately. So I swam in the ocean every day, talked to the moon, and raged against the Universe to please give me some answers. Yes, I'm Canadian. I can rage and say please at the same time.

When we ask these questions, we usually get answers. In fact, it's exactly this type of soul-searching question that brings on a spiritual awakening, whether we're ready for one or not, and mine was about to smash into me like a battering ram.

While I was in the Bahamas, I saw a picture of Jamie with a woman, posted only four days after I moved out. Seeing that photo really hurt. Was there no end to his cruelty? It's the people we trust the most who end up betraying us in the end. When you're falling in love, you can't imagine that person ever hurting you, and then one day, you can't remember a time when they didn't.

When I didn't comment on the photo, Jamie sent me a cryptic text instead. "Also . . . I don't think we should talk on FB anymore, so I removed you as a friend."

I hadn't heard from him in weeks, so I had no idea what he was talking about.

"I'm sorry. Was that text meant for me? We don't talk on FB."

"Yes, my new girlfriend likes to post pictures, and I'm trying to spare you from seeing them." Bam! He really liked to drop bombs on me. I mean, seriously . . . who does that? He obviously wanted to draw my attention to the photo so he could rub it in my face. When I called him out on it, he accused me of reading into things and told me it was "time to move on already." This from the man who cried over his wife for three years after their divorce.

I'd booked a trip to India while I was still at Jamie's (which made him jealous), so I knew texting me right before I left was another dig, and it worked. I was horrified that he'd replaced me so easily, and now he was rubbing it in my face, only he didn't stop there. His sister let me know she was blocking me on FB because Jamie told her too. In fact, he made his whole family block me. It wasn't enough that he broke my heart, kicked me out of his house, and treated me like shit for six months. For some reason, he still felt the need to punish me.

He erased me from his life and made sure his family did, too. I knew the real reason for doing that was that he didn't want his dirty little secret to get out. It was the same reason he'd never let his ex talk to me. She and I were the only people who knew he was bipolar, so he had to destroy us. I couldn't even imagine what he was saying about me to his family, and it hurt, because I loved his family. Not only did I lose my lover and my friend, I lost my entire tribe when he cast me out.

The good news is that I ended up having a wonderful time in India. The tour group was full of funny, easy-going people, exactly what I needed at that moment. There were two other single girls, and the three of us became friends. In fact, they were instrumental in my healing process because they let me talk about my heartbreak whenever I needed to (which was a lot) and offered me great advice in return.

We spent two weeks in northern India and two weeks in the south, and by the time I got home, I was a new person. I was still grieving and would be for a while, but I was in a much better head space. So it was time to turn my attention inward and find those answers I was so desperately seeking.

FORTY

Bali—January 2020

When I landed in Bali, my heart instantly expanded with joy. It was good to be back. I'd been here several times while working on ships, and the island was dear to my heart. The hotel was approximately forty-five mins north of Ubud, and by the time I got there, it was already dark. The staff greeted me with a refreshing glass of cold tea made from ginger, honey, and lemongrass. It was delicious, and exactly what I needed.

The hotel lobby had an open-air concept, with a beautiful view of the gardens which were currently dancing with butterflies. As the bellman escorted me to my room, I could see how spectacular the property was. It was built on the side of a mountain with narrow, winding streets that circled down to the creek.

When I got to my room, I knew I was in for a treat. It was magnificent. The ceiling had a thatched roof that must have been fifteen feet high, and in the center was a king-sized bed surrounded by sheer white curtains. In front were huge glass doors that led to a private balcony.

When I stepped outside, every bird, cricket, monkey, and housefly said hello, and I could hear water from a stream down below, although I couldn't see it through the dense foliage. I took a deep breath, closed my eyes, and welcomed the wonderful sounds. This jungle symphony was music to my ears, and I would have liked nothing more than to keep my windows open all night, except there weren't any screens, and I wasn't crazy about sharing my room with the bugs.

After a restless sleep, I got out of bed and walked over to the yoga studio for our first class. I confess I was a little nervous that a trip like this might attract a lot of skinny-poser-yoga types, but I had nothing to worry about. There were fifteen people in our group, and as I looked around I saw various shapes, sizes, and ages. Perfect.

I've always been athletic, but after three years with a busted hip, I had not only gained a ton of weight, but my muscles had atrophied from the lack of exercise. Although I'd been busting my ass at physiotherapy, the progress was slow, and I still struggled. It's part of the reason I chose this trip in the first place. Getting my strength back was important, as was losing the weight I'd gained.

Everyone seemed nice, and the yoga studio was exceptional. It had a thirty-foot ceiling with massive windows that were wide open, filling the room with fresh air and the sounds of the jungle. The sun danced on the hardwood floors, yet the temperature was still cool at this hour.

After yoga, everyone went to breakfast, where our guide asked us to introduce ourselves and express why we chose this particular trip. What's fascinating is that almost every person had a similar story to mine. They'd had a rough year; their lives were turned upside down, and they were here for some physical and spiritual pampering. I think in some way, all of us were going through major transitions. It felt like kismet.

Today was all about seeing the spiritual side of Bali, so after breakfast, we gathered near the temple and learned how to make offerings called *canang sari*. You can see these offerings all over Bali since the locals say their prayers at least three times a day.

When we finished our ceremony, we piled into two vans and headed to Ubud. Tirta Empul is a temple that was built in 962. It's a sacred place for the Balinese, and people come from all over the island to bathe in the healing waters. I had really been looking forward to this ritual, but when we got there the place was crawling with tourists. It wasn't exactly the peaceful experience I was hoping for, but I made the most of it.

The following day was pretty relaxing. Once again, we had an early morning yoga class, but with a different instructor. I loved starting my day with yoga and was already making plans to bring this practice home with me. After breakfast, we had a cooking class, and then we spent the afternoon by the pool, where I got to know my traveling companions.

That evening, we reconvened for a guided meditation. This was another first for me, and I was looking forward to it. During the meditation, I laid on the floor with my eyes closed while listening to the sounds of the jungle, and it was really amazing. Afterward, I felt totally at peace, and I decided this was another practice I wanted to take home with me.

The next day, we headed to Tabanan to meet a local healer. This was one of the reasons I'd booked this trip in the first place. So far, my doctors hadn't been much help with my hip, so I wanted to try a more holistic approach. I couldn't wait to see what the healer could do.

When we got there, we had a tour of the grounds, and then we gathered under a thatched roof while the priest gave the blessing. He was dressed all in white and had a very calm demeanor. After the ritual he made his way to several people, placed his hands on them, and chanted something under his breath. When he got to Savanna (another Canadian), I noticed tears streaming down her face. He was obviously tapping into something powerful, and I hoped she was getting what she came for. She was just as excited as I was to meet the healer.

When he finished with her, he made his way to several others but completely passed me by. I was surprised but waited patiently, thinking he'd circle back. After a few minutes, he turned to the guide and said something in Balinese. She told us the session was over unless anyone else needed him. My hand shot through the air like lightning.

He came over, asked what the problem was, and the guide explained it to him. He nodded, then put his hand on my lower back for about twenty seconds before removing it.

"Her lower back is blocked, but I can't fix her hip. She needs surgery."

I couldn't believe what I was hearing. The healer couldn't heal me? I was incredibly disappointed, and I fought to control the tears that gathered in my eyes. My emotions must have shown because the healer's expression suddenly softened as he moved towards me without saying a word. Once again, he put his hand on my lower back and closed his eyes. I could feel the heat coming from them as he prayed. He removed his hand and pointed to the floor.

"Can you lay down on your stomach?" he asked, and the guide interpreted. "May I touch you?" he asked once I was face down on the floor.

"Yes, of course."

And then he did something unexpected. He took his finger and poked me right in the tailbone. I don't think anyone had ever done that to me before. It was a strange sensation, to say the least. Once he found the bottom of my spine, he pushed it upwards and held it there.

"Does it hurt?" he asked.

"Yes, a little. But it's also relieving some of the pressure."

"Good." He held it for a minute, and then he spoke to the guide, who spoke to me.

"Do that every morning, and it will help, but it still needs surgery."

I thanked him for his time, but I was still disappointed. As he closed the session with chanting and prayers, tears streamed down my face. I didn't know where this flood of emotion was coming from, but try as I might, I couldn't stop it.

Everyone sat down for lunch, but I couldn't stop crying, and by this point I was pretty embarrassed. As everyone talked animatedly, I kept my face glued to my plate. I didn't know why this was hitting me so hard, but it felt like my last hope had been dashed, and I couldn't shake the feeling of despair that was washing over me.

After three years of stress, I guess I'd reached some kind of breaking point, but did it have to be in public? As I was telling myself to get it together, I suddenly felt a hand on top of mine. I looked up to see one of the ladies smiling at me.

"Are you OK?" she asked in a gentle voice.

"No. I'm really not," I said, embarrassed.

"Do you need a minute alone?" she asked, sympathetically.

"Yes, I do," I said as I got up to leave. I walked over to the garden and told myself to get it together. I was on vacation, for heaven's sake. Why was I crying like this?

After lunch, we drove to the Jatiluwih Rice Terraces, and by the time we got there, I was feeling much better. I was sitting beside a nice lady from Ireland, and we chatted the entire time. As we weaved our way through the lush mountains on our way to Pemuteran, the Irish lady and I continued talking until we reached the lake and everyone got out to stretch their legs. A couple of the girls came over to see if I was feeling better.

"What happened back there with the healer?" asked Savanna, the girl from Toronto.

As I told her what had happened, a tear rolled down my cheek. The girls looked at me with concern, and I started laughing as I wiped my tears away. "I swear I haven't been crying this whole time! I don't know why I'm so emotional today."

"Wait a second. The healer said he couldn't fix it? That doesn't sound right," said Savanna. "Why don't you let me look at it?"

"What do you mean?"

"I'm a reiki healer. I bet I can fix it," she said confidently. "I'll look at it when we get to Pemuteran and see what's going on."

"You do reiki? I've wanted to try that for a long time, but I can't seem to find a good reference."

"Perfect! Then it's meant to be," she said, smiling.

I smiled, too, but then I shook my head. "As much as I'd love that, I'm not letting you work while you're on vacation."

"No, really. I'd love to. I'm still new, and there's so much to learn, so I'm really interested in hearing your feedback. Plus I'd really like to prove that guy wrong." she said, giggling. Savanna was quiet, but she had a wicked side that

I really enjoyed. I was still hesitant because I know how much doctors suffer on trips once people find out they're doctors. They never get a minute's peace, and I didn't want to be that person.

"Seriously," she prodded, as if reading my mind. "You'd be doing me a huge favor."

"Well . . ." I said dramatically, "since you put it THAT way . . ." Everyone laughed.

"Yay!" said the other girls. "I've always heard about reiki, but I've never tried it."

"Me neither. You can be the guinea pig, Sage. You'll have to give us a full report when it's over."

FORTY-ONE

The next morning, several of us got up early so we could watch the sunrise before yoga. The class was a lot harder than the previous ones, and I found myself struggling to keep up. As usual, we were starving when it was over and looking forward to breakfast. I saw several girls sitting at a table, so I joined them. One of them was talking about being a healer, but she was just starting to come into her powers.

"I recently saw a channeler who told me I'm a teacher," I said as I sat down.

"Really? What did she have to say?"

I told them about Mother Earth clearing our karma back in 2012 and how it was up to us to heal our patterns and move on so we don't start a new cycle with the same old shit.

"Wasn't 2012 the year the Mayan calendar came to an end and everybody thought it was the end of the world?" asked one of the girls.

"Yes, but it was really the end of a cycle, not the end of the world," I said.

Savanna was staring at me like I'd grown another head. "Oh my gosh, you get it," she said in awe.

I smiled. I knew the feeling. That's how I'd felt when I'd had my session with Luna a few months ago. "I do."

"But you *really* get it!" she repeated, which made me laugh.

"I *really* do."

"That's so great! I never meet people who get it."

"How about sharing it with the rest of us," said one of the girls.

I turned to Savanna. "Maybe you should explain. You probably know more than I do."

"No! Please, I really want to hear what this channeler has to say."

I told them about the four issues everyone has, how each of our souls has an essence, and the things Luna said about my life in Mongolia. The girls had a steady stream of questions, so instead of telling them a little, I ended up telling them the whole story. That led to more questions about my life and childhood, so by the time we were done, they practically knew everything about me. The Coles Notes version, anyway.

One of the girls leaned forward. "Please tell me you're going to write a book about this. This is fascinating."

"I'm going to try," I said. It's nice that they didn't think I was crazy.

"This group of people, all being here at the same time—it's not random. Something big is happening. I can feel it. We all have something to learn from each other," said Savanna.

"It's nice having people to talk to about this. I still have so much to learn, and I'm obviously in the right company," I said, and then I turned towards Savanna. "What do you think about doing reiki after we come back from snorkeling? If you're still interested, that is."

"Hell yeah. Let's do it," she said, grinning.

"Are you sure? I still feel bad about asking while you're on vacation."

"Honey, you might be the teacher, but I'm the healer. It's my job. "

"Maybe we can do it on the beach, unless you need somewhere private."

"Nope, not at all. The beach is perfect. Oh man, I'm so excited to see where this leads us, especially after this conversation."

When we got back from snorkeling, everyone went to the pool to get drunk while Savanna and I headed to the beach. We found a couple of chaise lounges and put our stuff down.

"Before we get started, can you explain what reiki is?" I asked her.

"Sure. It's basically healing on a spiritual level. We all carry karma from different lifetimes into our physical bodies, and it can often manifest as pain or disease. I help by releasing the trapped energy. That's why I'm looking forward to doing it on you. I'm still new to it, and I'm *really* interested in hearing what you have to say. Should we get started?"

"Absolutely. What do I need to do?"

"Nothing. Just lay down and relax. I'll do my thing, and we can talk about it afterwards."

I laid down and closed my eyes. She stood behind me, and I felt her hands on top of my head. I felt heat, like when the priest touched my back. After ten minutes, I felt a slight tingling in my forehead, and then the back of my head became really itchy. She stayed there for about thirty minutes, then she put one hand on my stomach and one on my chest before gently touching the sides of my hips.

Next, she moved to my left knee and ankle, and then she asked me to turn over and placed her hands on my lower back. She stayed there for a long time, and then she was finished. The whole thing took about ninety minutes.

"So, tell me what you felt," she asked eagerly as she sat down.

I told her about the heat, the tingling in my eyebrows, and the need to scratch my head. "Sorry, I don't have much to report, but I feel like you have a *lot* to tell me. What's happening for you throughout this process? What do you see and feel?"

"Well, what I do first is ask permission to touch your body, like I did, and then I ask your soul for permission." She laughed then. "Oh man, if I thought *you* had a big personality, your soul's on a whole other level."

That wasn't surprising, but it was funny hearing it expressed like that.

"Most people's souls give me a quiet yes, but when I asked your soul, she was like YES!! PLEASE!!" She said this so dramatically that I burst out laughing.

"Great. My soul's a drama queen."

"It was all I could do not to laugh out loud!"

"Why didn't you?"

"I didn't want to scare you. Plus, I'm supposed to be doing this super serious thing."

"Fair enough."

"So first I did your head and what I felt there was a lot of anger and hate."

"Really? But I'm not an angry person at all."

"I know. I was really surprised, but it wasn't you. It was your inner child, and it was directed at your father."

"Really?"

"Oh yes. This was clearly anger at your father, and you know, I think that conversation we had at breakfast brought all that anger to the surface so it could be healed, which is why I felt it so strongly. You said you've done a lot of work to forgive your parents, and it showed, but the way he hurt you was so deep. Your anger was on a *soul* level."

"Of course. Betrayal by men was my old karmic pattern."

"Exactly. So I was removing the anger and hate in order to give your inner child a break. She's been holding onto it for so long."

"Because he never apologized when he had the chance."

"Yes, and maybe part of you felt like you didn't do it right. So I touched your head for a while, but mostly I was way *above* your head. I was talking to your soul, and we were basically having a conversation, but I kept hearing this message over and over. *It's not your fault. You did everything right.*"

"You mean when I was a child?" I asked, confused.

"Yes. Your soul is very powerful, and you're able to handle a lot of things, but this message kept repeating. It was very loud. I kept getting this pulsating sensation as I held this chakra, and I really needed you to understand the message so you could process it and move through it. Then I started to almost chant it. *You did everything right, you did everything right . . .* and then I got all these goosebumps behind my neck, so I knew it was working."

"Hmm . . . I wonder what that's all about? I know I took on the beatings. I know I rebelled eventually, and I was always haunted by the look on my father's face when I told him I hated him . . . but I never thought I did anything *wrong*."

"I wouldn't worry about it. It'll come to you later. That's how reiki works. As the energy starts moving, things will be revealed to you in the coming weeks, but they wanted to make sure you heard this message and that you *believe* it. *It's not your fault. You did everything right.*"

"Ok. I'll make sure I'm paying attention to any thoughts that come up."

"Good. So then I moved down to your belly, where I saw your inner child, and what's interesting is that she's dressed all in white, which signifies purity."

"Aren't most people's inner child dressed in white?" I asked. I remembered the shaman saying the same thing, that my aura was pure white. I kind of thought everyone had a white aura.

"Actually, I've never seen anything like it. Your inner child is *really* pure. Most people, even when I ask them to describe their inner child in my sessions or to draw them, they're always in color."

Not only was Savanna a healer, she was also a registered therapist, and I loved that she saw things from both the spiritual and scientific perspective. I think it's why she was so good at explaining things that I'd always found confusing in the past.

"Your inner child has this bubble around her that's also white, except it was starting to weaken because it was surrounded by so much darkness."

"Was she scared of it?" I asked. I remembered how often I felt scared as a child.

"No, she doesn't even know. She's completely innocent. They call it the *magical child.* The darkness is simply her environment, and she's never known anything different."

"Like when you're a kid and you think everyone's home is exactly like yours?"

"Exactly, but she's also powerful because you haven't allowed the darkness to penetrate your soul like some people do. Anyway, I was told to strengthen your aura because after this, you'll be processing, and I didn't want that darkness coming in and making it more difficult than it needs to be. Eventually, it lightened up, and then there was this smokey atmosphere left over. It's like the residuals of your past still hanging around, so there's something there that still needs work."

I was quiet for a minute and then something occurred to me. "After you remove that darkness, does it come back when you're not around? Like will I have to fight this over and over again?"

"No, that piece should never return; however, it depends on how you're able to integrate it into your life. Some people are slower, so they might need more sessions in order to fully release it because they're still holding on. But if you're open and know how to handle that release, then it shouldn't come back. Of course, if you let negativity and self-doubt come in, you open the door."

"That makes sense." This was a lot to process, but it did make sense.

"So, if you feel, say, self-doubt coming to the surface, then that's the new piece that needs to be healed. It was probably buried under the anger, and now it's coming to the surface because it wants you to deal with it."

"So, reiki peels away the layers one piece at a time."

"Exactly. But you have to be mindful, and you have to do the work. You can't just go to reiki and not follow up, because when healing is too easy, your soul doesn't learn."

Easy certainly wasn't my problem. In fact, very little was ever easy in my life.

"So, next I did your back, and it was really dark." She shivered suddenly.

"It was?" This is the part I'd been waiting for. My hip was busted, and it hurt a lot, but my lower back is what caused me the most pain.

"You know how you said at breakfast that you were part of an exorcism when you were twelve?"

"Yes."

"Well, some of those demons . . . when they left that man . . . they went straight to your lower back. Probably because you were so afraid, and they're attracted to fear. Anyway, those entities have been living there ever since."

I sucked in air. It's like someone had slapped me. There was that exorcism again. It just kept popping up lately. "Wait a minute. The pain hasn't always been there, though. In fact, my lower back's only been hurting since I injured my hip three years ago."

"That's because these things take time to manifest. It started as a seed, and it's been growing ever since. Your lower back was full of entities, and once that frequency was in your body, you kept attracting more. That's how the law of attraction works, until it started manifesting as pain.

"The fact that you hurt your hip, yet the pain was in your lower back . . . was right around the time you met Jamie, who's full of entities. Everything came full circle because the entities in your back recognized the entities in Jamie, who recognized the entities in your mother, so they were finally allowed to manifest themselves fully.

"That's why the pain has been so unbearable. Until you start to heal and change the frequency in your body, you'll keep attracting the same kind of energy. All of your relationships will continue to suck because that's what you're attracting until you raise your own vibration. Fear, anger, hate—these are low vibrations. Love, joy, laughter—these are high vibrations. Raise your vibration to that of love, and you'll attract better people."

She waited a beat while that sank in. This is what I loved about Savanna. She had a way of explaining things so they made sense. In the past, I'd found spiritual healers to be cryptic and lofty in their ideas. They'd say something, and if you didn't understand it right away, they moved on instead of explaining it in a simpler fashion. Savanna might have been a healer, but she was also a great teacher, and I was learning a lot from her.

"So your head was all about your dad, but your back was all your mom. It was incredibly powerful. In fact, I thought I was going to vomit. I was fighting these entities as I tried to remove them, and I just kept saying, 'Get out of here you fuckers because I'm not going anywhere, so you can do whatever you want.'"

I blinked several times, but I was speechless. Is this what her life was like? I swear, meeting Savanna was like meeting Morpheus, and right about now, I was wishing I hadn't taken the red pill.

"The darkness started coming up, and at first it entered my head and got stuck there, then it got stuck in my throat, and that's when I felt like throwing up. I could have spent a lot more time on you, but I was getting tired."

"Oh my God, Savanna."

"Yeah, I was gagging the whole time." She made a face. "Think of it as a window that gets splattered with mud, then more mud piles on top of that. So what I do is remove the layers of mud one layer at a time. Once I broke through, I saw a white light up your tailbone. It started off really dark, but then I finally saw the light coming through."

"I wonder if that's why the priest stuck his finger on my tailbone yesterday," I said, putting it all together. I remembered him saying my lower back was blocked.

"Maybe. It makes sense. It was all black, and it was starting to spread like tentacles across your lower back." She made a face, and I could tell she still felt it.

"Maybe that's why I couldn't stop crying after he touched me. He probably stirred things up, but then he didn't remove it, and that's what gave me that huge emotional outburst."

"Oh yeah, could be," she said brightly.

I'm not gonna lie. This conversation was freaking me out. I mean, what was I supposed to do with this information? My deepest, darkest fears were coming true. Entities were real.

"So what happens now? Did you get rid of them?" I asked anxiously.

"Not yet. I weakened them, but they're still there, and they're still fighting. The darkness *never* stops fighting. I did the best I could, though. This struggle's been going on for so long. They especially like to attack at night when you're sleeping. That's when we let our guard down."

Good Lord. Was *I ever going to sleep again?* I wondered.

"When we sleep, we're in this weakened state, and that's when the darkness tries to get in. So far, they've never succeeded because you're incredibly strong, and so is your soul, but they are, too, so you have to be mindful. Actually, your inner child has done a lot of the work. She's been fighting them off since you were twelve."

My mind was going a thousand miles an hour as I tried to process this information. I wasn't exactly sure how I felt about all this. It sounded crazy, yet I knew with every fiber of my being, it was true. I closed my eyes for a second and listened to the sound of the waves, which had a calming effect on me.

"When I get home, I'll continue working on you. These entities are too strong for me to deal with right now. I need to be in my own space, surrounded by my crystals and stuff. I'll be able to finish the work when I'm more protected."

"You mean you're going to drop this bombshell, and now I have to live with this information until you get home? How am I supposed to sleep? Oh my God, I suddenly hate having my own room. Can we put the lid back on this Pandora's box, please?"

She laughed. "You're strong, and you have a strong soul. You're entirely capable of fighting these entities on your own. We all are, but first you need to heal so you can stand in your own power. Once you find your sovereignty, they won't be able to scare you anymore."

"Thank you, Savanna. I mean it. This is a game changer."

"You're welcome. I hope it helped. Actually . . . how's your back feeling?"

"You know . . . now that you mention it, my back feels great. You did it!"

"Yay!" We both clapped. It's funny how similar we were. Not only was she a fellow Canadian, but she was Serbian, and her name was Savanna Popovic. We had the same heritage, the same initials, we both had bipolar mothers, and we could pass for sisters. The Universe really does move in mysterious ways. I threw my arms around her and gave her a big hug. After three years of living in pain, I was finally free, and it was all because of her.

Forty-Two

After my session, I went to my room to shower before heading to dinner. When I got there, the girls immediately asked how it went. I hesitated at first because I knew how crazy it sounded, and then I decided to tell it like it is. The truth was all I had.

"Wait a minute," said one of the girls, holding up her hand. "You mean to tell me you saw an exorcism when you were twelve?"

"Yah, please expand on that," said another girl.

I told them about the church and that fateful night that had haunted me for years. By the time I was finished, their mouths were hanging open. I knew the feeling.

"Your *parents* did that to you? But you were so young!"

"Holy crap, Sage. That's quite a story. No wonder you're supposed to write a book. I also have childhood trauma, but I never talk about it. I don't even know *how*. I can't believe how open and brave you are. It's really inspiring."

There were tears in her eyes, and I could see that she was in pain. Was this the reason I had to write a book and share my story with the world? Would my experiences help people like her? Because that was a worthy cause and all the inspiration I needed.

As the conversation moved on to other things, I suddenly overheard a young man on the other end of the table say something about how much it pissed him off when straight people go to gay bars. "It's one of my biggest pet peeves," he said loudly. "They don't belong, and we don't want them there."

I don't know why this caught my attention, but it did, and it seriously offended me. I had spent the better part of the nineties in gay bars. What the hell was this youngster talking about?

"Sorry to interrupt, but did you just say straight people don't belong in gay bars? Why would you say that?"

Holy shit. I should have kept my mouth shut because he suddenly lashed out with so much rage, I physically recoiled. "Because *your kind* isn't welcome!" he sneered at me.

My *kind?* Was this guy for real? As you can imagine, we ended up having a massive argument. Even though he *really* pissed me off, I spoke very calmly, trying to diffuse the situation, except he was hell bent on making a scene.

He went on and on, attacking me and talking in circles (like drunks do), and the more he talked, the more irritated I became because he was acting just like Jamie. He wasn't listening at all. He spewed anger and hatred, and he wasn't even making sense. Still, I remained calm, although what I really wanted to do was go all Gen X on his ass and throat punch the spoiled little shit for taking the freedoms my friends and I had fought for for granted.

Eventually, it came out that he'd grown up in the midwest, where he was shunned for being gay, and although I understood his pain, I failed to see how it was my fault. What's really amazing is that he couldn't even see how he'd become the very thing he hated. *He* was now the intolerant one. What's also incredible is that even though there were six people at the table, all of his anger was aimed at me. There I was, attracting the crazies again.

When I finally got to my room, I was seething. I replayed the conversation as I thought about all the things I had wanted to say but didn't. How *dare* that little shit lecture me. There are thousands of people who fought for many years against all kinds of prejudices, and I'm proud to say I'm one of them. Have we really been forgotten? And is that what we did to the generation that came before us?

I tried to sleep, but I couldn't. I couldn't shake my anger, yet I knew he was young and drunk, and that his misguided beliefs came from his own pain, so I decided to send him love, understanding, and healing because I'm a good person. Of course I don't downshift that quickly, so my thoughts went something like this: fucking little piece of shit . . . peace, love, healing . . . asshole, son of a bitch . . . peace, love, understanding . . . I know. I'm far from perfect, but at least I was trying.

When I wasn't thinking about him, I was thinking about my conversation with Savanna. The reality that demons/entities/darkness can live inside your body without you even knowing it was something I was happy not knowing. My worst fears were coming true. What was I supposed to do with that? On the one hand, it was such a relief that she'd fixed my back; on the other hand, I was seriously freaked out.

The next morning, I dragged myself out of bed and got ready. When I walked into the restaurant, Mr. Anti Straight People was already there. He was sitting at a table by the buffet, so I decided to say hello. I didn't want any weirdness between us, and I was hoping, now that he was sober, that he'd realize what an ass he'd been the night before. I was trying to give him an out.

As I walked past his table, I made a point of catching his eye and saying "good morning" in a friendly manner. He looked straight at me, then dramatically turned his head in the other direction without saying a word. I sighed. My mother does that.

I filled my plate with tropical fruit and made my way to a table near the beach. Soon, I was joined by Savanna and two other girls.

"So, how did you sleep last night after our session?" Savanna asked.

"Um . . . not very well."

"Oh no. What happened? What's going on?"

"The weirdest thing happened last night. I had this intense argument with Toby after dinner. It went on forever, and try as I might, I couldn't escape it."

"What? Why?" I filled her in on what happened.

"Spoiled little shit," she mumbled. "They always take everything for granted."

"Yes! Thank you for agreeing with me. It was weird, though. He wouldn't stop attacking me no matter what I said, and even though there were several people at the table, it was like all his rage was aimed directly at me."

She started laughing. "That's amazing!"

I raised an eyebrow. "I'm glad you're amused, but I promise you, I was not."

"Yes, but don't you find it interesting that I just finished removing all that anger from your head and the first thing that happens is this? The darkness wanted to replace the anger with more anger. Don't you see? This was a test, and you passed it."

"Oh, wow. I never thought of it like that. Although I'm not sure I passed the test. I was pretty angry and ended up thinking about it all night. No matter how much I tried to shake it off, I couldn't. He really got under my skin."

"Yes, but even through your anger, you recognized Toby's pain, and you sent him love and healing."

"True . . . but I also wanted to throat punch him."

She laughed. "That's ok. You're allowed to have your emotions, and you're allowed to react to them. You're human. We all are. In fact, you *should* acknowledge your emotions because that's the only way to heal them—by walking through them, not around them. They call it spiritual bypassing. Burying them is exactly what creates issues later on. The trick is not to take his anger on because it belongs to him and has nothing to do with you. He needs to heal that himself. In the end, though, you sent him love and healing, which means you transcended the anger, and *that* was the lesson." She smiled. "You did good. You should be proud of yourself. Healing's a process, not a straight line."

On the drive to Sanur, Savanna and I had an interesting conversation. I found it fascinating that we both had bipolar mothers, yet we'd lived such different experiences. I hadn't realized that the illness could manifest itself in such different ways.

All of my experiences with mental illness were so extreme, it surprised me to learn that it wasn't always like that. It made sense that a quiet person might show symptoms in a completely different manner than someone with a big personality.

That evening, we went shopping, and after treating ourselves to ice cream, we headed back to the hotel. It was only nine, but neither of us had gotten any sleep the night before, and we were exhausted. We talked outside her room for a few minutes, and then we said goodnight.

I slept soundly, but around 5 a.m. I woke up to go to the bathroom. I didn't have to be up for another hour, so I headed back to bed. Still freaked out by recent events, I put one hand on my stomach and one on my heart. Then, I asked Spirit to wash me in white light, like Savanna had taught me. Next, I thanked the Universe for protecting my mind, body, and spirit while I slept.

As I laid in bed, I was suddenly struck by a memory from childhood, one I'd forgotten long ago—one that made me feel ashamed. As this memory played out, I thought about what Savanna had said. *It's not your fault. You did everything right.* I figured this memory was surfacing for a reason, so I decided to dig deeper. It was obviously significant. I just wasn't sure why.

You did everything right. The words came to me again, then out of nowhere I started crying. In my mind, I was right there, feeling the emotions I'd felt that day. My whole life I had been told I was exactly like my father, and I'd often wondered if that meant being abusive as well. I was so worried that when I was thirteen I vowed never to have children, just in case. I was determined to stop the cycle of abuse. Over the years, that vow cost me several relationships and a lot of pain.

You did everything right. I kept hearing it over and over again, and then I remembered what Luna had said during my reading. "You're not an abusive person. You're NOT. You're not abusive, aggressive, or cruel. We want that to be very clear. You're not ANY of those things. It's really important you understand that."

At the time, I'd thought it odd because it came out of nowhere, but now I understood. She must have been talking about this same memory. I'd obviously been carrying this shame for a long time, without even knowing it.

"I want to speak to my inner child," I said out loud. I had no idea what I was doing. I was going purely on instinct, but it felt like the right thing to do.

"It's not your fault," I told her, "and you're nothing like him. You wouldn't have been abusive. You wouldn't have been cruel. You would have been a great mother because you're caring, kind, and understanding. The things that happened were not your fault. *You did everything right.*"

Tears streamed down my face, and I released all of my shame and anger with them. This is exactly what Savanna had been talking about. She said reiki would stir things up and bring them to the surface so they could be healed. She told me to surrender to the process, so that's what I did. I allowed my tears to flow, and then I asked Archangel Raphael to assist me with this healing.

After a few minutes, I remembered what she'd said about the anger towards my father. I figured that while I was at it, I should address this as well, especially since the darkness was trying so hard to bring more anger into my body.

"I want to speak to my father!" I demanded. I don't know who I was asking, or if anyone was even listening, but it seemed like the right thing to do. Then I started talking to him. I told him everything I hadn't had the chance to say while he was alive. Things I'd never had the courage to say.

"We were just children!" I shouted. "You were supposed to protect us! Instead you beat us and criticized us. You damaged us beyond belief. You never saved us from that evil woman. You always took her side, no matter what she said or did. She continuously made you choose between us and her, and you *always* chose her! You never apologized for any of it, and even though I know you regretted it for the last twenty years, you *still* never said a word.

"I could see the regret in your eyes, yet you were selfish until the very end. You were on your deathbed, and you *still* couldn't apologize. You couldn't give me that one thing, the closure I needed so badly. You selfish fucking man!" I screamed at the ceiling. "Don't tell me you had no idea what was going on.

She was your wife! You believed every word she said, and you beat us for it. We were just children!!!"

By now, I was sobbing so hard I was actually convulsing on the bed. Snot was running down my face, and I thought for sure I'd wake up the neighbors. This probably went on for thirty minutes before I started to calm down. Once my breathing returned to normal, I spoke again.

"I forgive you, Dad. I forgive your soul because I now understand what kind of family you grew up in, and I know you're a product of your environment and that you were a victim just like us. I don't excuse you or your actions, but I do forgive you. I forgive you for all of it."

All of a sudden, I stopped crying as a feeling of extreme calm washed over me. My body stopped shaking, and my breathing returned to normal. I laid there for several minutes as I tried to digest what was happening. Releasing all of that pain and anger made me feel so much lighter! In fact, I felt amazing, like a heavy weight had been lifted. One I didn't even know I was carrying.

"Holy shit," I said to the empty room. "So . . . that just happened." And then I giggled because I felt positively giddy. *Is this what healing feels like?* I wondered, *because I'm pretty sure there's a lot more where that came from.* There were a lot of people I needed to forgive, including myself, for making so many bad decisions in the first place.

By now, it was time to get up, so I got ready and went out to join the rest of the group. We walked along the beach until we came to a really cool yoga studio. It had an open air concept, but what made me laugh was their pet cow, who was tied to a post outside.

The teacher was excellent, and I really enjoyed the class, the sound of the waves as they gently lapped the shore, and the occasional mooing of the cow. It was my favorite class yet, and when it was over I felt so grounded. I could feel the energy flowing through my body, like it was no longer blocked, and it felt amazing. I knew yoga was supposed to do that, but this was my first time feeling it in motion.

There was a new hop in my step as I walked back to the hotel, and after a massive breakfast, I decided to swim in the ocean. I wanted to cleanse my energy and rid myself of any residual anger that might be hanging around. I remembered how the shaman had taught me that when I lived in Cancun, and I was grateful for these spiritual tools.

After my swim, I sat on the beach contemplating my morning and thinking about what came next. Tomorrow, I'd have to check out of this hotel and make my way to the other side of town, where I'd rented an Airbnb for three weeks. I was happy I had another three weeks in Bali before I had to leave. Perhaps I could use this time to write the outline for my memoir.

I thought about Savanna, and I was grateful that I'd met her on this vacation. I learned so much from her in such a short period of time, and now I understood why Luna had sent me here. I had no idea how to write a book or where I was supposed to begin, so I decided to follow Luna's advice. She told me not to worry about the story, just start at the beginning and simply write my experiences until they were finished. I took a deep breath, filling my lungs with air as the sun warmed my skin, and then I picked up my pen . . . and started writing.

Author's Note

First, I'd like to say thank you for reading my story. When I got home from Bali, several things happened at once. It was mid-February 2020, and only a few weeks later, the world shut down. Then I lost my job, and I was completely isolated, which meant I had nothing but time to write this book and heal. Two years to be exact. Just like Luna said.

That peace I'd been searching for my entire life? I found it. Learning that the Universe wasn't doing this *to* me, but that I was doing it to myself, was a hard pill to swallow, but am I ever glad I did. I might have taken the long way around, but I finally got here, and I can't wait to see what happens next.

Love is the highest vibration, and when we learn to love ourselves, we attract light instead of darkness. Good relationships instead of bad. It's our job to heal this planet and spread the love, and it starts by healing *you*.

I spent so many years feeling like I was broken, but it's only when we break that a crack appears and the light has a place to enter. Being broken is the first step towards healing if you let it be. Wounds are portals to healing, so *break*, I say. Break wide open, and let the light in.

Gratitude

I have several people to thank for helping me on my journey. Caroline: thank you for walking the seawall with me and being my sounding board. Chelle: thank you for suggesting my character's name. Sidney: thank you for walking me through our childhood. I know it was hard. Savanna: thank you for holding my hand when I was scared. Dad: thanks for letting me know that it's OK to tell this story. When you said you wanted others to learn from your mistakes, it was everything.

To my editor, Grace: thank you for steering me in the right direction and helping me get rid of the noise. You're an amazing editor who asked all the right questions. Chantel: thank you for your attention to detail, and I'm sorry for the Canadian spelling! Abigail and her team at Printopya: I love the cover art. You really nailed it! Thank you for your infinite patience with this first time author.

Bailey: You were the first person to read this, and I'm glad it brought you healing. It was the encouragement I needed to keep going.

For those of you interested in your own healing, I'm working on a workbook called *Lost In The Overwhelm*. It will be available in the spring of 2025 and will be full of useful and practical tools. Feel free to join my Facebook page for all the latest updates.

Facebook Page: @Sovereign & Sage

Manufactured by Amazon.ca
Acheson, AB

14736244R00201